Academic Advising

New Insights for Teaching and Learning in the First Year

Mary Stuart Hunter
Betsy McCalla-Wriggins
Eric R. White
Editors

 National Resource Center for The First-Year Experience® and Students in Transition

 National Academic Advising Association

Cite as:

Hunter, M. S., McCalla-Wriggins, B., & White, E. R. (Eds.). (2007). *Academic advising: New insights for teaching and learning in the first year* (Monograph No. 46 [National Resource Center]; Monograph No. 14 [National Academic Advising Association]). Columbia, SC: University of South Carolina, National Resource Center for The First-Year Experience and Students in Transition.

Sample chapter citation:

Darling, R., & Woodside, M. (2007). The academic advisor as teacher: First-year transitions. In M.S. Hunter, B. McCalla-Wriggins, & E. R. White (Eds.), *Academic advising: New insights for teaching and learning in the first year* (Monograph No. 46 [National Resource Center]; Monograph No. 14 [National Academic Advising Association]; pp. 5-17). Columbia, SC: University of South Carolina, National Resource Center for The First-Year Experience and Students in Transition.

ISBN 978-1-889-27155-2

Additional copies of this monograph may be obtained from the National Resource Center for The First-Year Experience and Students in Transition, University of South Carolina, 1728 College Street, Columbia, SC 29208, Telephone (803) 777-6029, Fax (803) 777-4699; or from the National Academic Advising Association, Kansas State University, 2323 Anderson Avenue, Suite 225, Manhattan, KS 66502, Telephone (785) 532-5717, Fax (785) 532-7732.

Special gratitude is expressed to Barbara F. Tobolowsky, Associate Director, for project management and copyediting; to Inge Kutt Lewis, Editor, for copyediting and proofing; to Michael Abel, Editorial Assistant, for copyediting and proofing; to Asheley Bice, Editorial Assistant, for copyediting and proofing; to Tracy L. Skipper, Editorial Projects Coordinator, for proofing; and to Erin M. Morris, Graphic Artist, for layout and design; all at the National Resource Center for The First-Year Experience and Students in Transition.

Library of Congress Cataloging-in-Publication Data

Academic advising : new insights for teaching and learning in the first year
/ Mary Stuart Hunter, Betsy McCalla-Wriggins, Eric R. White, editors.
     p. cm. -- (The first-year experience monograph series ; no. 46)
(NACADA Monograph Series ; no. 14)
  Includes bibliographical references.
  ISBN-13: 978-1-889271-55-2
  ISBN-10: 1-889271-55-1
  1. Counseling in higher education--United States. 2. College student
development programs--United States. 3. College freshmen--United States.
I. Hunter, Mary Stuart. II. McCalla-Wriggins, Betsy. III. White, Eric R.
(Eric Robert), 1944- IV. National Resource Center for the First-Year
Experience & Students in Transition (University of South Carolina).
LB2343.A294 2007
378.1'94220973
                         2006100834

Contents

Contents

Section Three: Critical Issues and Strategies for Advising Diverse Populations of First-Year Students

Contents

Notes From the Editors

Mary Stuart Hunter, Betsy McCalla-Wriggins, and Eric R. White

Today's higher education landscape is far different from what it was 10 years ago. Higher education has become much more accessible, and students are bringing more racial, ethnic, and cultural diversity to the college community. While students' expectations for academic success have increased, they also report a lower level of academic engagement (Sax et al., 2004). In addition, parents are more involved than ever before (see chapter 2). As students change, so do programs, curricula, and institutions. Academic advisors are in a unique position to deal with both the changing student population and the evolving institution. As a result of their individual interactions with students and their role as student advocates, they are able to identify and respond to changing student needs. In addition, academic advising initiatives have adjusted quickly to the changing institutional landscape. In 1995, the National Resource Center for The First-Year Experience and Students in Transition and National Academic Advising Association (NACADA) collaborated to publish *First-Year Academic Advising: Patterns in the Present, Pathways to the Future*. This monograph provides information on the theoretical and practical components of student-centered academic advising. In addition, it suggests strategies that, when employed on a campus, will likely improve academic advising. In the intervening decade, many new ideas and strategies for advising first-year students have emerged. This volume attempts to bring advising into a new era within a new framework.

Grounded in the philosophy that academic advising is a form of robust one-on-one teaching, this monograph attempts to view advising from this new perspective, one that brings advising to the center of institutional mission and activity. Light (2001) suggested that "good advising may be the single most underestimated characteristic of a successful college experience" for students (p. 81). Higher educators everywhere will agree that student learning is a common goal across all institutional types. We contend that the academic advising relationship is where some of the best teaching and learning can occur within the academy. It is our hope that this monograph will challenge all readers to see the tremendous potential that academic advising has for educating today's college students.

The monograph begins with a section on the foundations of academic advising in the 21st century. In the first chapter, Ruth Darling and Marianne Woodside address teaching and learning activities in a learning paradigm for advising that serves as a framework for the entire monograph. Jennifer Keup and Jillian Kinzie's chapter follows and highlights current national information about today's students, which helps to inform advisors in shaping the educational process of new college students.

Section two of the monograph includes topics inherent in a comprehensive approach to academic advising. In chapter three, Christine Johnston and Betsy McCalla-Wriggins describe an advanced learning process that identifies learning patterns and suggest practical strategies for incorporating this process into initiatives for advising first-year students. Joanne Damminger then asserts in chapter four that students' self-assessment is a key component in academic advising and that the power of self-assessment should not be underestimated.

In chapter five, Wes Lipschultz and Mike Leonard examine how the current and future uses of technology have the potential to enhance the advising-teaching connection and increase communication between students and advisors. Next, Jim Black examines the importance of advising during the period between students' acceptance to an institution and the first few weeks following matriculation. In chapter seven, Stuart Hunter, Jean Henscheid, and Michelle Mouton address several venues where advising occurs beyond the academic advisors' offices: first-year seminars, learning communities, and early alert programs. In the final chapter in section two, Vicki McGillin and Charlie Nutt tackle the complex topic of advising assessment by addressing both the measurement of effectiveness and quality of first-year advising and student learning outcomes.

The third section of the monograph focuses on critical issues and strategies for advising diverse populations of first-year students. In chapter nine, Penny Rice and Sharon McGuire discuss first-year adult students. In chapter 10, Evette Castillo focuses on students of color, highlighting the status of several micro-populations of students in higher education and discussing varied cultural contexts and critical issues specific to these student populations. In the next chapter, Dick Vallandingham addresses the special characteristics and needs of students with disabilities. In chapter 12, Marion Schwartz focuses on the unique needs of honors students. In chapter 13, Melinda McDonald and George Steele assert that more than any other group of first-year students, undecided students perhaps benefit the most from academic advising in a learning paradigm. In the following chapter, Ruth Darling and Melissa Smith examine first-generation college students and their unique characteristics, needs, and expectations. To conclude this section on critical issues and strategies for advising diverse populations of first-year students, Casey Self presents current information on advising lesbian, gay, bisexual, and transgender first-year students

The monograph concludes with a chapter that sets out challenges for academic advising at colleges and universities in the 21st century along with a set of specific recommendations for an individual advisor to consider in developing and/or enhancing an academic advising program for first-year students. Finally, we charge all those who believe both in the importance of academic advising and the first year of study to maintain the highest professional standards so that the very strongest foundation for student success in college can be established. In so doing, higher educators will ensure that all first-year students are given the opportunity to learn from their college experience, to achieve their potential, and, ultimately, to be successful life-long learners and citizens.

References

Light, R. J. (2001). *Making the most out of college: Students speak their minds.* Cambridge, MA: Harvard University Press.

Sax, L. J., Hurtado, S., Lindholm, J. A., Astin, A. W., Korn, W. S., & Mahoney, K. M. (2004). *The American freshman: National norms for fall 2004.* Los Angeles: University of California, Higher Education Research Institute.

Section One

Foundations for Academic Advising in the 21st Century

Chapter One

The Academic Advisor as Teacher: First-Year Transitions

Ruth A. Darling and Marianne Woodside

Academic advising plays a vital role in supporting student learning on a college campus. It is essential that advisors take on a teaching role with students from the students' initial interactions with an institution in their first year through graduation. One of the primary objectives for academic advisors, as teachers, is creating a teaching-learning relationship with students and aiding their growth and development. It begins in those first meetings where students share their stories with advisors about their transition from high school to college and from home to the university and advisors help them make sense of those experiences. As we work with students and listen to their stories, academic advisors are challenged to teach students how to discover what they need to manage the first year, how to meet those needs, how to cope with the rigor of college-level learning and the structure of curricular requirements, and how to construct an educational plan built on principles of higher learning and academic success.

This chapter will describe the knowledge base upon which academic advising is built and introduce two models (i.e., model of transition and novice-to-expert model) that provide practical ways academic advisors can engage in the teaching role as they help first-year students make the transition to college. The models provide a framework for advisors to consider how they fulfill their role as teachers in a learning/student-centered context, what they need to learn about and from the students, what first-year students should learn from the advising experience, and how advisors assess students' learning. We conclude the chapter with guidelines for academic advisors that are framed within the context of teaching and learning and shape the experience of academic advising for both the student and advisor.

Academic Advising as Teaching

Baxter Magolda's (2000b) work on constructivist teaching provides insight into how advisors might think about their role as teachers. She asserts that approaching teaching and learning from the constructivist perspective requires a new way of thinking about knowledge, authority, learners, and teachers. "Guiding students to author their own knowledge in the context of existing knowledge recognizes that knowledge is socially constructed by knowledgeable peers" (Baxter Magolda, 2000b, p. 98). First-year students make meaning of their new experiences and create a changed reality as they develop new relationships, move through the events of the first year, and react to those events. New knowledge is constructed as a result of these relationships and interactions. Using this construct, advisors as teachers partner with first-year students as they engage in the process of constructing new knowledge and making new meanings of their experience.

As students share their stories with academic advisors, the advisors begin to understand the specific goals, challenges, problems, and background of each student. The students' stories also serve as the beginning point for students' learning to navigate the unfamiliar campus culture. Ignelzi (2000) states,

> Education isn't simply presenting more adequate information in an effective manner; it is a process that must incorporate the developmental readiness of the student and must construct a developmental bridge between the students' current way of understanding and the new way, thus providing a path on which to cross over. (p. 6)

When considering academic advising as teaching, Ignelzi's (2000) comments suggest that academic advisors teach students how to actively engage with their learning and the campus culture. The success of first-year students depends on advisors' understanding the various and diverse experiences that shape students' lives. Through a process and relationship grounded in teaching and learning, advisors work with students to create a bridge facilitating the transition from high school or work through the first year of college. Advisors must focus on understanding how to create intersections in the teaching, advising, and learning process that allow students to become fully engaged in their undergraduate experience, the curriculum, and in their pursuit of life-long learning.

The literature in academic advising provides the advising practitioner with various definitions and approaches to advising, including frameworks that place advising within the context of teaching and learning. For example, Crookston (1972) defined the role of advising as developmental. Developmental advising facilitates the student's rational processes, environmental and interpersonal interactions, behavioral awareness and problem-solving, decision making, and evaluation skills. He proposed that advising is essentially a teaching function and is based on a negotiated relationship between the student and the advisor with varying degrees of learning for both the student and the advisor. O'Banion (1972) asserted that the purpose of academic advising was to help students choose a program of study, which would serve them in the development of their full potential; thus, placing academic advising as a necessary and central activity in the process of education. He further defined the process of advising as occurring in five hierarchical steps: (a) exploration of life goals, (b) exploration of vocational goals, (c) program choice, (d) course choice, and (e) course schedule.

The need for academic advisors to consider the developmental readiness of students is widely represented in the literature as summarized by Creamer and Creamer (1994). Drawing on numerous articles that focus on developmental advising and student development theory, the authors define the task of developmental advising as the "use of interactive teaching, counseling and administrative strategies to assist students to achieve specific learning, developmental, career and life goals" (p. 19). Using this framework, academic advisors are caring in their relationship with students, working to support developmental growth, and assessing the effectiveness of advising through its developmental impact on students. Also, Gordon (1988) asserts that developmental advising is "the vehicle most likely to succeed" in teaching students the decision making skills necessary to make academic and career decisions (p. 108). The problem-solving activities, present in the developmental advising process, not only help students make choices but also contribute to the development of critical-thinking skills.

Expanding on the concept of academic advising, Frost (1991) defines academic planning as a teaching/learning process during which advisors help students identify a mission and objectives, consider alternatives, and arrive at informed decisions about their academic futures. Frost reinforces the concept that academic advising is a shared relationship where both student and advisor have responsibilities. Academic planning "not only assists students in making immediate choices, but also contributes to the teaching role of advising by serving as a model for future behavior" (p. 20).

Academic advisors are challenged by several authors to consider various student transitions (i.e., adjusting to the rigor of college learning, dealing with failure, deciding on a major, navigating institutional policy and procedures) as discussion points where learning best takes place (Chickering, 1994; Laff, 1994). Laff questions the idea of developmental advising as being too centered on stages of development and suggests that it is the transition between those stages where learning and growth occur. "Development is driven when our interactions bring up experiences that do not fit our expectations—we make mistakes when our ways of thinking about things do not account for new, different, or unexpected experiences" (p. 47). And, building on the idea of students in transition, Chickering makes use of Ann Lynch's moving in, moving through, and moving out construct as a way to think about the various transitions in a student's life and the role of the academic advisor. Chickering suggests that by helping students recognize the importance of pursuing lifelong learning, advisors "will strengthen student motivation for tackling diverse opportunities" resulting in effective transitions (p. 51).

All first-year students experience a significant transition into college. The following discussion introduces two models of transition (i.e., model of transition and novice-to-expert model) that are useful in two ways. First, these models provide a foundation for understanding the first-year experience. Second, using the models as approaches for teaching through the advising process, academic advisors and students can acquire the knowledge about the transition and skills needed to better negotiate the first year. Furthermore, by working with the academic advisor, the students learn how to use the models to work through the first-year transition.

With increased knowledge and insight, those engaged in academic advising can move toward understanding the relationships and connections not only among events and choices students make but also among how they learn and construct their world and their student identity. Building upon the ideas of academic advising as teaching and a constructivist approach to academic advising, these models or tools for advising address the transition issues of the first-year college student and place the advisor in the teaching role. The first, model of transition, describes the context of the first year. The second applies a well-developed model of novice-to-expert to the first-year experience. Both models support academic advisors as they teach students about the transitions during the first year and empower students to assume responsibilities for their academic careers and beyond.

Model of Transition

One way of explaining transition is to describe the context in which it occurs and explore the relationship between the past and the present (Figure 1). In this model, concentric circles describe the core of the individual and the factors of influence (Bronfenbrenner, 1979; Woodside Paulus, & Ziegler, 2005). The four concentric circles represent the individual, the past social experiences, the past education and work experiences, and the current first-year experience. The two arrows represent the direction of change. One arrow begins from the outer circle, the

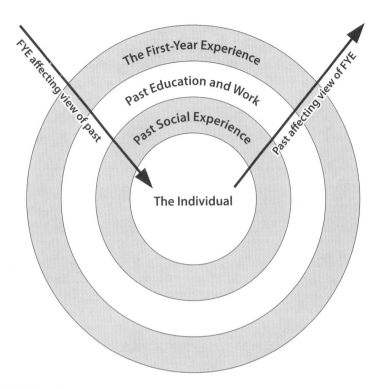

Figure 1. Model of transition.

first-year experience, and extends to the inner circles to the variables that form the core of the individual. A second arrow begins within the individual core and extends outward to the last circle, the first-year experience.

The Individual

The core of the concentric circle addresses the question, Who am I? It is the variables and components that define the individual including temperament; personality traits; aptitudes; health; emotional stability; and other factors including race, gender, gender orientation, and ethnicity.

Past social experiences. This circle represents the influences such as family, childcare, neighborhood, school, religious institutions, social organizations, and other social contexts.

Past education and work experiences. This circle signifies the wide variety of experiences where the individual assumes the role of a student or worker. This role can include early interactions with parents, childcare, pre-school, and other formal educational experiences or later interactions with work, colleagues, or career. Students gain knowledge, skills, and values in these settings that contribute to academic preparedness.

The first-year experience. This circle represents the experiences of the first-year student on the college campus. It encompasses pre-enrollment activities such as applying, being accepted, and attending orientation. It also includes establishing a class schedule, beginning the term, attending classes, studying for classes and exams, and completing the first year. From the moment students apply to college, they enter the fourth circle, the first-year experience. To make sense of and negotiate this environment, students use who they are and their past experiences, represented by the first three circles. In other words, they use the past to help negotiate the college world they encounter, especially when something in their college experience captures their interest. However, knowledge from these first three circles is not all they need.

The Arrows

The first arrow, moving from the core to the outer circle, represents how students use who they are and their past to understand college life. For example, if students were academically successful in high school, they will begin college by using tested study approaches. The second arrow, moving from the outer circle to the inner core, represents how the first-year experience alters how students view their past. For example, at the individual level, a shift from dependence to independence begins to occur. Experience in the college environment helps the individual to see past experience, past education, and work in a different light. For example, an understanding of and relationship with parents may alter. Previous educational experiences may provide a solid foundation for the college experience or may become irrelevant.

How can the academic advisor use this model to support the transition of the first-year student? According to constructivist teaching principles and academic advising practice, it is the responsibility of the academic advisor to teach students how to navigate this new environment, to help them describe this new situation, and to help them gain new skills and new understandings. Acquiring new knowledge, skills, and understandings allows them to effectively navigate the transition.

During first-year advising, the teaching role in academic advising is traditionally restricted to providing information about the curriculum and the collegiate environment. This new model focuses on helping students understand their past experience and their new world; access what knowledge, values, and skills they already have to support the transition; and assess what new knowledge, values, and skills they need to function effectively in the collegiate setting. The challenge for academic advisors is teaching students how to discover what they need to manage this first year, how to meet those needs, and how to help them follow through once they have these insights.

In summary, the model of transition is intended to explain the difficulties, challenges, and anxieties that first-year students experience. The model also reinforces the concept that change is bidirectional: Students use their past to make meaning of their first-year experience, and their perception of the past changes as they make the first-year transition. The early college experience (first day, week, month, or six months) now influences the meaning of the experience and perception of the first three foundation circles. They create for themselves new patterns and new designs—a different worldview.

Novice-to-Expert Model

Studies about how individuals progress from the early stages of their learning, or making meaning of new subject matter, through a stage of competence, and finally to the stage of expert exist for a variety of disciplines such as nursing, counseling, computer science, physics, teaching, and others (Atherton, 2003; Cooper, 2003; McClam & Puckett, 1991). Dreyfus and Dreyfus (1986), using their understanding of computer science and philosophy, developed a five-stage model that helps describe the experience of the first-year student as a novice. We see the purpose of academic advising as moving the first-year student, over a period of years, from *novice*, with little understanding and skills to master the new situation, to *expert*, with complete mastery of the situation. The advisor as teacher helps the first-year student begin to master the environment—academics, social/daily living, emotions, finances, and relationships with advisors and teachers.

How does the academic advisor use this model to help students in their first year? The advisor, in the teaching role, provides the information through discussion or one-on-one interviews that help students assess their status as novices. The student, using the information from the advising session, applies this new understanding to college learning and the campus environment. How does the novice-to-expert model describe the first year and its challenges (Table 1)? Each stage is described and defined by the tasks that need to be mastered.

Novice

During this time, the first-year student is a beginner within the institutional context. To function successfully as a novice and to provide a foundation that allows movement to advanced beginner, the student needs rules and plans to follow. At this time in the student's development, there is a limited ability to assess various situations and to act outside the rules. This is the just-tell-me-what-I-need-to-do phase of the novice-to-expert model. Although this may run counter to many theories that encourage students to become good problem-solvers, students cannot solve problems until they learn the rules and understand at least one strategy that will work for them. Students need to know the resources available to them and how to use them appropriately.

Advanced Beginner

As advanced beginners, students have spent some time on campus and have begun to see how rules and plans work. They can actually use the rules and plans in multiple situations and are beginning to see that many situations are complicated with multiple variables to consider. Although they consider multiple variables, each of these choices looks the same to the students. This is the too-many-choices stage.

Competent

As students consider multiple variables in their situations, they marvel at the choices they have. In contrast to the advanced beginner, the competent considers multiple variables as broadening rather than confusing. They can plan for both the short term and the long term and are able to link the two approaches to planning. They are still using procedures and rules, but this time they use them to their advantage. This is the I-know-where-I-am-going stage.

Proficient

As they begin to view their academic career as one part of their life plan, students in the proficient stage develop an ability to make their own rules and guidelines for achieving academic success. The term, success, broadens to include careers, leadership, social competency, friendship, dating, and for some marriage and family. Students can assess their own academic journey in light of traditional models and the experiences of others. When making decisions, they use the guidelines they have developed and that work for them. The student continually modifies these guidelines. This is the campus-serves-me stage.

Table 1
Novice-to-Expert Model

Stage	Characteristics of the Stage	Characteristics of the College Student/Environment	Academic Advisor's Role
Novice "Just tell me what to do"	Follows rules and plans. Limited ability to assess situations. Limited ability to act outside the rules.	**Environment:** Entering a new culture. Learning a new language. Discovering new ways to live. **Academic:** Adjusting to different expectations for academic performance. Adjusting to diversity of teaching styles, classroom settings, and cultural backgrounds of teachers. **Social/Daily Living:** Affiliating with different peer groups. Establishing new routines. Making decisions about their own priorities. Becoming responsible for activities of daily living. **Emotional:** Being "on their own." Being away from home. Changing relationship with family and home/community. **Financial:** Working to support college education/expenses. Working to support their families. **Relationship with advisors and teachers:** Paying attention to these experts. Wanting answers.	Provides information, structure, serves as a navigator or a guide, teaches student about the environment and culture.
Advanced Beginner "Too many choices"	Follows rules and plans based upon variables. Limited ability to assess situations. All variables have same importance.	**Environment:** Beginning to be able to negotiate their environment. **Academic:** Adjusting to type of study choices expanding. Seeing increasing number of career options. **Social/Daily Living:** Experiencing consequences of choices concerning health and wellness, study habits, and relationships. **Emotional:** Beginning to see multiple possibilities for personal growth. Feeling frustrated by complexity of choices.	Helps students learn to realistically assess alternatives, outline choices and possibilities, review consequences of decisions.

Table 1 continued p. 12

Table 1 continued

Stage	Characteristics of the Stage	Characteristics of the College Student/Environment	Academic Advisor's Role
		Financial: Feeling overwhelmed by financial responsibility. Being over-committed financially. **Relationships with advisors and teachers:** Seeing advisors and teachers as experts. Wanting these individuals to help them list choices they have. Not wanting experts to tell them what to do.	
Competent "I know where I am going"	Can work with multiple variables. Can plan actions that relate to short and long terms plans. Can use procedures and rules to solve problems.	**Environment:** Navigating the environment. Teaching others how to succeed. Connecting with experiences outside their environment that relate to their current academic focus. **Academic:** Having determined a direction for academic planning. Having made a comprehensive academic plan. Having mastered the academic skills necessary to be successful. **Social/Daily Living:** Associating with a peer group or connecting to campus organizations and activities. Being able to manage their daily life and its demands. **Emotional:** Establishing solid relationships. Becoming confident in their role as a college student. **Financial:** Understanding financial commitments. Balancing school and work. **Relationships with advisors and teachers:** Engaging in collaborative discussion of alternatives and possibilities. Sharing responsibilities.	Helps students articulate possible goals, objectives and outcomes, discusses multiple options, collaborates with students to help them find their own path.
Proficient "School serves me"	Can see the "big" picture. Can distinguish important variables. Views situations that do not fit the rules or the plan.	**Environment:** Making college environment a part of their identity. **Academic:** Seeing the academic plan as a means to a larger end. Actively developing skills that will support a transition to work.	Shares in the learning process with the student, helps students achieve their own goals within the college environment,

Table 1 continued

Stage	Characteristics of the Stage	Characteristics of the College Student/Environment	Academic Advisor's Role
	More ease of decision making. Uses guidelines for actions within a specific context.	**Social/Daily Living:** Seeking opportunities to learn outside the classroom. Managing their daily life and its demands. **Emotional:** Actively searching for experiences that challenge their view of the world. **Financial:** Constructing a plan to pay off debts incurred during the college years. Connecting finances to future work and career plans. **Relationships with advisors and teachers:** Seeing advisors and teachers as resources and mentors.	helps students begin to expand beyond college environment, supports students in their decisions.
Expert "Beyond the university"	Does not need rules or guidelines. Relies on a deep understanding of a situation. (intuitive). Analysis useful in novel situations. Can envision multiple possibilities.	**Academic:** Completing specific degree requirements. Making plans for professional education or the world of work. Using college education on a daily basis. Being reflective of the experience of learning. **Social/Daily Living:** Moving their focus away from campus in their daily lives. Integrating what they have learned in their day-to-day activities. Managing change and moving through transitions. **Emotional:** Feeling a sense of self-efficacy beyond the campus. Reflecting on the meaning of college for them. **Financial:** Integrating financial considerations as a part of holistic thinking about the future. **Relationships with advisors and teachers:** Considering teachers and advisors as points of reference for a shared experience.	Articulates student's strengths, reflects with the student about learning experiences, discusses possibilities for future studies and plans, supports student's plans for transition from college to next phase of learning or work.

Expert

Comprehension and creativity are the activities that mark the expert stage of development. The student fully understands the institutional system and negotiates it with ease. Although the student does not use problem-solving in the sense of earlier stages, the student is able to progress using an internal sense of understanding. Interestingly enough, if the student is confronted with a novel situation, the student uses the approaches of a novice. This is the beyond-the-campus stage.

The stages of novice-to-expert provide both the academic advisor and the student a way to think about the stages of mastery of a situation and challenges a college student may experience. Most first-year students understand that they are in a novel situation that will challenge their current understanding of an educational and social experience.

For most students, the model provides hope that there is life beyond the first year. The students can anticipate that they will be able to master the institutional environment and use it to develop confidence, widen their social experiences, and challenge and expand their thinking.

Implications for Practice

As the academic advisor assumes the teaching role, using the constructivist framework of teaching and learning described in the introduction, there are three guidelines that are helpful to consider. These are described within the context of academic advising and integrated with the model of transition and novice-to-expert model. The guidelines and suggestions for practice are discussed in relationship to the transition needs and learning of first-year college students.

Guideline #1: Place the Student at the Center of Advising.

Academic advising first and foremost focuses on the individual student and how the student learns and acquires new knowledge. Baxter Magolda (2001a) asserts, "individual learning and knowledge claims are grounded in how the individual constructs knowledge" (p.1). With this statement, Baxter Magolda articulates an epistemological claim about how individuals learn, placing the student at the center of the learning activity. This notion rejects lecturing to or filling students up with knowledge—models of teaching that are prevalent on many campuses. Rather, the focus of academic advising becomes helping each individual understand his or her own collegiate experiences and build his or her own sense of reality in the college world.

Implications for academic advising for the first-year student. As mentioned previously, the academic advisor tries to build a bridge for students who are in transition from high school and home to the collegiate environment. If the advisor is to support the transition, then he or she must understand the students' world. The advisor should establish an environment where students can explore the meaning of college, the challenges of the first year, their strengths and weaknesses, and how the college curriculum may influence their success in the first year.

Use of the models. The model of transition helps students understand themselves better. Students examine how their backgrounds contribute to their own understanding of the college experience. This model provides a tool for students to explore, within and outside the advising appointment, the influences that support and define the first-year experience. Using the model of transition allows the advisor to understand students on more realistic terms, enabling the advisor to tailor academic advising to meet individual needs.

The novice-to-expert model provides a framework for the academic advisor that affirms that students are in transition and that the collegiate experience is a novel one. It also helps first-year students understand and accept that collegiate life is dynamic and that personal, academic, and professional goals and experience change with time.

Guideline #2: Learning Is Linked to Self-Concept.

How students handle the transition from high school to college is linked to their sense of self that has been formed by internal and external influences (Baxter Magolda, 2000a; Ignelzi, 2000; Kegan, 1994; Love & Guthrie, 1999). The stronger the internal influences, the more students are able to define what they know in terms of their own experience and their own reasoning. For some, what others think strongly influences how they think about themselves (Weiten & Lloyd, 2006). Cognitive theorists agree that, in early stages of development, students turn to authorities for answers. As students develop cognitively, they begin to see multiple perspectives, engage in critical thinking, and look within themselves for answers to difficult questions (Baxter Magolda, 2000a; Gilligan, 1982; Kohlberg & Hersh, 1977; Perry, 1970/1999).

Implications for academic advising for the first-year student. Academic advisors expect to work with first-year students with a wide range of self-identities. Early in the first year, students may see academic advisors and teachers as authority figures. Academic advisors need to promote less dependence upon authority and encourage students to look within for support. For students who are looking to authority, academic advisors should try to provide some alternatives and help students make choices. For those first-year students who are already using internal sources of affirmation, academic advisors are able to provide information, help students generate alternatives, and encourage students to explore options, and weigh their decisions.

Use of the models. The model of transition provides a place for the student to examine his or her life and the external and internal influences on the sense of self. During this process, the students begin to place themselves within a personal context. This is a starting point to begin the development of a strong self-image based upon self-assessment.

The novice-to-expert model provides the academic advisor with an opportunity to help the first-year student become aware of the types of information and the kind of questions needed to understand the first-year experience. Advisor and student can explore the culture that defines the context of the first-year experience. By looking together at the tasks in which the novice must engage, the academic advisor can provide information and guidance, serve as a teacher/guide within the new culture, and facilitate a discussion where both first-year student and advisor are experts. By using both models, the academic advisor encourages students to think critically about themselves within the context of their learning and academic career.

Guideline #3: Learning Is a Process.

Students evolve through stages of development as they begin to understand that knowledge is complex. They begin to seek multiple perspectives, explore information within context, and make meaning of their experiences based upon a reflective process. Within the context of academic advising, some of the most successful learning occurs when advisors pose provocative questions or tasks and help students consider the significance of these questions or tasks (Bain, 2004). Because the focus is on the student experience, the students are more likely to engage in the topic of transition. Academic advisors use the models to help students discover their place in the transition from high school to college.

Implications for academic advising for the first-year student. The academic advisor focuses on both the present and the future, providing students with a broad view of the first-year experience. They also help students connect their learning to the curriculum and the collegiate environment and understand what the advising/learning process brings to their experience.

Use of the models. The model of transition grounds the first-year student in the present, but it is also a framework for the future collegiate career. As the academic advisor helps the student use the four concentric circles to articulate his or her background, the student becomes aware of past learning and development. The advisor makes the case for viewing this first year as a continuation of that same learning process. The model also presents a portal for viewing the future. Once the first year is complete, it becomes part of the fourth circle; the individual is able to incorporate the first-year experience into the past, which is used to guide the student in their second year. Understanding that this first-year experience provides a foundation for the next year's work may help provide relevancy and immediacy to the advising process. Since knowledge building is developmental, it is critical to engage the student in discussions concerning the knowledge gained and the knowledge needed for future collegiate success.

The novice-to-expert model helps place the first-year experience within the context of the comprehensive collegiate experience. The advisor uses the novice-to-expert model to assess where the first-year student is within the developmental framework and to assure the student of future learning and development. The lack of confidence that being a novice may generate will give way to growth and then mastery of the campus environment. Using the comprehensive picture, the academic advisor provides a longer-term perspective beyond the first year. In addition, the advisor projects how the advising relationship will change as the needs of the student changes beyond the first year.

By using both models, the academic advisor encourages students to think critically about their academic career. Students move beyond facts, rules, and regulations as they evaluate and synthesize their place in the transition. In this way, the academic advisor transmits or teaches the knowledge, insights, and skills of academic planning to the student.

Summary

Using the guidelines and models based on the constructivist perspective of teaching and learning, academic advisors help students reflect upon their current experiences, provide a road map for student learning and development, and project a way students can think about their futures. We believe that the implications for practice meet five goals that support student transition throughout the first-year in college. During the process of academic advising, where the student is the focus of the learning experience, (a) the first-year student's experience is normalized, (b) the student has a set of frameworks to think about college learning and the first-year experience, (c) the student better understands the problems faced by most first-year students as well as personal issues, (d) the academic advisor is actively engaged in teaching, and (e) the student understands better how to interact with advisors as teachers during the first-year transition and beyond.

References

Atherton, J. S. (2003). *Docio: Competence, proficiency, and beyond.* Retrieved June 21, 2004, from http://www.doceo.co.uk/background/expertise.htm

Bain, K. (2004). What makes great teachers great? *The Chronicle of Higher Education, 50*(31), B7. Retrieved January 13, 2004, from http://chronicle.com

Baxter Magolda, M. B. (2000a). Editor's notes. In M. B. Baxter Magolda (Ed.), *Teaching to promote intellectual and personal maturity: Incorporating students' worldviews and identities into the learning process* (New Directions for Teaching and Learning, No. 82, p. 1). San Francisco: Jossey-Bass.

Baxter Magolda, M. B. (2000b). Teaching to promote holistic learning and development. In M. B. Baxter Magolda (Ed.), *Teaching to promote intellectual and personal maturity: Incorporating students' worldviews and identities into the learning process* (New Directions for Teaching and Learning, No. 82, p. 88–98). San Francisco: Jossey-Bass.

Bronfenbrenner, U. (1979). *The ecology of human development.* Cambridge, MA: Harvard University Press.

Chickering, A. W. (1994). Empowering lifelong self-development. *NACADA Journal, 14*(2), 51-53.

Cooper, A. (2003). *From novice to expert. Professional learning cannot be hurried.* Retrieved March 21, 2005, from http://www.theschooldaily.com/

Creamer, D. G., & Creamer, E. G. (1994). Practicing developmental advising: Theoretical contexts and functional applications. *NACADA Journal, 14*(2), 17-24.

Crookston, B. B. (1972). A developmental view of academic advising as teaching. *Journal of College Student Personnel, 13*(1), 12-17.

Dreyfus, H. L., & Dreyfus, S. E. (1986). *Mind over machine: The power of human intuition and expertise in the era of the computer.* Oxford: Basil Blackwell.

Frost, S. H. (1991). *Academic advising for student success: A system of shared responsibility* (ASHE-ERIC Higher Education Report No. 3). Washington, DC: The George Washington University, School of Education and Human Development.

Gilligan, C. (1982). *In a different voice: Psychological theory and women's development.* Cambridge, MA: Harvard University Press.

Gordon, V. N. (1988). Developmental advising. In W. R. Habley (Ed.), *The status and future of academic advising* (pp. 107-118). Iowa City, IA: The ACT National Center for the Advancement of Educational Practices.

Ignelzi, M. (2000). Meaning-making in the learning and teaching process. In M. B. Baxter Magolda (Ed.), *Teaching to promote intellectual and personal maturity: Incorporating students' worldviews and identities into the learning process* (New Directions for Teaching and Learning, No. 82). San Francisco: Jossey-Bass.

Kegan, R. (1994). *In over our heads: The mental demands of modern life.* Cambridge, MA: Harvard University Press.

Kohlberg, L., & Hersh, R. H. (1977). Moral development: A review of theory. *Theory into Practice, 16*, 53-59.

Laff, N. S. (1994). Reconsidering the developmental view of advising: Have we come a long way? *NACADA Journal, 14*(2), 46-49.

Love, P. G., & Guthrie, V. L. (1999). *Understanding and applying cognitive development theory* (New Directions for Student Services, No. 88). San Francisco: Jossey-Bass.

McClam, T., & Puckett, K. S. (1991). Qualities of effective supervision: Changes in novices' perceptions. *Human Services Education, 12*(1), 13-23.

O'Banion, T. (1972). An academic advising model. *Junior College Journal, 42*(6), 62-69.

Perry, W. G. (1999). *Forms of intellectual and ethical development in the college years: A scheme.* San Francisco: Jossey-Bass. (Original work published 1970. New York: Holt, Rinehart, & Winston)

Weiten, W., & Lloyd, M. A. (2006). *Psychology applied to modern life: Adjustment in the 21st century* (8th ed.). Pacific Grove, CA: Wadsworth.

Woodside, M., Paulus T., & Ziegler, M. (2005). The experience of helping. *Human Service Education, 25*(1), 9-26.

Chapter Two

A National Portrait
of First-Year Students

Jennifer R. Keup and Jillian Kinzie

Ｎew students enter college and are immediately challenged to make important decisions about their educational journey. They have to select courses, determine when to schedule these classes, and consider which enriching experiences to participate in, including informal socializing, student employment, and campus organizations. Among the first staff members new students interact with about these issues are academic advisors. In fact, the quality of academic advising is the most powerful predictor of satisfaction with the college environment (National Survey of Student Engagement, 2001).

Further, advisors are more equipped to facilitate the intellectual and personal development of students and improve the quality of their educational experiences when they are aware of the extent to which students are likely to participate in educationally purposeful activities, interact with faculty and advisors, and take advantage of academic support services during their first year of college. An enriched understanding of the backgrounds and patterns of academic and personal engagement of first-year students nationally provides the context in which to enhance the role of advising as a teaching and learning process and to explore the experiences of students at individual institutions. It also furnishes a framework for increasing advisors' appreciation of the potential for campus level student data to inform their work with first-year students. Therefore, the purpose of this chapter is to highlight general information about students today, elaborate on our wide empirical base of information about students' educational experiences, and ultimately, help inform the advisor-student relationship and emphasize its role in shaping the educational process of new college students.

Given the proliferation of data collection instruments and analytical methodologies, we are now able to assemble a more accurate and comprehensive picture of the experiences and development of first-year college students than we have in previous decades. Thanks to large national databases such as the Department of Education's National Center for Educational Statistics (NCES) and the U.S. Census Bureau, we have empirical information about who students are prior to their entry to any specific college or university, the demographic composition of entering classes, and patterns of institutional enrollment. Further, recent data sets drawn from the Cooperative Institutional Research Program (CIRP) at UCLA, namely the Freshman Survey and Your First College Year (YFCY) survey, coupled with data collected via the National Survey of

Student Engagement (NSSE) out of the Center for Postsecondary Research at Indiana University provide a comprehensive portrait of the first-year experience at four-year institutions nationally. Responses to the partner instrument to the NSSE for two-year institutions, the Community College Survey of Student Engagement (CCSSE), provide insight into the transition experiences of those students who are attending two-year institutions for their first-year of college. Please see the chapter appendix for more specific information about these national student surveys and the samples used for the findings reported in this chapter.

Who Is Going to College?

The students who are currently entering into the educational process have been described as Millennials, Generation Y, Generation neXt, Boom Babies, and Echo Boom (Daniel, Evans & Scott, 2001; Howe & Strauss, 2000; Levine & Cureton, 1998; Newton, 2000). Indeed, they represent a new breed of students with more racial, ethnic, and cultural diversity; higher expectations of their own skills and abilities; and more educated and involved parents than ever before (Astin, Oseguera, Sax, & Korn, 2002; Howe & Strauss; NCES, 2005; U.S. Census Bureau, 2005). Generational perspectives, subjective observations, and impressions from popular culture offer a provocative stimulus for discussions about the characteristics, interests, and needs of today's undergraduates. When combined with the substantial empirical information on new students, we find a considerable mass of data on first-year college students of the new millennium.

Demographic Composition of College Enrollments

Age of Entering College Students

Many more students than ever before are entering college. U.S. Census Bureau (2005) data show that there has been continued growth in the general population between the ages of 18 and 24 since 1993. As such, higher education is experiencing the entry of increasingly larger cohorts of traditionally aged college students, while the percentage of entering college students over the age of 25 has remained relatively constant over the past 25 years, representing approximately one third of all college students. Although older undergraduates are more likely to be enrolled in community colleges, a significant proportion of the student population at two-year institutions is also of traditional age (Horn, Peter, & Rooney, 2002). Since these enrollment trends are expected to continue well into the next decade, higher education advisors must be prepared to serve the needs of a growing number of traditionally aged students in the coming years.

Gender

One of the largest shifts in higher education is taking place with respect to gender. According to more than 35 years of trends data collected via the CIRP Freshman Survey (Astin et al., 2002; Sax et al., 2004), the proportion of female incoming students has grown from less than half in 1971 to approximately 55% of new students nationwide today. In an extension of these trends, women are expected to continue to outpace men in enrollments and outnumber them on college campuses such that gender differences on two- and four-year colleges and universities across the country will favor women by nearly 2.8 million students by 2013 (NCES, 2005; U.S. Census Bureau, 2005).

Also according to CIRP trends data, college-going women have experienced gains in educational aspirations as well as representation. Although fewer than half of women expressed an interest in pursuing a graduate degree in 1966, three quarters of female first-year students aspire to such degrees today. First-year men experienced much smaller gains in their educational aspirations during this time and actually become *less* interested in pursuing medical and law degrees (Astin et al., 2002). As such, we may see the "feminization" of several historically male academic disciplines as first-year men migrate out of pre-law and pre-med majors and women move into these fields of study.

These trends indicate that women in the current cohorts of incoming students may express educational interests and require academic guidance in ways that their predecessors did not. Further, female students' aspirations for graduate school may need to be supported from the beginning of their undergraduate experience in order for them to turn into reality and for women to make greater strides in graduate school enrollment overall.

Racial, Ethnic, and Cultural Composition

We also see increasing racial and ethnic diversification of the collegiate student body nationally. Although the majority of the college-going population at four-year institutions is still White/Caucasian, new NCES (2005) data indicate that nearly 30% of undergraduates attending college today are members of minority groups as opposed to 1971 when CIRP data showed that students of color represented less than 10% of first-year students (Astin et al., 2002). Most notably, non-white Hispanic[1] students experienced the largest gains of the various ethnic groups over the past decade while African American and Asian students experienced more modest increases during that same time period and currently represent 10%, 13%, and 7% of the college student population, respectively (U.S. Census Bureau, 2005). Given that the overall trend of racial/ethnic diversification is expected to persist, campus personnel must continue to work toward shaping a truly multicultural college environment that facilitates diversity experiences for all students. However, it is important to acknowledge variation in these statistics by region of the country, especially in the western United States where minority students are rapidly becoming the majority, and by institutional type, particularly in two-year colleges where minority students still make up a larger percentage of the student population than at baccalaureate-granting institutions (NCES, 2005).

Beyond the issue of racial/ethnic categorization, it is interesting to note that students are increasingly from multicultural home environments than in previous years. For example, in 2003, 22% of all college students were from families in which at least one parent was born outside of the United States (U.S. Census Bureau, 2005), and the percentage of students in elementary and secondary schools who speak a language other than English at home had increased by 10 percentage points in 25 years (NCES, 2005). As such, it is critical that higher education professionals consider issues such as multiple language acquisition or English as a second language as well as cultural norms and expectations that are present in home environments, which can have important implications for some students' assimilation into higher education and achievement in college.

Economic and Cultural Capital

According to CIRP Freshman Survey data, the percent of students who enter four-year colleges and universities with "major" financial concerns increased from 8% in 1966 to a high of 19% in the mid-1990s and currently hovers at approximately 15% (Astin et al., 2002; Sax et al., 2004). Since many students chose to attend two-year colleges for financial reasons, the CIRP statistics on students at four-year institutions are only a conservative estimate of financial concern among the college-going population at large.

The implications of these data are fully apparent when one considers the significant differences in college matriculation rates among low-, middle-, and upper-income students. Of particular importance is the fact that low-income students suffer a disadvantage at every point in the pipeline of higher education. More specifically, they attend college at much lower rates than those students with high incomes, their enrollment appears to be increasingly concentrated at two-year institutions, and they graduate at much lower rates than their high income peers (Choy, 2002; Gladieux & Swail, 1998).

While financial resources often are a critical component of college student success, the cultural capital gained from previous generations' college attendance also represents an important resource to the college-going population. Recent NCES (2001) data show that students whose parents did not go to college make up a growing proportion of the undergraduate population. These data also indicate that first-generation students generally report lower educational expectations, are less prepared academically, and receive less support from their families in planning and preparing for college than their peers whose parents attended college (NCES, 2001). First-generation students are more likely to enter higher education through the community college sector. However, students entering baccalaureate-granting institutions show that the educational achievement of these students' parents has increased during the past three decades. This is particularly true of these students' mothers whose own academic and professional achievements have significantly narrowed the gap in educational levels between fathers and mothers and placed them in higher status professions (Astin et al., 2002).

These findings suggest that students from lower socioeconomic backgrounds may be especially at risk and in need of additional guidance from peers, faculty, and staff to navigate an already challenging transition to college. Similarly, first-generation status may also alert academic advisors to a sub-set of the entering student population who may need more specific attention or interventions, particularly at community colleges. However, it should also be noted that the increasing educational levels of the parents of students in four-year colleges and universities can generate high familial expectations and involvement in the students' transition to college. Managing the pressures generated by educated parents may require advisement, albeit of a different nature, for non-first generation students as well.

Educational Characteristics of Entering College Students

In addition to the increased diversity of students' personal background, there have also been significant shifts in the educational background of today's entering first-year students, including intellectual preparation, interests, and engagement.

Pre-College Academic Engagement and Performance

One of the most sustained and dramatic changes among entering college students over time is in their level of academic engagement in high school. Perhaps it would be more accurate to reference this trend with respect to *disengagement* since aggregate responses to several measures on the CIRP Freshman Survey indicate that first-year students who are entering four-year colleges and universities appear to have been less academically engaged in high school than ever before (Sax et al., 2004). For example, just under two thirds of students nationally indicated that they had frequently or occasionally come late to class during their last year in high school. Similarly, more than 40% of students also report feeling frequently "bored in class" during their senior year in high school. Further, those who report that they "overslept and missed class or an appointment" in high school has increased from 20% in 1968 to approximately one third of all students currently entering four-year colleges and universities (Astin et al., 2002; Sax et al., 2004).

Students entering four-year institutions today also report spending less time on their studies in high school than previous cohorts of new students. As shown in Figure 1, only one third of entering college students report studying or doing homework six or more hours per week as seniors in high school. Despite the reduction in time devoted to schoolwork, high school grades continue to soar. In the late 1960s, just less than 20% of entering first-year students reported average grades of A while approximately 23% reported average grades of C or lower; today, A grades outnumber C or lower grades by a ratio of more than eight to one (Astin et al., 2002; Sax et al., 2004). In further corroboration of these CIRP Freshman Survey trends, more than half of respondents (55%) to the High School Survey of Student Engagement (HSSSE) reported they devote a total of three hours or less per week to preparing for all of their classes and that they do not have to work very hard to earn good grades (Getting Students Ready for College, 2005). Since there is no evidence that students today are actually achieving at higher levels than those in the past, this increase in grades may actually reflect grade inflation. In fact, national indicators suggest that, generally, the level of achievement is down, and the 2001 national survey of college faculty conducted by the Higher Education Research Institute shows that only one third of college professors nationwide believe that their students are well prepared academically (Lindholm, Astin, Sax, & Korn, 2002).

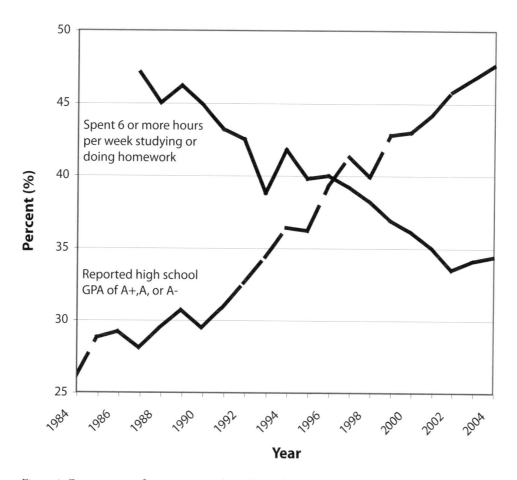

Figure 1. Convergence of time spent studying/doing homework and academic achievement.
Source. Astin et al., 2002; Sax et al., 2002; 2003; 2004.

One of the implications of the combination of high grades and low levels of engagement in high school is that these unproductive academic and behavioral patterns established in elementary and secondary school often persist through the college years. Even more importantly, they can have a profound influence on what students think is expected of them in college (Kuh, 2005) and perceptions of their own academic skills. For example, CIRP Freshman Survey trends show that students are increasingly optimistic about their chances for success in college and have record high levels of academic self-confidence. More specifically, nearly 60% of today's entering students expect to earn at least a B average in college, compared with only one third of the cohort from 1972 when this survey question was first introduced. In addition, more than 20% also expect to graduate from college with academic honors.

While optimism is certainly a good thing, there is concern that students are entering college with an inflated sense of their ability to earn good grades and therefore will put less effort into their studies but still expect to earn the kind of grade point averages that they received in high school. Also important to consider is the disillusionment and discouragement that may result from unmet expectations, especially because many of today's students may not realize that their expectations for academic achievement relative to their skills and/or work habits are, indeed, unrealistic. These statistics suggest that one pressing challenge for academic advisors is to help students redefine what it means to be a "good student" and gain a realistic understanding of what it will take to succeed in college as opposed to high school standards.

Field of Study

In addition to the gender migration in and out of specific fields of study that we mentioned earlier, first-year students overall are also considering different majors and career fields than they have in the past. Most recently, entering college students have shown a slightly increased interest in educational programs and careers in health/medicine and in teaching (Sax et al., 2004) with a decrease seen in majors such as business and engineering. This is particularly interesting given that comparative analyses of the academic performance of 12th graders nationally conducted by the National Assessment of Education Progress (NAEP) show that current cohorts of entering college students are better prepared than their predecessors with respect to mathematics, a pre-requisite for many of the majors (NCES, 2005). Similarly, interest in more traditional liberal arts majors (e.g., English, mathematics, social sciences, and history) has been generally declining. As such, academic advisors may need to help students gain an appreciation for the humanities and liberal arts and understand the function and relevance of the elements of the general education curriculum related to liberal arts education.

What Is the Transition Experience of First-Year Students?

Entry into college is one of most important developmental transitions in students' lives. This fact becomes even more significant when one considers that the majority of entering students at four-year colleges and universities are 18-24 years old, which represents a particularly important phase of students' lives with respect to their intellectual, moral, and identity development (Evans, Forney, & Guido-DiBrito, 1998; Upcraft, 1989). Further, since more than 75% of students attending four-year colleges and universities plan to live in campus housing (Sax et al., 2004), it also represents the first time that many of them will live away from home. Students attending two-year colleges face their own challenges. Almost 60% of these students report that they work in excess of 20 hours per week, and more than one third spend 11 hours or more a week caring for dependents, thus making it difficult to balance college, work, and family commitments (Community College Survey of Student Engagement, 2005). In addition, many students in both the two- and four-year sectors are entering college marginally prepared, while others are going to school while working full-time jobs, and many have little understanding of what it takes to succeed in college. However, regardless of their personal background or individual experiences prior to college, all of them will go through the process of adjustment to their new lives as college students.

Personal Challenges in the First Year

Perhaps not surprising in such a significant time of flux, many students experience challenges in their transition to college. The nature and outcome of these trials has important implications for students' emotional well-being, feelings about campus community, satisfaction with college, academic performance and success, and, ultimately, their persistence to the second year and beyond. Since campus personnel, including academic advisors, serve as a critical resource to help students overcome these obstacles, it is important to understand as much as we can about the specific nature of students' concerns and challenges.

Financial Concerns

Since the mid-1980s, increases in tuition and fees have exceeded inflation and growth in median family income. At the same time, less financial aid comes in the form of grants, and more students and their parents are securing loans to cover college costs (College Board, 2003; King & Bannon, 2002). Since students and their parents are paying a larger portion of the costs of college and the costs are greater, it is not surprising that financial concerns topped the list of first-year student challenges. Data from the 2004 national administration of YFCY indicate that more than two thirds of new students at four-year colleges and universities have at least some concerns about their ability to pay their college expenses, including nearly 20% who report that were "not sure they will have the funds to complete college." To address this concern, 29% of these first-year students have an on-campus job, 24% maintain employment off campus, and slightly more than 5% work for pay both on and off campus. Student employment is a fiscal necessity for many entering college students and can be structured so that it is a meaningful component of a successful learning experience (Astin, 1993; Pascarella & Terenzini, 1991), but we must also face the potentially negative impact it may have on first-year students. At a time when important academic and personal patterns are being formed (Schilling & Schilling, 1999, 2005), more than 20% of students report that their job responsibilities interfere with their coursework at least occasionally.

Social Integration

While it is secondary to the issue of finances, students also express concern with respect to integrating into the social fabric of the campus. Nearly half of respondents to the 2004 YFCY indicate that they feel lonely or homesick at least occasionally and just fewer than 40% feel worried about meeting new people on an occasional or frequent basis. These findings may represent expected responses of a primarily residential student population at four-year colleges who are adjusting to a new institutional environment. However, a more concerning statistic is that one third of these students regularly feel isolated from campus life. This statistic is particularly troubling when one considers that many theories of student development, adjustment, and retention highlight involvement, integration, and engagement as critical component of student success (e.g., Astin, 1984; Kuh, 2005; Pascarella & Terenzini, 1991, 2005; Tinto, 1993).

For a small contingent of new students, the issue of balancing familial ties and obligations with their new life as college students further complicates social integration into campus life. This can prove to be an important element of their first-year experience and one that needs to be considered in their academic planning and success. According to the 2004 YFCY, approximately one third of students entering four-year colleges at least occasionally feel the need to "break away from their family in order to succeed in college." More than 17% of YFCY respondents feel that their family responsibilities "interfered with their coursework" at least occasionally during the first college year. However, since fewer than 10% of these same students report devoting three or more hours per week to household or childcare duties, YFCY data suggest that these family demands are more complex in nature. Not surprisingly, these statistics are much larger for commuter students than they are for those who live on campus (Keup & Stolzenberg, 2004).

Pre-College Expectations Versus the Reality of the First Year

In addition to facing financial, social, familial, and personal challenges upon entry to college, students must also face how the reality of the first year lives up to the expectations that they had formed about college, particularly with respect to their academic success. Expectations play an important role in the experience of new students because they serve as a filter through which students evaluate and make sense of the information they are presented, and also shape subsequent behaviors and experiences (Feldman, 1981). From the perspective of the institution, expectations provide clues about how students will interact with peers and faculty members, behaviors that directly affect achievement and satisfaction with college. For example, if a new student does not expect to talk with a faculty member or advisor about career plans or take part in study abroad programs, chances are that opportunities to pursue these activities will be overlooked. In sum, expectations influence the types of opportunities students pursue and, thus, are an important factor in shaping student success in the first year of college.

The longitudinal data collected via the 2003 CIRP Freshman Survey and 2004 YFCY indicate that students at baccalaureate-granting institutions generally reported very high expectations for the college environment. However these analyses also identify specific areas where entering college students overestimate college experiences. For example, 97% of first-year students in the 2004 YFCY sample predicted that there was at least "some chance" that they would earn at least a B average in college. While an impressive proportion of the sample actually achieve at this level during the first year (i.e., 79%), 18% of these students do not perform to their own standards and are likely disappointed by this outcome. Drawing from the College Student Expectations Questionnaire (CSXQ) and the College Student Experiences Questionnaire (CSEQ) to conduct similar comparisons, Kuh (2005) reports that a wide gap exists in terms of the degree to which students expect to partake in educationally productive activities and their actual use of campus academic support services, such as writing centers, and their contributions to class discussions in the first year.

Comparisons between CIRP Freshman Survey and YFCY data also show that involvement in cocurricular activities during the first-year tend to be far lower than students' initial expectations. In particular, there are disparities of approximately 15 percentage points between expected levels of involvement and actual participation in varsity athletics and volunteer work. Further, greater than 20 percentage-point differences are noted for comparisons of expectations and first-year engagement in fraternities and sororities, participation in student clubs and groups, and student employment. While students are far less engaged than they expected in these more formal cocurricular pursuits, the first-year experience does live up to their expectations with respect to informal socializing, including developing close friendships and cross cultural/racial interactions.

Overall, these findings suggest that students' expectations generally exceed the reality of their experience during the first year of college. Since student satisfaction with college and their overall success appear to be influenced by the extent to which their expectations for campus life correspond with what they experience early on (Braxton, Hossler, & Vesper, 1997), information about student expectations provide valuable feedback for campus personnel to consider when creating first-year programming, policies, and interventions. As such, it appears that a priority of first-year support systems should be to help new students cope with the reality of a potentially challenging transition experience in light of their unrealistically high expectations and help them find opportunities to meet their expectations in the second year and beyond (Keup & Stolzenberg, 2004).

Health and Well-Being

Perhaps as a result of coping with these challenges, first-year students are also facing significant issues related to their physical and, particularly, emotional well-being. As CIRP trends show, students' self-ratings of their emotional health and self-understanding are at all time lows (Astin et al., 2002). However, 2003 CIRP Freshman Survey and the 2004 YFCY data reveal that while approximately one quarter of all students frequently feel overwhelmed as seniors in high school, this statistic swells to 40% during the first year of college for students at four-year institutions. In addition, 12% of students frequently feel depressed during their first year of college, an increase of five percentage points from self-reports of high school experiences with depression. Further, students are engaging in stress reducing and leisure activities (e.g., exercising and sports, reading for pleasure) less often and drinking and partying more regularly during the first year of college than they did in high school. These decisions may help at least partially explain why students' self-ratings of their physical health experience a slight decline during the first year of college and approximately one quarter shared that they at least occasionally worried about their health. Overall, these statistics suggest that the current population of incoming students may need additional guidance on how to make healthier life choices and about the utilization of campus services that are designed to support emotional and physical well-being during the transition to college.

Academic and Intellectual Experiences

Among the more important things institutions should know to provide a quality first-year experience and effective academic advising is what new students actually do in terms of their academic experiences during the first year and their levels of involvement in educationally purposeful activities. Extensive research indicates that good educational practices in the classroom and interactions with others, such as faculty and peers, are directly related to high-quality student outcomes (Kuh 2003, 2005; Pascarella & Terenzini, 2005). As such, information on these activities can then be used to help direct students' efforts and energy toward appropriate tasks and behaviors and to engage them in educationally purposeful activities at high levels.

Academic engagement and performance during the first year. First-year students' participation in course-related learning activities is important to understanding their level of academic engagement. Course-related learning activities include what students do in and outside of class, such as the time students spend preparing for class, the extent to which they prepare multiple drafts of a paper or assignment, and the frequency with which students work with peers inside and outside of class to prepare assignments. Table 1 illustrates some of the specific activities in which students are highly engaged and those that yield lower levels of involvement.

Table 1

Academic Engagement Among First-Year Students

At least half of all students reported that they engaged in the following activities "often" or "very often":

Worked on a paper/project that required integrating ideas or information from various sources

Used e-mail to communicate with an instructor

Asked questions or contributed to class discussions

Discussed ideas from readings or classes with others outside of class

Received prompt feedback from faculty members on academic performance

Included diverse perspectives in class discussions or writing assignments

---

At least one-third of students had no experience in the following activities:

Participated in a community-based project as part of a course

Worked with faculty members on activities other than coursework

Tutored or taught other students

Source. 2004 National Study of Student Engagement (NSSE); *N* = 85,000

Time on task is a key feature of effective educational practice (Chickering & Gamson, 1987). Quite simply, what students put into their education determines what they get out of it. The amount of time first-year students spend preparing for class, which includes studying, reading, writing, doing homework or lab work, analyzing data, rehearsing, and other academic activities, is a simple indicator of students level of academic engagement. Although conventional wisdom suggests that students should spend two hours outside of class for every one hour in class, the reality is that the majority of full-time, first-year students at four-year colleges and universities are spending less than half the recommended time, or about 13 hours or less a week on their course work. While CIRP Freshman Survey and YFCY data show that students spend significantly more time studying and doing homework the first year of college than they did as high school seniors, both YFCY and NSSE data show that fewer than 10% of full-time, first-year students dedicate the suggested number of hours per week to preparing for class. Filling the void of time dedicated toward studying and other academic activities, NSSE data show that full-time, first-year students spend an average of 12 hours a week relaxing and socializing (e.g., watching TV, partying), about 5 hours per week participating in cocurricular activities, between 3 to 5 hours per week in a job either on or off campus, about 4 hours a week commuting to class, and about the same amount of time caring for dependents. In total, these non-academic activities account for about 44 hours a week of students' time outside of class.

Community college students are spending even less time preparing for class, more time caring for dependents, and almost no time in college-sponsored activities. Among full-time students with fewer than 30 credit hours earned at community colleges, only 30% spend more than 10 hours per week preparing for class. About 80% of full-time community college students report no involvement in cocurricular activities and more than two thirds are spending between

1 to 5 hours a week commuting to and from classes (CCSSE, 2005). Combined, these data demonstrate that community college students are dedicating very little time to two important learning activities, studying and involvement in cocurricular learning experiences. Despite the real demands placed on community college students, considerable encouragement and support should be provided to help students realize the educational benefits of reallocating their time. Even small increases in time spent on these activities might greatly enrich the quality of students' learning in two-year institutions.

How students spend their time is also related to their class attendance patterns, the extent to which they report coming to class unprepared, and how often they turned in late or sub-par assignments. Specifically, NSSE data show that about 60% of first-year students acknowledge that they "sometimes" come to class unprepared, and YFCY data show that the same proportion of students regularly come late to class. CCSSE findings are similar, with about 57% of students at two-year institutions reporting that they "sometimes" come to class unprepared. In addition, over one third of 2004 YFCY respondents "frequently" or "occasionally" skip class and a similar proportion of first-year students at least occasionally turn in course assignments that, in their opinion, do not reflect their best work.

In addition to their individual choices, the amount of academic activity that represents collaborations with peers is less than optimal. Fewer than 40% of first-year students are frequently working in or outside class with peers on assignments at four-year institutions. CCSSE data indicate that although about 45% of students at community colleges report that they worked with peers during class, only 21% of students at two-year institutions report that they frequently work with other students outside of class to prepare class assignments. Furthermore, fewer than half of YFCY respondents state that they often participated in group discussions during class, just 16% report working on group projects on a frequent basis, and 12% indicate that their classes frequently included student evaluations of each other's work. These data show that most first-year students are having limited experiences with collaborative learning overall and suggest that it is particularly limited outside of the classroom. As such, students may need to be more actively encouraged to foster this element of their educational experience both inside and outside the classroom during the first year and beyond.

The gap between the amount of time students are advised to study and the actual time students spend both individually and collaboratively on course-related learning activities, combined with students' admissions about coming to class unprepared portrays a troubling image of time on task. Getting students to dedicate the time necessary preparing for class is a critical aspect of student success. Time devoted to preparing for class, cocurricular activities, and on-campus work, is positively related with other engagement items and self-reported educational and personal development growth. Furthermore, despite spending insufficient time studying according to faculty standards, a large majority of students feel at least somewhat successful adjusting to the academic demands of college, are earning good grades, and experience only very slight decreases in their GPA as compared to high school. This suggests that grades may not help motivate students to spend more time studying. Instead, students might need to be more purposefully guided by faculty and academic advisors to understand the relationship between time allocation and academic performance, educational gains, and future success.

Participation in enriching educational experiences and utilization of academic resources. Enriching educational experiences can be defined as learning opportunities inside and outside the classroom that augment the academic program. For example, internships, first-year seminars, service-learning, study abroad, and participation in a learning community represent such enriching first-year programs, resources, and experiences. Involvement in these complementary activities is positively associated with student learning and development.

Among the most common of these educational experiences for today's undergraduates is engagement in diversity activities and interactions. Given the recent demographic shifts in the pool of high school graduates, it is perhaps not surprising that the current cohort of entering college students are interacting with peers who are different from themselves more frequently than previous generations of students. In fact, the highest proportion of first-year student engagement in enriching activities is related to diversity experiences. Further, while many other areas of the college experience pale in comparison to students' pre-college expectations, students "socializing with someone of a different race or ethnicity" is one area where students' first-year experiences live up to their high expectations. Specifically, slightly more than 50% of first-year students report having had serious conversations with students who are very different from themselves, and with students of a different race or ethnicity, "often" or "very often." As such, it is important for academic advisors to build upon this momentum to engage in cross-cultural interaction and to continue to urge students to take part in diversity experiences in the college environment. Further, it is critical for institutional staff and administrators to help shape meaningful informal and formal opportunities for this type of interaction.

Although data on students' diversity experiences is positive, there are several other opportunities for enriching educational experiences that are woefully underused by our current population of first-year students. For example, while a majority of students who responded to the 2004 YFCY indicate that they participated in a first-year seminar, only very small percentages of first-year students enrolled in learning communities (7%) and honors courses (10%). Further, significant proportions of students at four-year colleges and universities admitted to having no experience with several support services at the university that would facilitate an enriching educational experience, including tutoring and other academic assistance (32%), programs offered by the career center (42%), and psychological counseling services (65%).

Among the most underused educational enrichment opportunities for first-year students are hands-on approaches to learning such as internships, community service, and study abroad programs. These enriching educational experiences provide unique opportunities for students to synthesize and apply their knowledge, which makes learning more meaningful and, ultimately, more useful because what students learn becomes a part of who they are (Kuh, 2003). As might be expected, NSSE data suggest that only small percentages of first-year students have the opportunity to participate in activities like internships (6%) and study abroad programs (2%), and data from the 2003 CIRP Freshman Survey and 2004 YFCY show a precipitous decline in students' participation in service activity from high school to college. However, NSSE and the CIRP Freshman Survey also assess first-year students' intent to participate in these activities. For example, approximately three quarters of 2004 YFCY respondents indicate that there is at least "some chance" that they will participate in volunteer or community service work. Further, data collected via the 2004 NSSE show that more than 75% of first-year students plan to take part in an internship or practicum and approximately 40% plan to study abroad during college.

These data indicate that students may be underusing important curricular and cocurricular opportunities for enriching educational experiences during the first year despite their intentions to take part in them during college. Therefore, it is critical for academic advisors to inform new students of opportunities for enriching educational experiences, capitalize on students' early interest in engaging in these activities, and encourage participation in these meaningful experiences in order to create a strong foundation of engaging practices for the remainder of the students' college career.

First-Year Support Networks and Resources

Students perform better and are more satisfied at institutions that cultivate positive working and social relationships among different groups on campus. More than 60% of first-year students perceive the quality of their relationship with peers as generally friendly and supportive. First-year students had slightly less positive views about the quality of their relationships with faculty and administrative personnel. About 50% of entering students find faculty members available, helpful, and sympathetic, while about 41% find administrative personnel and offices helpful, considerate, and flexible.

Given these student perceptions of support at the institutional level, it is important to ask to whom do students *actually* turn for support during this critical time of adjustment to college? According to several higher education researchers, fellow students are one of the most important influences on student outcomes in college (e.g., Astin, 1993; Pascarella & Terenzini, 1991, 2005). Data on first-year interpersonal interactions from the 2004 administration of YFCY reveal that friends are called upon to provide the most support. Nearly 95% of survey respondents feel at least somewhat successful developing close friendships with students and, as illustrated in Table 2, they are interacting with these peers more often than anyone else during the first year of college. More than 80% of respondents to the 2004 YFCY report that they communicate in person, via phone, or electronically with close friends at their institution on a daily basis. These data also show that some students also are relying on the support of peers who do not attend their same college; approximately one third of 2004 YFCY respondents report daily interaction with friends at other institutions. Finally, while more than 60% of YFCY respondents attend colleges greater than 50 miles from their homes, more than one third of students report daily interactions with members of their family.

In addition to interactions with their peers and family, regular contact with faculty is an important factor in student success (Astin, 1993; Kuh, 2003; Pascarella & Terenzini, 2005), particularly when one considers that many college professors serve as formal or informal advisors to first-year students. Although new students are typically encouraged to get to know members

Table 2

Interpersonal Interactions of First-Year College Students

Percent of first-year students who interacted at least monthly with:	
Faculty during class or office hours	53.5
Other college personnel	41.7
Faculty outside of class or office hours	39.7
Academic advisors	28.8
Percent of first-year students who interacted daily with:	
Close friends at this institution	81.9
Close friends not at this institution	37.4
Family	34.9

Source. 2004 Your First College Year (YFCY) Survey; N = 30,547

of the faculty, interact with them in and outside class, and visit during office hours to discuss assignments and seek feedback on their academic performance, few first-year students are realizing the full potential of faculty-student interactions. Slightly more than half indicate that they communicate with faculty during class or office hours at least monthly and nearly 40% report similar interaction with professors outside of class or office hours (Keup & Stolzenberg, 2004).

Data collected by the 2004 National Survey of Student Engagement (NSSE) illustrate the types of interactions that students are having with faculty. For example, about half of first-year students report that they "often" or "very often" discuss grades and assignments with their instructors. However, fewer than 15% of first-year students report that they discuss ideas from readings or classes with faculty members outside class, and fewer than one eighth report working with faculty on activities other than coursework (e.g., committees, orientation, student life activities). Although 56% of first-year students report receiving prompt feedback from faculty on their academic performance, this number could be higher since timely and apt feedback is so critical to setting expectations, informing students when they need to seek assistance, and helping them improve. NSSE and CCSSE results on these indicators of student-faculty interaction are comparable, with community college students reporting only slightly less involvement with instructors on activities outside of class. Other statistics raise the question about the quality of these interactions, including the fact that only 22% of the 2004 YFCY sample felt completely successful getting to know faculty during the first year, 17% of these students felt unsuccessful in this area, and more than one quarter of YFCY respondents at least occasionally felt intimidated by their professors.

As shown in Table 2, regular contact with academic advisors is even less common. While nearly all of the 2004 YFCY survey respondents indicate that they used academic advising at least once a term, just under half of the students completing the 2004 NSSE report that they even "sometimes" talk about career plans with a faculty member or advisor and less than 30% of the 2004 YFCY sample interact with their advisors even on a monthly basis. While more than 60% of students at community colleges report that advising services are very important to them, more than 35% report that they rarely or never use academic advising or planning services (CCSSE, 2005). Part-time students at two-year colleges report even less use of these campus services. While these data reveal institutional variation, it remains a challenge for advising personnel at all colleges to encourage more students to take part in this positive educational experience and reap the corresponding benefits of a quality advising relationship.

Although infrequent, nearly two thirds of students responding to the YFCY indicate that they are satisfied with academic advising services, and one third report that these interactions provide guidance about their educational program at least occasionally. Conversely, of the proportion of students at two-year colleges who took advantage of advising services, only a quarter indicate that they are very satisfied (CCSSE, 2005). The *quality* of academic advising is one of the strongest influences on students' perceptions of institutional support, and their level of interaction with faculty members and overall satisfaction with their college experience are the most powerful predictors of satisfaction with the college environment. As a result, these statistics provide important feedback for campus educators. For example, the gaps between utilization and satisfaction, point to a key opportunity for intervention for advisors at community colleges. Given the percentage of students at two-year institutions who expect to transfer to a four-year institution, it is essential that these students have more satisfactory and productive interactions with advisors.

Implications for Academic Advising

The national picture of incoming cohorts of college students has important implications for advisors. Overall, these data offer valuable feedback to academic advisors about the previous experiences and present needs of new college students. The more advisors take into consideration what is known about the characteristics, expectations, and behaviors of first-year students the more effective they will be in encouraging students to take advantage of the activities that contribute to learning and development.

First, student demographic characteristics, national survey data, and assessments of the skills and expectations students bring to the college campus should inform advising practice. Demographic and pre-college information about students can be used to paint a portrait of the incoming class, and more importantly, to identify specific student needs and areas for intervention by advisors. Advisors should know where their students are from, their preferred learning styles, their talents, and when and where they need help. Institutions and advisors need to take advantage of the wealth of information available about students at a national and institutional level and use this information to meet students where they are, help them develop high expectations for their performance, and appreciate the skills and behaviors necessary for academic success in college.

Second, given what is known about the range of expectations students bring into college, advisors may need to assess the degree to which they are equipped to help students cope with potentially unmet expectations, understand the academic challenges of college, and provide students with the resources to manage multiple demands upon their time and sources of stress. Academic advisors might team up with faculty teaching first-year seminars and counselors to provide more integrated support for new students. In addition, given that first-year students already rely heavily upon the support of peers, academic advisors also may want to partner with upper-class peer mentors as part of the support structure that they offer new students.

Third, to make progress towards realizing the view of advising as teaching, advisors need to fully acknowledge their role in educating students about what it takes to succeed in college. Advisors can use national findings and institutional data to demonstrate to students the relationship between dedicating more time to academic work and enriching educational experiences, intellectual gains and cognitive development, and future success. As such, advisors have the potential to challenge students about the time they spend on academic work, ask questions about their levels of involvement in educational purposeful activities and make suggestions. They can help establish high but attainable expectations for students and make explicit what students need to know and do to be successful.

Finally, academic advisors are encouraged to work with their institutional research offices to gain access to data about the student experience. Knowing students pre-college experiences, and more importantly, where the college experience falls short of what students need in terms of their participation in enriching experiences and time on task, can suggest a course of action for advising. Armed with these data, advisors become particularly effective at facilitating the persistence and success of first-year students to the second year and beyond.

Summary

These statistics drawn from national data are intended to help us better understand the pool of current undergraduates as well as the elements of their transition to college that are particularly salient to the educational experience fostered by academic advisors. While the broad scope of national data are informative, they do not replace a more specific understanding of the characteristics and experiences of students at particular institutions. As such, the content of this chapter is intended to help identify questions and topics to ground inquiry at the institutional level, provide a framework for assessment at respective campuses, and offer a context in which to understand the results of analyses using local information such as the data maintained by the admissions or registrar's offices, or drawn from institutional administrations of national surveys or home-grown assessment tools. In other words, the summary that follows is purely a starting point for advisors in their work with first-year students:

◇ Today's students are more racially, ethnically, and culturally diverse than previous generations. Further, larger percentages of students entering higher education today come from a multicultural home environment where English is a second language.

◇ The trend of more women entering higher education has continued. One significant correlate of greater representation of women in higher education has been an increased interest in graduate study among entering female college students, particularly in the previously male-dominated fields of law and medicine.

◇ Currently, larger numbers of traditional-aged, full-time, and first-generation students are entering colleges and universities across the country than ever before.

◇ Today's high school students are less academically engaged and spend less time on task than their predecessors, especially during senior year in high school. However, in spite of their academic disengagement in high school they receive higher grades, thereby creating unrealistic expectations for success in college among the pool of entering college students.

◇ There is evidence that students' patterns of academic disengagement are continuing through the first year of college, including limited time on task and low levels of experience with collaborative learning.

◇ Financial concerns top the list of challenges that current first-year students face in their transition to college. Perhaps related to this circumstance, more students in four-year institutions are pursuing employment as students than ever before and a high proportion of community college students work more than 20 hours a week. These levels of employment can have a profound impact on students' curricular and cocurricular engagement during the first year and their adjustment to college overall.

◇ Students are entering college with record low levels of emotional health and self-understanding, which continue to decline during the first year of college. Two potential correlates of this shift in emotional health are the fact that students (a) drink and party more frequently and (b) exercise less often and admit to low levels of physical health.

◇ Although there are a host of human resources available to entering students in their transition to college, first-year students most often turn to their peers for assistance, particularly at four-year institutions. As such, peers are one of most important influences for first-year students. Community college students report high levels of collaboration with peers in class, suggesting that instructor-directed group activities have greater significance for student learning at two-year colleges.

◇ Students are underusing some important programs and support services during the first year and are, therefore, missing out on some key educationally enriching experiences such as involvement in learning communities, internships, service-learning, and academic assistance programs.

◇ The quality of the academic advising experience is one of the most powerful predictors of engagement in and satisfaction with the college environment, yet first-year students report limited contact with faculty and academic advisors, report varying degrees of satisfaction with this interaction (particularly at community colleges), and thus may not be reaping all the educational benefits of advising.

Notes

[1]While the name for this racial category is often "Latino," the demographic data from this chapter are drawn from U.S. Census data, which uses the term "Hispanic." The original terminology was maintained in reporting these data.

References

Astin, A. W. (1984). Student involvement: A developmental theory for higher education. *Journal of College Student Personnel, 25*, 297-308.

Astin, A. W. (1993). *What matters in college? Four critical years revisited*. San Francisco: Jossey-Bass.

Astin, A. W., Oseguera, L., Sax, L. J., & Korn, W. S. (2002). *The American freshman: Thirty-five year trends*. Los Angeles: UCLA, Higher Education Research Institute.

Braxton, J., Hossler, D., & Vesper, N. (1995). Incorporating college choice constructs into Tinto's model of student departure: Fulfillment of expectations for institutional traits and student withdrawal plans. *Research in Higher Education, 36*(5), 595-612.

Chickering, A., & Gamson, Z. (1987). Seven principles' for good practice in undergraduate education. *AAHE Bulletin, 39*(7), 5-10.

Choy, S. (2002). *Access and persistence: Findings from ten years of longitudinal research on students*. Washington, DC: American Council on Education.

College Board. (2003). *Trends in student aid*. Washington, DC: Author.

Community College Survey of Student Engagement (CCSSE). (2005). *Engaging students, challenging the odds*. Austin, TX: The Community College Leadership Program, The University of Texas at Austin.

Daniel, B. V., Evans, S. G., & Scott, B. R. (2001). Understanding family involvement in the college experience today. In B. V. Daniel & B. R. Scott (Eds.), *Consumers, adversaries, and partners: Working with the families of undergraduates* (New Directions for Student Services, No. 94). San Francisco: Jossey-Bass.

Evans, N. J., Forney, D. S., & Guido-DiBrito, F. (1998). *Student development in college*. San Francisco: Jossey-Bass.

Feldman, D. C. (1981). The multiple socialization of organization members. *Academy of Management Review, 6*, 308-318.

Getting students ready for college: What student engagement data can tell us. (2005). The High School Survey of Student Engagement. School of Education, Indiana University Bloomington.

Gladieux, L. E., & Swail, W. S. (1998). Financial aid is not enough: Improving the odds of college success. *College Board Review, 185*, 16-21, 30-31.

Horn, L., Peter, K., & Rooney, K. (2002). *Profile of undergraduates in U.S. postsecondary institutions: 1999–2000* (NCES 2002–168). Washington, DC: National Center for Education Statistics, U.S. Department of Education, U.S. Government Printing Office.

Howe, N., & Strauss, W. (2000). *Millennials rising: The next great generation*. New York: Vintage Books.

Keup, J. R., & Stolzenberg, E. B. (2004). *The 2003 Your First College Year (YFCY) survey: Exploring the academic and personal experiences of first-year students* (Monograph No. 40). Columbia, SC: University of South Carolina, National Resource Center for The First-Year Experience and Students in Transition.

King, T., & Bannon, E. (2002) *The burden of borrowing: A report on the rising rates of student loan dept.* The State Public Interest Research Group Higher Education Project. Retrieved from http://www.pirg.org

Kuh, G. D. (2003). What we're learning about student engagement from NSSE. *Change, 35*(2), 24-32.

Kuh, G. D. (2005). Student engagement in the first year of college. In Upcraft, L. M., Gardner, J. N., & Barefoot, B. O. (Eds.), *Challenging and supporting the first-year student: A handbook for improving the first year of college* (pp. 86-107). San Francisco: Jossey-Bass.

Levine, A., & Cureton, J. S. (1998, May/June). Collegiate life: An obituary. *Change, 12-17,* 51.

Lindholm, J. A., Astin, A. W., Sax, L. J., & Korn, W .S. (2002). *The American college teacher: National norms for the 2001-02 HERI faculty survey.* Los Angeles: UCLA, Higher Education Research Institute.

National Center for Education Statistics (NCES). (2001). *Students whose parents did not go to college: Postsecondary access, persistence, and attainment.* Washington, DC: Author, U.S. Department of Education.

National Center for Education Statistics (NCES). (2005). *The condition of education, 2005.* Washington, DC: Author, Department of Education. Retrieved June 2, 2005, from http://www.nces.ed.gov//programs/coe

National Survey of Student Engagement (NSSE). (2001). *Improving the college experience: National benchmarks of effective educational practice.* Bloomington: Indiana University Center for Postsecondary Research.

Newton, F. B. (2000). The new student. *About Campus, 5*(5), 8-15.

Pascarella, E. T., & Terenzini, P. T. (1991). *How college affects students.* San Francisco: Jossey-Bass.

Pascarella, E. T., & Terenzini, P. T. (2005). *How college affects students: A third decade of research* (vol. 2). San Francisco: Jossey-Bass.

Sax, L. J., Astin, A. W., Lindholm, J. A., Korn, W. S., Saenz, V. B., & Mahoney, K. M. (2003). *The American freshman: National norms for fall 2003.* Los Angeles: UCLA, Higher Education Research Insititute.

Sax, L. J., Lindholm, J. A., Astin, A. W., Korn, W. S., & Mahoney, K. M. (2002). *The American freshman: National norms for fall 2002.* Los Angeles: UCLA, Higher Education Research Insititute.

Sax, L. J., Hurtado, S., Lindholm, J. A., Astin, A. W., Korn, W. S., & Mahoney, K. M. (2004). *The American freshman: National norms for fall 2004.* Los Angeles: UCLA, Higher Education Research Institute.

Schilling, K. M., & Schilling, K. L. (1999). Increasing expectation for student effort. *About Campus, 4*(2), 4-10.

Schilling, K. M., & Schilling, K. L. (2005). Expectations and performance. In M. L. Upcraft, J. N. Gardner, B. O. Barefoot, & Associates, *Challenging and supporting the first-year student: A handbook for improving the first year of college* (pp. 108-120). San Francisco: Jossey-Bass.

Tinto, V. (1993). *Leaving college: Rethinking the causes and cures of student attrition* (2nd ed.). San Francisco: Jossey-Bass.

Upcraft, M. L. (1989). Understanding student development: Insights from theory. In M .L. Upcraft, J .N. Gardner, & Associates, *The freshman year experience* (pp. 40-52). San Francisco: Jossey-Bass.

U.S. Census Bureau. (2005). *School enrollment—Social and economic characteristics of students: October, 2003.* Washington, DC: U.S. Department of Commerce.

Appendix: Description of National Surveys and Student Samples

Cooperative Institutional Research Program (CIRP) Freshman Survey

Since 1966, the Cooperative Institutional Research Program (CIRP) has administered the Freshman Survey to profile the background characteristics, attitudes, values, educational achievements, expectations, and aspirations of new students entering colleges across the country. Although the principal purpose of the CIRP Freshman Survey is to conduct longitudinal studies of college students' development during the undergraduate years by means of follow-up surveys, the entering freshman surveys themselves have yielded an extremely interesting and informative portrait of the changing character of American college students. The trend data generated by these consecutive annual surveys not only reflect changes that directly affect higher education, but also can be viewed as indicators of how our society is changing (Astin et al., 2002).

The CIRP trends data reported in this chapter represent the weighted responses of hundreds of thousands of students entering between 200 and 400 baccalaureate-granting institutions nationwide each year. The perspectives of entering college students in this chapter are drawn from the weighted responses of more than 275,000 students to the 2003 administration of the Freshman Survey at 413 four-year colleges and universities nationally. Additional information on the CIRP Freshman Survey is available at http://www.gseis.ucla.edu/heri/freshman.html

Your First College Year (YFCY) Survey

Developed in collaboration with the Policy Center on the First Year of College, YFCY is administered through the Cooperative Institutional Research Program (CIRP) at UCLA. While it may be used as a stand-alone instrument, YFCY was designed as a follow-up to the CIRP Freshman Survey, thereby enabling institutions to identify features of the first year that encourage student learning, involvement, satisfaction, retention, and success. As a longitudinal follow-up, YFCY provides an assessment of the academic and personal development of students over the first year of college. The YFCY data reported in this chapter are based upon the responses from approximately 32,000 students who completed the instrument in spring 2004. Longitudinal findings regarding student change and development since entering college are derived from more than 21,000 students who completed both the 2003 CIRP Freshman Survey and 2004 YFCY. While these data are not nationally representative, they include students from all four-year institutional types, controls, and selectivity levels as well as a wide range of institutional sizes to provide an informative portrait of the first-year experience at large. More information about YFCY can be found at http://www.gseis.ucla.edu/heri/yfcy

National Survey of Student Engagement (NSSE)

The National Survey of Student Engagement (NSSE) is designed to obtain, on an annual basis, information from four-year colleges and universities nationwide about student participation in programs and activities that institutions provide for their learning and personal development. The results provide an estimate of how undergraduates spend their time and what they gain from attending college. Survey items represent empirically confirmed "good practices" in undergraduate education. That is, they reflect behaviors by students and institutions that are associated with desired outcomes of college. The NSSE data reported in this chapter are based on responses from more than 85,000 randomly sampled first-year undergraduate students who completed the instrument in 2004 at more than 480 four-year colleges and universities. This data offers a national picture of the quality of first-year students experience in undergraduate education. More information about NSSE can be found at www.nsse.iub.edu

Community College Student of Student Engagement (CCSSE)

Similar to NSSE, the CCSSE provides information on student engagement, a key indicator of learning and, therefore, of the quality of community colleges. CCSSE asks questions that assess institutional practices and student behaviors that are correlated highly with student learning and student retention. Although major objectives of the NSSE and CCSSE are similar, there are important differences in the sampling and survey administration procedures. CCSSE was administered in spring 2005 during class sessions at CCSSE member colleges. Data reported in this chapter are from about 136,000 students, with fewer than 30 credit hours completed, from more than 257 community colleges. More information about CCSSE can be found at www.ccsse.org

Section Two

Comprehensive Approaches to Academic Advising

Chapter Three

The Power of Personalized Learning Patterns in Academic Advising

Christine Johnston and Betsy McCalla-Wriggins

The goal of both advising and teaching is to support students as they learn. Defining what we want students to learn is often discussed in conversations on accountability, assessment, and learning outcomes. "We are all, as colleagues and educators, now accountable to students and society for identifying and achieving essential student learning outcomes and for making transformative education possible and accessible for all students" (Keeling, 2004, p.1).

If we are to look at learning as the goal of teaching through the advising process, then this question must be asked, "What is learning and how does learning occur?" For the purpose of this chapter, learning will be defined as "the ability of individuals to take in the world of stimuli which surrounds them, to make sense of it, and to respond to it in appropriate ways" (C. Johnston, personal communication, July 13, 2003).

By understanding how students learn, we can structure our interactions to help students make sense of the world around them, and significantly increase the opportunities for learning to occur. We can also empower them to take responsibility for their own learning which is fundamental to the development of intentional lifelong learners in the 21st century (AAC&U, 2002).

This chapter will discuss an advanced learning process, entitled aptly, the Let Me Learn Process, which identifies learning patterns. Practical suggestions of how advisors can use this process with first-year students will be described, and evidence will be presented to demonstrate the power of this advanced learning process. Finally, recommendations are presented about how to incorporate this process into initiatives for first-year college students.

An Advanced Learning Process

Students receive and act on information based on the combinations of their learning patterns. Below is an example of a common task for all students, registering for classes, described in four ways that reflect different learning patterns. Advisors should read through each version and identify which approach resonates with them.

One set of instructions explains registration in a step-by-step fashion, organizing and numbering all items that need to be completed. Another set of instructions explains the process in a very exact, specific, detailed manner. A third approach would have the advisor showing the student a web page with links to the Advisement Center and Registrar's page. Still another explanation would simply tell the student to follow the directions on the web to register. Each approach is equally valid, but students may prefer one method over another. When directions are offered in a less preferred manner, then there is a greater probability that students will begin the college experience with some degree of anxiety. Their reaction may be, "If I can't even understand how to register for classes, how will I ever be successful in a college-level course?"

Individuals usually present information in the manner in which they prefer to receive it. It is helpful to examine and reflect on how advising information is presented in first-year orientation programs, as well as in other first-year initiatives on campus. Which approach is most often used? Is that approach the one understood by most students? This chapter will present information that will assist advisors in finding the answers to these questions.

In the 90s, Johnston began exploring how to give students and educators information about their learning processes along with a common vocabulary so that they could communicate their learning experiences more effectively. In order to capture the degree to which individuals use their learning processes, Johnston and Dainton developed The Learning Connections Inventory (LCI), a 28-item Likert-style (from 1 never to 5 always) instrument that reports the degree to which individuals use each of the four learning patterns. Johnston and Dainton's (2005) development of the instrument (tested on 9,000 children and adults) revealed that each learner uses (a) sequence, (b) precision, (c) technical reasoning, and (d) confluence. The LCI reports the patterns as four different scale scores, each representing the degree to which a person uses a learning pattern first, as needed, or avoids its use altogether. If a person's learning pattern is at the "use-first" level, the individual responds instinctively and automatically. If scores are at the "as-needed" level, the individual uses these patterns when the situation calls for that particular approach. If the scores of a pattern are at the "avoid" level, this means that the individual does not naturally draw on this approach and normally feels some anxiety if those patterns of behavior are required for a task.

There is no genetic, gender, or cultural predisposition to any particular set of learning patterns. It is important to understand that working within each of the patterned processes are three distinct operations: (a) cognition (thinking), (b) conation (doing), and (c) affectation (feelings). For a complete explanation of this, refer to Johnston's *Unlocking the Will to Learn* (1996) and *Let Me Learn* (1998).

Learning Patterns

The following descriptions briefly explain the thinking, behaviors, and feelings associated with each of the patterns. However, this relatively simple bulleted list should not belie the complexity of the interaction of the patterned processes within the learner.

The *sequential pattern* is that aspect of learning that needs to follow step-by-step directions, organize and plan work carefully, and complete the assignment free from interruptions. At the use-first level, sequence involves the following thoughts, actions, and feelings:

◇ I want clear directions.
◇ I want time to do my work neatly.
◇ I like to do my work from beginning to end.
◇ I don't want to change direction after I have begun a project.
◇ I want to know if I am meeting the instructor's or my boss's or my teammates' expectations.

Learners who avoid sequence do not value directions, and neither plan nor live by a schedule. They also find following directions confusing and, maybe, even frustrating.

The *precise pattern* is that aspect of learning that needs to process detailed information carefully and accurately, take detailed notes, know exact answers, and write in a highly specific manner. Precise learners have the following thoughts, actions, and feelings:

◇ I want complete and thorough explanations.
◇ I ask a lot of questions.
◇ I like to answer questions.
◇ I need to be accurate and correct.
◇ I like many details.
◇ I like test results.
◇ I seek written documentation of my success.
◇ Words are my friends.

Students, who avoid precision, rarely read for pleasure and do not attend to details. Memorization for these students is tedious and a waste of time.

The *technical reasoning pattern* requires practical application and relevance to any learning task. It is the non-verbal process, which sees the mechanics of operations, the function of pieces, and needs to work hands on, unencumbered by paper-and-pencil requirements. The technical reasoning pattern is not reflective of the technology industry. It is that component of the learning pattern that seeks practical application, solves problems, and understands how mechanisms operate. Technical reasoning provides thoughts, actions, and feelings similar to those described below.

◇ I don't like to write things down.
◇ I need to see the purpose of what I am doing.
◇ I like to work by myself.
◇ I like to figure things out.
◇ I don't like to use a lot of words.
◇ I look for relevance and practically.
◇ If it's broken, I'll fix it.

Students who avoid technical reasoning do not take things apart to understand how they work; they hire others to do building and repair work. Problem-solving is done with others, not alone.

The *confluent pattern* of learning is that aspect that avoids conventional approaches, seeks unique ways to complete any learning task, begins work before all directions are given, takes risks, and allows for failure and starting again. The learning processes of confluence involve the following thoughts, actions, and feelings:

◇ I don't like doing the same thing over and over.
◇ I see situations very differently than others do.
◇ I like to do things my own way.
◇ I don't like following the rules.
◇ I enjoy using my imagination.

For students who avoid confluence, taking risks seems foolish and wasteful to them. They would rather not make mistakes than have to learn from them. They are more careful and cautious in making life decisions.

A more detailed chart that describes how learners think, feel, behave, and speak based on a use-first-and-avoid pattern is included in Tables 1 and 2.

Bridge learners are those who use all patterns as needed without a clear use-first level preference. They learn from listening to others and interacting with them. Sometimes, they feel like a jack of all trades and a master of none, but they also find they can blend in, pitch in, and help make things happen as a contributing member of any group. They lead from the middle by encouraging others rather than taking charge of a situation.

If three or more patterns are employed at the use-first level, the students are *strong-willed learners*. They prefer to work alone so that they can control the plan, the ideas, the talk, the decisions, the process, and the outcomes. They lead from out in front, and sometimes, others find it hard to follow their lead.

Tools to Support the Let-Me-Learn Process

Advisors may find that the students with whom they have the greatest rapport may very well have learning patterns similar to their own. Advisors should consider these additional questions: How do advisors communicate with their students, both verbally and in writing? What learning patterns do students use first? Are students in specific majors more likely to have certain learning patterns? What could happen when students select a major or area of study that draws on a learning pattern that they avoid? The Let-Me-Learn (LML) process provides tools to help advisors find the answers to the above questions.

Learning Connections Inventory

The Learning Connections Inventory (LCI) provides the most specific information on how advisors and their students process information through the four learning patterns. While the paper version of the LCI needs to be validated by trained staff, the online version self-validates and generates a report geared specifically to the individual. More specific information about the LCI is available at www.lcrinfo.com. However, advisors can begin to implement the concepts that support this process through other methods as well. For example, advisors can identify students' learning preferences from reviewing their class notes and by observing their behavior in a group. Responses to and types of questions asked (or not asked) in an advising session can also give some indication of their use-first patterns as well as what they avoid (see Tables 1 and 2). With this information, an advisor can change the way he or she responds to the student to be more effective. Advisors can also help students look at classroom assignments to determine what is being required by the instructor and then work with students to develop strategies so they can appropriately respond to those requirements.

Advising Strategies Using the LML Process

At the beginning of this chapter, four examples of directions that might be given to students about registration were listed. The different directions are read, heard, and understood through the different learning processes of your students. See Table 3 for suggestions on how to more effectively communicate with students in advising sessions based on their preferred learning style.

Table 1

Indicators of Students' Use-First Levels

How I think	How I do things	How I feel	What I might say
Sequential			
I organize information. I mentally categorize data. I break tasks down into steps.	I make lists. I organize. I plan first, then act.	I thrive on consistency and dependability. I need things to be tidy and organized. I feel frustrated when the game plan keeps changing. I feel frustrated when I'm rushed.	Could I see an example? I need more time to double-check my work. Could we review those directions? A place for everything and everything in its place. What are my priorities?
Precise			
I research information. I ask lots of questions. I always want to know more.	I challenge statements and ideas that I doubt. I prove I am right. I document my research and findings. I write things down.	I thrive on knowledge. I feel good when I am correct. I feel frustrated when incorrect information is accepted as valid. I feel frustrated when people do not share information.	I need more information. Let me write up the answer to that. I'm currently reading a book… Did you know that…? Actually…
Technical			
I seek concrete relevance–what does this mean in the real world? I only want as much information as I need–nothing extraneous. How does this work?	I get my hands on it. I tinker. I solve the problem. I do!	I enjoy knowing how things work. I feel self-sufficient. I feel frustrated when the task has no real-world relevance. I do not feel the need to share my thoughts.	I can do it myself! Let me show you how… I don't want to read a book about it, I want to do it! How can I fix this? I could use a little space…
Confluent			
I think outside the box. I brainstorm. I make obscure connections. Unique ideas.	I take risks. I am not afraid to fail. I try new things. I might start things and not finish them. I will start a task first, then ask for directions.	I enjoy improvisation. I feel comfortable with failure. I feel frustrated by people who are not open to new ideas. I feel frustrated by repetition.	Why do we have to do it that way? Can we try this? Let's bend the rules. I have an idea… I have another idea…

Table 2

Indicators of Students' Avoid Levels

How I think	How I do things	How I feel	What I might say
Sequential			
These directions make no sense! I did this before. Why repeat it? Why can't I just jump in?	Avoid direction; avoid practice. Can't get the pieces in order. Ignore table of contents, indexes, and syllabi. Leave the task incomplete.	Jumbled Scattered Out of synch Untethered/Unfettered Unanchored	Do I have to do it again? Why do I have to follow directions? Does it matter what we do first? Has anybody seen…?
Precise			
Do I have to read all of this? How am I going to remember all of this? Who cares about all this stuff?	Don't have specific answers. Avoid debate. Skim instead of read. Take few notes.	Overwhelmed when confronted with details. Fearful of looking stupid. Angry at not having the "one right answer!"	Don't expect me to know names and dates! Stop asking me so many questions! Does it matter? I'm not stupid!
Technical			
Why should I care how this works? Somebody has to help me figure this out! Why do I have to make something; why can't I just talk or write about it?	Avoid using tools or instruments. Talk about it instead of doing it. Rely on the directions to lead me to the solution.	Inept Fearful of breaking the object, tool, or instrument. Uncomfortable with tools; very comfortable with my words and thoughts.	If it is broken, throw it away! I'm an educated person; I should be able to do this! I don't care *how* it runs; I just want it to *run*!
Confluent			
Where is this headed? Where is the focus? What do you mean, imagine?	Don't take social risks. Complete one task at a time. Avoid improvising. Seek parameters.	Unsettled Chaotic No more change or surprises, please!	Let's stay focused! Where did that idea come from? Now what? This is out of control!

Table 3

Advising Strategies Using the Let-Me-Learn Process

For highly sequential students	For highly precise students	For highly technical students	For highly confluent students
Advisors can...			
Make sure that all directions are clearly stated step-by-step.	Make sure that directions contain detailed information.	Make sure that students understand the real-life consequences of not following up on the advisement tasks.	Anticipate that some students will avoid reading or following directions; help them to understand when it is optional or imperative for them to do so.
Provide a model or sample.	Provide additional references or URLs for independent information gathering.	When possible, demonstrate the practical application of the material provided.	Make sure that the student has opportunities for risk-taking.
Expect to repeat the directions more than once.	Anticipate requests for detailed information about directions.	Provide opportunities to learn and to be assessed through hands-on activities and/or problem solving.	Understand that some students will profit from making mistakes.
Allow adequate time for students to fill out forms.	Anticipate requests for detailed explanations of concepts, procedures, and narratives.	Anticipate that some students would prefer to figure out their career path and courses through trial and error.	Negotiate alternative ways for completing advisement tasks.
Remain on topic.	Expect to observe the student writing down everything that is said during the session.	Anticipate that some students will take minimal notes and will need coaching to meet your expectation for completing required paper work.	Anticipate that some students will have difficulty completing repetitive tasks.
Use numbered sequences when listing items in a sequential order	Expect to help students balance a compulsion to gather information against the requirements of meeting deadlines.	Be practical. Couch your questions so that they do not appear to be overly personal. Allow the student his/her personal space. Get to the point of the advisement session. Make the time worthwhile. The students need to leave the session with practical advice and insights.	Anticipate that some students will generate ideas and grasp the larger picture, but may be perceived as not pulling their own weight with the tedious parts of follow-up work and meeting deadlines.

Understanding Assignments

When students and faculty have similar learning patterns, students will understand the assignments and be able to complete them in ways that are acceptable to the instructor. However, this is not always the case. There may be times when students are stymied by an instructor's projects and find themselves frustrated because the assignment is unclear to them so that they have difficulty meeting the expectations of the instructor. Most importantly, not understanding a student's learning preference is not just a problem for the student. The following comments reflect this situation. Students say, "Dr. X is a lousy teacher/ advisor. I just cannot understand what he wants or expects me to do." Instructors/advisors would comment about the same students, "They just don't get it. No matter how I try to explain it, they're just not working hard enough or putting enough effort into completing the assignment or gathering more information as I have directed." Before learning about the advanced learning process, one specific instructor used these words to describe students who had learning patterns different from his:

> I used to think some students were just dense, uninterested, or at the very least unmotivated. I judged students who didn't ask questions as less academic. I thought students who did assignments in a unique way were the brightest. I couldn't have been more wrong. Now, I know they simply learn differently than I do. (D. Stoll, personal communication, November 16, 2005)

Rather than be frustrated, a useful tool for advisors is the word wall (Table 4). It assists advisors in communicating more effectively with students based on the students' learning preferences.

Table 4
Word Wall

Sequential cue words		Precise cue words	
alphabetize	order	accurate	explain
arrange	organize	calibrate	facts
classify	outline	certainty	identify
develop	plan	describe	label
distribute	put in order	detail	measure
group	sequence	document	observe
in a series	show a sample	exact	specific
list	show an array	examine	write
Technical cue words		**Confluent cue words**	
assemble	erect	brainstorm	improvise
autonomy	experience	carefree	incredible
build	figure out	create	independent
concrete	illustrate	different	invent
construct	just do it	dream up	risk
demonstrate	make	far-fetched	take a chance
draw	problem-solve	ideas	unique
engineer	tools	imagine	unusual

Advisors can also use the word wall to help students identify the patterns reflected in the assignment given in any class. When students understand their personal learning processes, they can direct their patterns in such a way to be able to take specific action. Using the knowledge of learning patterns and cue words (as seen in the word wall), students can decode assignments, objectives, or the task at hand. They can look for key words within a set of directions and engage specific patterns (i.e., sequential, precise, technical, or confluent) to accomplish the task.

For example, if the task is to "write in bulleted form a brief technical description of the newly developed circuitry board," sequential learners may only see the word "write" and reject the entire assignment because they are not precise learners. But, if they overcome the initial rejection and translate the assignment into sequential cue words (i.e., substituting the word "write" with "list," then they will succeed.

Using Patterns With Intention

Sometimes, assignments may require students to use a pattern they avoid or a pattern that is not their primary one. Table 5 gives advisors and students specific strategies to use when an assignment or project calls for a learning pattern that students avoid. These are called forge strategies (Table 5). For example, if I avoid any pattern, I may need to forge (pull up) its use. Table 6 identifies strategies when a pattern is not called for in an activity and the advisor and/or student need to tether (pull back) their primary pattern. For example, when I use a pattern first in a situation that does not call for it, I may need to tether (pull back) its use. Sometimes, if I use a pattern as needed, I may need to intensify (turn it up a little) its use.

A good example of the effects of personalized strategies used by students aware of their learning processes comes from a conversation overheard between two students who were discussing the challenges of their organic chemistry class. One student said there was no way he could understand the text.

He said, "I'd start to read and the words would just swim in front of my face. I thought 'What is this guy talking about?'"

The second student responded, "Oh, I loved the text. It saved my life! I don't know what I would have done if I hadn't been able to read and re-read his lecture. But that kit we had to buy. Now that was useless."

"Useless?" the first student responded, "That saved my life! When I couldn't understand a word I was reading, I would take out the kit and build the model. Then I could make the words on the page make sense. In fact, I asked the instructor if I could use the kit during exams. See, if I can build a model of the problem we are supposed to solve, then I can solve the problem, and explain my thoughts on paper."

The two students grinned at each other, and began to laugh, as they realized that they both were solid learners who had very different approaches to learning (C. Johnston, personal communication, July 10, 2005).

Evidence to Support Advanced Learning Process

When educators take the time to inform students about their learning patterns, they can expect measurable results. In studies completed at Foothill College in Los Altos Hills, California, and at Cumberland Community College in New Jersey, students whose advisors and instructors used this advanced learning process as a part of their instruction and advisement had a significant increase in student retention.

Table 5

Strategies to Help Forge Patterns

Sequential	Precise	Technical	Confluent
Read the directions carefully.	Take my time and carefully read over all of the information.	Be willing to show others what I know by demonstrating something or building it.	Think of something unusual for real life and then stretch it to be imaginary.
Mark off each step as I go.	Read the subtitles to know where to gather information.	Use whatever tools are given to me to show what I know.	Be willing to take small risks with new ideas.
Look for words that ask for me to respond using a specific order or organization.	Don't trust my memory, and write it down!	Remind myself that I can learn from experiences, so observe and absorb the experience as it is occurring.	Be willing to do a skit with other people to show what I know.
Double-check my work for completeness.	Look for words that ask for important facts or details.	Check if I can work with someone who uses technical as needed.	Take my time to think of ways to do assignments in a unique or different way.
Make sure that I follow the key directions step-by-step.	Answer questions using at least two full sentences.	Look for words that ask me to build or make something.	Ask others for ideas to get started.
Make sure that I do not start something until I have all of the directions or unless I have permission to try a different approach.	Double-check my work for accuracy.	Think about how I can apply this to my life.	Be willing to learn about things in creative, fun, and entertaining ways.
Work to follow through with one project from beginning to the end.	Whenever possible, ask questions about things of which I am not sure.	Stick with the task until I can make it work.	Look to see if I can work with someone who uses confluence as needed.
Check if I can work with someone who uses sequence as needed.	Check if I can work with someone who uses precision as needed.	Communicate through action.	Work to make connections in order to see the big picture.

Table 6
Strategies to Help Tether Patterns

Sequential	Precise	Technical	Confluent
When the directions are not clear, think of an assignment that was similar to the current task and make up my own directions.	Answer the question first and add detail if there is time.	Take short breaks to refresh and keep motivated.	Remember that not everyone likes change.
Think through the steps carefully before asking what I am to do.	Remember that not everyone communicates in words.	Remember that I can communicate using words.	Don't get discouraged if my idea is not used.
Take a deep breath when plans change and take the risk to not be in control for the moment.	Think about the question before I ask. Sometimes I already know the answer (trust myself).	Know that when I work with others they have something to teach me, too.	Make sure to follow the assignment's objectives and, if I'm not sure, ask.
When there is a time limit, don't panic and place a star by the most important areas that need to be double-checked.	Remember to allow others to share their information.	Try to connect with the task faster rather than mulling for a long period of time.	Work to not wait until the very last minute. This will give me time to make corrections and allow it to be more complete.
Remember that not everyone has the same plan as I.	Don't get hung-up on inaccuracies. Correct them and move on.	Remember that I have something that is valuable to teach others.	Allow others to share their opinions.
Allow wait time for others to respond.	Remember that there are times when I don't have to prove my point.	If I can't get it to work and there's a time limit, ask for help.	Remember that others may need help "seeing" my idea and its connections to the task.
Don't panic when the final product doesn't look like the example.	Seek to prioritize the amount of information that needs to be shared out loud or on paper.	Keep in mind that not everything has a purpose or has to work.	Stick to the task; don't let my mind wander.
Look to see if I can work with someone who uses sequence as needed.	Look for body language that suggests I am giving too much information.	Don't be afraid to share your thoughts or ideas.	Remember to rehearse before I express.

In 1996-1997, an average of 68% of the students at Foothill College completed courses, and 35% persisted from fall to spring quarter. These figures are consistent with national retention data (Astin, 1993; Tinto, 1993). After being exposed to the LML process in their career and entry-level courses (i.e., composition, math, world language, and basic skills) and licensure courses in pharmacology, dental hygiene, and veterinary technician, 88% of the 469 students completed the courses. That is a marked improvement from the average course completion rate before the intervention. One previously disengaged student said, "Lately, I have been studying with a partner, and that has been very helpful. I am able to learn more with the help of other people's patterns." Among students, there was also a realization that the LML Process had transferability, both to other courses and to work situations. In the second year of the study, 87% of the 769 students completed their courses, and 92% received transferable grades. Again, this shows a sustained improvement from the 68% retention rate prior to using the LML process (Pearle, 2002).

Student exit data at the community college in New Jersey revealed similar results. Of the 330 first-year students surveyed at the conclusion of their courses in which the LML process was integrated into the instruction, 60% reported that knowing their instructor's teaching/learning patterns contributed to their ability to perform up to expectations in the class. Sixty-one percent said they had been able to use knowledge of their learning patterns in other classes as well as outside of the classroom. Sixty-two percent reported, "The LML process has helped me in becoming a better student" (Dainton, 2004, p. 13). A particularly interesting point is that, of the 330 students who found themselves in courses in which this study was being conducted, 35 reported they had considered dropping the class but decided not to, because of the influence of the LML process on the learning environment and the instructor's sensitivity to their learning processes.

This process was also included as part of a Visions of the Future learning community for undeclared first-year students at Rowan University in New Jersey. Students who participated reported that it was helpful not only in understanding the teaching styles of their professors but also in understanding their friends and roommates (Braun, 2005).

Another first-year student who used this process in class explained that it really helped him understand that he was "not weird." This particular student is highly confluent and loves literature and discussing the new and varied thoughts expressed in many of the books he read his first semester at the university. When returning home for his first visit, his family asked what he had learned, and he began to share some of the ideas he had been exposed to in his literature class. The response from his family was, "Didn't you do anything?" Based on his new knowledge of learning patterns, he understood that most members of his family are highly technical and that to them "learning" was "doing something." Rather than feeling defensive, he realized the reason for their differences and understood that both views were equally valuable, just different (B. McCalla-Wriggins, personal communication, November 2, 2005).

How to Incorporate LML Into First-Year Advising Activities

Regardless of the setting where interactions with students take place, there are multiple ways to incorporate this advanced learning process into the first year of college.

Individual Advising Sessions

When meeting with students individually, discussing their learning patterns can reinforce the impact of their patterns both in and out of the classroom. It also provides an opportunity to help students develop specific strategies that they can use when situations and tasks require them to tether and/or forge their patterns. As students learn to intentionally make choices and change their behaviors, they begin to feel very empowered. The Career and Academic Planning Center at Rowan University developed a brochure, included in the chapter appendix, which is a useful learning pattern reference for students. It provides a way for advisors to structure their conversations so students can develop individual short- and long-term goals, career exploration options, and personal learning success strategies.

Professional Development Activities

Incorporating learning pattern information into the professional development activities for faculty and full-time advisors, academic and student affairs staff, as well as peer advisors, tutors, and residence assistants provides a strong foundation for the entire campus to support students' learning. It gives everyone a new vocabulary through which to communicate. Most importantly, the more frequently students reflect on and discuss their learning patterns and the strategies needed to be successful in various settings, the more likely this information will be incorporated into their lives.

First-Year Orientation Programs

It is beneficial for students to take the LCI as part of a first-year testing/placement program and have the results explained at first-year orientation. Programs for parents on learning patterns can help reinforce this approach to learning and also give parents and students insights into why they may have had difficulty communicating. As advisors meet with new students at orientation and subsequent follow-up advising sessions, they can further discuss learning patterns and how that knowledge can be used in the classroom, in interactions with roommates and classmates, as well as in exploring appropriate academic and career options.

First-Year Seminars and Other First-Year Courses

Having information about their own and their students' learning patterns can be especially helpful to faculty. It provides an opportunity to discuss how the faculty members' learning patterns play out in both how they teach and the type of assignments they create. Faculty can also coach students with different learning patterns to respond in ways that will allow them to be more successful and create teams that draw on the strengths of all the students. If students take the online version of the LCI, a system can be created that allows the faculty to have access to their reports and to see their scores in graph form.

Introduction to the Major and Career Decision making Classes

Looking at various majors and careers through the lens of learning patterns is valuable. For example, if students are considering accounting as a major but find the precision requirements of the accounting profession a problem, it is helpful to discuss aspects of a profession that may not match the students' preferred learning pattern. It does not mean that these students should give up their goal to become accountants; rather, they will frequently need to forge those patterns that they naturally would avoid. Likewise, for students who rely heavily on their confluence, a career in the arts could draw on that learning pattern.

As is suggested by the ideas presented above, there are endless possibilities to using learning pattern information to support student success. However, as with any new initiative, there are challenges and opportunities. One very effective approach is to gather those on your campus who are truly interested in the transformative learning model discussed in *Learning Reconsidered* (Keeling, 2004). Representatives from both academic and student affairs need to be included in this conversation because learning occurs at multiple locations, settings, environments, and times on our college and university campuses.

Conclusion

The impact that our learning patterns have on how we understand and respond to each other begins with the old adage: Know thyself. It begins by capturing an individual's mental process as he or she engages in the act of learning. As the processes "speak" to each other, they chatter, argue, and negotiate. When used skillfully, they support one another in achieving the intended learning outcomes. When learners understand their mental processes, they can develop personal strategies to overcome otherwise defeating behaviors.

As advisors working with first-year students, we have the unique opportunity to interact with students at the very beginning of their higher education experience. What we choose to include in the activities, programs, small-group discussions, advising sessions, and classes during those first critical weeks can have a significant impact on whether our students are retained and persist to graduation.

As we teach first-year students through the advising process, we can help them develop personal learning strategies that guide their actions. We must understand what is being asked in a specific situation and act with intention to coax students' learning patterns to formulate reasonable and appropriate responses and help them find a career path that matches, compliments, and enhances their learning processes. The aim of advising then becomes teaching an individual to make adjustments: adapt, improvise, overcome. For as much as we attempt to make the first-year experience a foundation upon which students will develop a strong sense of belonging and efficacy, we miss the mark when we fail to recognize that entering students bring not only their hopes, dreams, aspirations, prior education, and experiences to the campus, but also bring their learning patterns.

As advisors, we should consider how students' lives can be changed if they possess the tools and language to successfully communicate with others. Just as students who have knowledge about their learning patterns can take responsibility for their own learning and create strategies to be successful, we, as advisors working with first-year students, can take the lead in moving our institutions to where the focus is truly on learning and the student.

References

Association of American Colleges and Universities (AAC&U). (2002). *Greater expectations: A new vision for learning as a nation goes to college*. Washington, DC: Author.

Astin, A. W. (1993). *What matters in college: Four critical years revisited*. San Francisco: Jossey-Bass.

Braun, J. T. (2005). *Enhancing the efficacy of a college learning community through teaching metacognition*. Unpublished master's thesis, Rowan University, Glassboro, NJ.

Dainton, G. (2004). *Executive summary: A study of Cumberland County Colleges' use of Title III funding to raise student achievement*. Turnersville, NJ: LCR, LLC.

Johnston, C. (1996). *Unlocking the will to learn*. Thousand Oaks, CA: Corwin Press.

Johnston, C. (1998). *Let me learn*. Thousand Oaks, CA: Corwin Press.

Johnston, C., & Dainton, G. (2005). *The learning connections inventory*. Turnersville, NJ: Learning Connections Resources.

Keeling, R. (Ed.). (2004). *Learning reconsidered: A campus-wide focus of the student experience.* Washington, DC: American College Personnel Association and National Association of Student Personnel Administrators.

Pearle, K. (2002). *Metacognition as vehicle for organizational change: How "thinking about thinking" and intentional learning break the mold of "heroic" teaching in higher education.* Unpublished doctoral dissertation, Rowan University, Glassboro, NJ.

Tinto, V. (1993). *Leaving college. Rethinking the causes and cures of student attrition* (2nd ed.). Chicago: The University of Chicago Press.

Online Resources

Let Me Learn
   www.letmelearn.org
Learning Connections Resources
   www.lcrinfo.com/index.shtml

Appendix

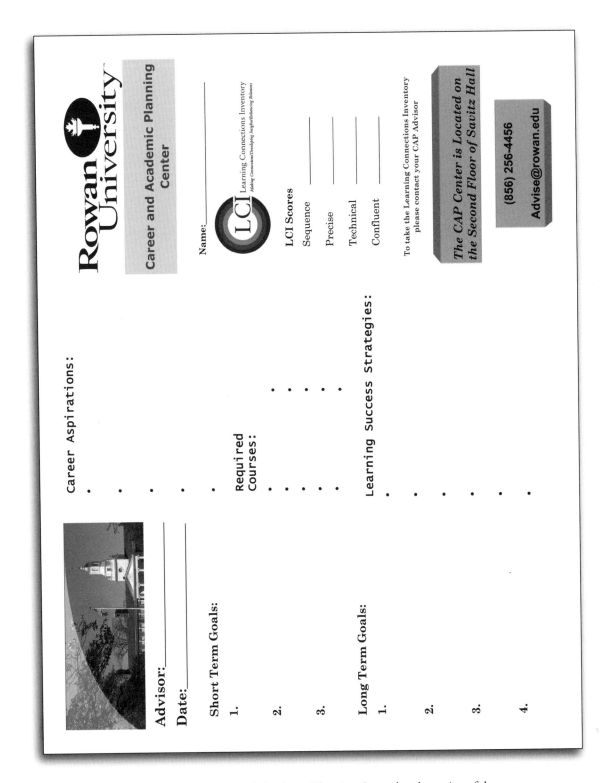

Figure 1. Rowan University's Career and Academic Planning Center brochure: A useful pattern reference for students.

When I Have a Use First Pattern

Sequential

1. I want clear directions.
2. I need step-by-step directions.
3. I want time to do my work neatly.
4. I like to do my work from beginning to end.
5. I want to know if I am meeting the instructors or my team mates' expectations.

Precise

- I want complete and thorough explanations.
- I ask a lot of questions.
- I like to answer questions.
- I need to be accurate and correct.
- I like test results. I seek written documentation of my success.

Technical

▶ I don't like to write things down.
▶ I need to see the purpose of what I am doing.
▶ I like to work by myself.
▶ I like to figure how things work.
▶ I don't like to use a lot of words.

Confluence

- I don't like doing the same thing over and over.
- I see situations very differently than others do.
- I like to do things my own way.
- I don't like following the rules.
- I enjoy taking risks.

Use First Intentional Learning Strategies

Sequential
- Make sure that directions are clearly stated step-by-step
- Ask for a model or sample
- Take time to develop a plan

Precise
- Make sure that directions contain detailed information
- Look for words that ask for important facts or details
- Focus on the lecture and not note taking

Technical
- Make sure you understand the relevance of the assignment
- Demonstrate the practical application of the material
- When you think you are done writing, write more!

Confluence
- Negotiate alternative ways for completing an assignment
- Don't get discouraged if my idea is not used
- Stick to the task, don't let my mind wander

When I Have an Avoid Pattern

Sequential

1. Avoid direction; avoid practice.
2. Can't get the pieces in order.
3. Ignore table of contents, indexes, and syllabi.
4. Leave the task incomplete.

Precise

- Don't have specific answers.
- Avoid debate.
- Skim instead of read.
- Take few notes.

Technical

▶ Talk about it instead of doing it.
▶ Avoid using tools or instruments.
▶ Rely on reading or writing to find a solution.
▶ Enjoy working in teams or groups.

Confluence

- Don't take social risks
- Complete one task at a time
- Avoid improvising
- Seek parameters

Avoid Intentional Learning Strategies

Sequential
- Double check your work to make sure it is complete
- Make a list of your priorities
- Check-off completed tasks

Precise
- Don't trust your memory, write things down
- Answer questions using three full sentences
- If you have any doubts, ask questions for clarification

Technical
- Try communicating with fewer words and more action
- Practice using tools to see what they can do
- Just do it!

Confluence
- Ask others for ideas in order to get started
- Be willing to "let-go" and learn from a unique perspective

Frequently Asked Questions

Q: What is different about Learning in college?

A: Learning is more than getting one right answer. Learning is being able to take in a situation and figure out what is expected—how to respond and succeed. Consequently we learn in many different ways and in many different situations.

Q: Why is it important to understand how I learn?

A: To be successful in whatever we do, we need to understand *how* we learn and then make our learning work well for us. Why? Because if we can't take in the world around us and make sense of it, we are not going to be successful.

Q: How do I use my mind with intention?

A: That is the key. When a person understands the way that their mind translates data collected by their brain (learning patterns) they can identify and decode the challenges that confront them, then balance and apply their learning patterns to overcome that challenge. In order to be successful in any endeavor we need to understand our individual learning, the system we are working in, the learning patterns of the people we work with and the task at hand. Use this understanding of yourself and the learning pattern charts to understand the learning patterns of your instructors and to decode their assignments.

For More Information on Learning Patterns Please go to:

www.Letmelearn.org

And

www.LCRinfo.com

Chapter Four

Self-Assessment: Relevance and Value in First-Year Advising

Joanne K. Damminger

Self-assessment is the exploration of one's abilities, interests, needs, and values and is essential for college students' self-awareness, understanding, educational choices, and informed career decisions. It is critical for higher education persistence and graduation that new students recognize the connection between the educational process of advising, designed to facilitate academic success and lifelong achievement, and career decision making regarding courses, majors, and future career aspirations. Self-assessment cannot be left to chance but must be intentional, organized, and communicated to the student. Meaningful interpretation of assessment information by a trained advisor/counselor can be helpful to students' decisions and also determine the readiness of students to make such decisions (Herr, Cramer, & Niles, 2004). Self-exploration is a key component of self-assessment because first-year students must first understand themselves in order to design educational experiences that meet short- and long-term goals for college and beyond.

Exploration of self, majors, and careers should be embedded in the curriculum, programming, and college experiences. It is through such experiences that students come to recognize the relevance and benefits of becoming intentional learners who take responsibility for their learning, academic decisions, overall development, and lifelong pursuits. Light (2001) points out the interrelatedness of advising and other choices for student involvement and first-year experiences. Self-assessment assists students in making choices that are interesting and motivating. As Light contends, students who seek involvement in activities related to interests are more likely to be satisfied and remain committed.

Know Thyself: The Necessity for Self-Assessment

Most first-year students spend very little time thinking about their interests, abilities, and values. The answers to questions such as "What would you do if you could do anything you wanted?" and "How would you spend your time if you could choose?" help students to identify their interests and what they may enjoy doing in the future. However, students often try to choose majors and career goals based on what their families think, or parents chose, or what will allow them to have the greatest earning potential. Although these values can be considered in the decision making process, the recognition by first-year students of strong skill areas, weaknesses, and core values regarding the world of work is equally important.

Therefore, it is necessary for new students to increase their self-knowledge through the process of self-assessment. Self-assessment is a process that includes recognizing its value, learning about various exploratory tools, choosing and completing assessment instruments, participating in the interpretation process, and reflecting on resulting data to transform them into beneficial information.

Intentional advising is an approach that supports building relationships, assesses advisees' needs, and works to provide for those needs. Such intentional advising incorporates frequent meetings, establishes rapport, builds relationships, and interacts in caring ways (Creamer & Scott, 2000; Jeschke, Johnson, & Williams, 2001; Light, 2001). Assessment needs to be introduced and recommended to every new student by the advisor and not left to student initiative alone. Students who learn about themselves and make informed choices will benefit from their courses and college experiences.

These components of effective advising demonstrate the connection between advising, assessment, student development, and teaching. Advising, as teaching, involves intentional growth activities and measurable outcomes (Crookston, 1972; O'Banion, 1972). First-year advising must include opportunities for self-reflection and deliberate discussion. The concept of advising as teaching extends far beyond course selection (O'Banion, 1994), and the advisor is the conduit in making sense of reflective thoughts and changing those thoughts into action for students.

From Theory to Practice

One of the most widely known student development theories by Chickering and Reisser (1993) relates student development to seven vectors of development with student identity as a fundamental feature. Three vectors relate closely to academic advising: (a) developing competence, (b) developing autonomy, and (c) developing purpose (Frost, 2000). Student development research suggests that a multitude of academic, social, emotional, physical, and interpersonal experiences contribute to the development of the individual student. Higher education professionals must be sensitive to the developmental level of students and provide students appropriate challenges and support for them to reach the next developmental stage. In the first year, advisors should consider advisees' levels of development and the need for additional self-awareness through assessment. Emerging theories of advising and career choice suggest that selection of career interventions must be designed for the student rather than the student fitting into prescribed interventions. This constructivist and postmodern approach to advising and career decision making encourages advisors to actively construct relevant educational experiences and career plans with students (Niles & Harris-Bowlsbey, 2005).

Involving students both in and out of the classroom reflects the value of creating learner-centered campuses interested in educating the whole student (Sandeen, 2004). The focus on learning acknowledges that learning and development are one and the same. In order to provide a comprehensive higher education experience that emphasizes preparing students to become lifelong learners and engaged citizens (Keeling, 2004), faculty and student affairs professionals, particularly as it concerns advising, must collaborate.

Part of a comprehensive educational experience is intentionally increasing self-knowledge because it is essential in our daily functioning and decision making. When looking closely at career-development guidelines developed by the National Occupational and Informational Coordinating Committee (NOICC, 1989) and America's Career Resource Network (n.d.), the first set of competencies needed for adults to choose and sustain productive careers focuses on self-knowledge and personal and social skill sets. The first of these competencies highlights skills for understanding oneself and developing and maintaining a positive self-concept. It includes the necessity to understand abilities, interests, and personal and work values as higher education seeks to provide for the education of the whole student.

Academic advising is one component of the higher education experience that can be shared and constructed by the advisor and advisee, and fosters the development of the whole student. Effective advising calls for frequent interaction that builds a relationship and creates a bond that is believed to far surpass the benefits of prescriptive advising. Prescriptive advising, defined as advising that results in simple and quick course selection with little or no relationship building, can fail to assess students' developmental level and needs (Crookston, 1972; Jeschke et al., 2001; O'Banion, 1972). Frequent advising sessions, which include self-exploration as well as discussion of current course content and its relationship to subsequent choices and desired outcomes, demonstrate the power of advising as teaching and not as isolated sessions designed for course selection alone.

Academic advising that is planned, intentional, on-going, and provides ample opportunities to meet and engage in advisor-student interaction in caring ways is teaching. Teaching can be defined as any experience between the teacher and student that contributes to the development of an individual and can be assessed. Therefore, the benefits of this model of advising (i.e., shared interaction between advisor and student, mutual respect, awareness, and intentionality of one's actions and behaviors, problem-solving processes, and decision making skills) can be viewed as teaching (Crookston, 1972).

Advisors working with first-year students need to approach the advising session with a lesson plan in mind. The plan is to build rapport with new advisees, diagnose immediate needs, and set goals to satisfy needs. Often the primary objective of the first advising meeting is to discuss courses and the registration process for second semester. However, to effectively satisfy the needs of first-year students, initial advising should include a discussion of the student's level of self-awareness and how such awareness of interests, values, and abilities can affirm or negate thoughts about majors and future occupations. In introductory advising sessions where this discussion naturally unfolds, advising becomes teaching. Students learn the value of self-assessment by acknowledging their current thoughts and incorporating them in decision making about courses, activities, majors, careers, and campus activities.

In all advising sessions, advisors need to incorporate open-ended questions to determine students' needs and levels of self-awareness. These questions may be very simplistic but cause student reflection on the core of career choice and satisfaction. They can include: "What are you interested in? What are you passionate about? What majors and careers are related to topics and situations that you find interesting and exciting?" The answers to these questions and the resulting conversation need to define self-assessment; explain the myriad paper, electronic, and Internet self-assessment tools; and allow students to choose the most appropriate tools for beginning or continuing the assessment process. Students can then complete the chosen self-assessment instruments, attend follow-up interpretation meetings with the advisor, and begin to use the information for decision making. Interpretation of results of any self-assessment instruments may be the most valuable part of the advising/teaching process because a trained and experienced counselor can assist a student in connecting the scored results with their own thoughts, wishes, and intentions.

These initial and subsequent advising sessions must have pre-determined outcomes that are important for all first-year students. These student outcomes include, but are not limited to, students' (a) increased self-awareness; (b) understanding majors of interest and associated programs of study; (c) possible course selections and reasons for choices; (d) knowledge of how and where to get more information about self, major, and careers; and (e) need for follow-up appointments.

At many institutions, the intentional advising as teaching concept is not clearly understood and often underutilized. Perhaps, the best models are those that integrate advising and self- and major exploration into the curriculum of a major or program. To facilitate such reflection, at a mid-sized public institution in the mid-Atlantic region of the United States, self- and major exploration was embedded in the curriculum of the business program. The resulting Career Development Program (Rowan University, 2005a) required that all first-year business majors attend a Career Center workshop about their major and self-exploration as well as complete the ORA (Organizational Renewal Associates) Personality Profiler (CollegeBoard.com, 2005). The assessment results and corresponding worksheets were evaluated by the professor for course credit. This procedure required that all business students learn more about themselves, their major, and the business specialization they were pursuing. The results were amazing as some students realized which specialization within business was most appropriately matched to their skills, values, and interests, and others learned that business was not a well-matched major for them at all. The Career Development Program also included requirements for junior and senior business majors including résumé writing and interview preparation, which were also embedded in junior and senior course curricula.

Assessment also needs to be embedded in first-year courses, support programs, and other areas of college curriculum and should match the needs of each particular campus. Another first-year program at the same public institution embedded first-year assessment and major exploration into a comprehensive first-year learning community for undeclared students (Rowan University, 2005b). The learning community comprised two linked courses, grouped housing, mentoring, and major and career exploration. As part of the learning community required meetings, students completed learning preferences, interests, values, and skills inventories to learn more about themselves, their learning patterns, and possible majors. Research on the effectiveness of the program showed that students felt one of the most valuable components was the required self- and major exploration. In students' interviews, community members commented that they would not have pursued such assessment opportunities on their own even if they knew they existed. However, students found the self-exploration extremely helpful in their choice of majors and in narrowing down occupations to explore (Damminger, 2004).

Similar programs are in effect at other institutions such as the First-Year Learning Community at Indiana University-Purdue University Indianapolis (IUPUI). All students are required to take a first-year seminar, which embeds self, major, and career exploration in the course content. Over a 13-week period, first-year students assess their interests, values, skills, and personalities using various instruments such as the Merkler Interest Inventory and the Keirsey Temperament Sorter. Additionally, they participate in interactive activities to investigate majors and careers (J. Pedersen, personal communication, August 20, 2005).

Self-Assessment Components: Interests, Skills, and Values

The first year of college is one of tremendous exploration, learning, and reflection. An area of critical importance in the exploration process is self-knowledge. Growing self-awareness is important for students' development and critical to effective advising. Assessment can be described as collecting data about a person with the use of formal or informal instruments. Students will find it easier to make informed decisions about course selection, majors, and careers if they obtain knowledge about themselves as students and learners in their own educational process.

Self-assessment could be considered a primary goal of first-year student orientation programs and first-year seminar courses.

Self-assessment includes awareness of one's interests, abilities, values, and learning patterns and their connection to course selection, choice of major, and occupational aspirations. First-year students seldom have this awareness and often do not know where to find help or fail to take the time to seek assistance. These students have never thought deeply about questions such as "What are my skills?" or "What do I like?" A provocative question, "How would you spend your time if you won the lottery and never had to work for money?" can nudge students into realizing what they like to do and where their interests lie. These thoughts need to be explored and can be initiated in the first advising session. Students need to reflect on their passions, abilities, and core values when they discuss first- and second-semester courses, majors, and jobs in which they are interested. Such advising sessions assist new students in making the powerful connections between themselves, course selection, well-matched majors, and future career goals.

Learning About Interests

An integral ingredient in effective decision making regarding future goals is knowing one's interests or being aware of what one likes and dislikes. This increased awareness is invaluable in assisting first-year students to jump-start their major and career exploration. Students, who assess their interests, find the process helpful in making informed educational and occupational decisions (Hansen, 2005). This assessment can be initiated with activities such as listing and sharing "20 Things I Like to Do." Such awareness often serves as a starting point in narrowing down majors and occupations to research.

While there are many variables to interests, the three major components are "personality, motivation or drive, and self-concept" (Brown & Lent, 2005, p. 281). Most self-assessment inventories include a component about interests and often suggest tasks related to a specific area of work and ask students to identify if they would like or dislike the task. These data are used to pair career areas with students' interests.

Both internal and external factors contribute to one's vocational interests. Additionally, various career development theories emphasize the extent to which such factors affect one's thoughts. Social Cognitive Career Theory stresses the role of external forces such as the family, school, and peer groups on one's interest. Gottfredson's Theory of Circumscription and Compromise focuses on self-concept and the effects that gender, prestige of occupation, and field of work have on career decision making (Brown & Lent, 2005). Super's Life-Span, Life-Space Theory is a developmental approach to career interventions and highlights the effect of various roles on a person's self-concept throughout one's life span (Niles & Harris-Bowlsbey, 2005). Trait and factor career counseling theories such as Holland's Theory of Type purport that interests are a manifestation of one's personality, and successful choice can result if personality type is well-matched to the work environment (Niles & Harris-Bowlsbey). There are many instruments that are beneficial in assessing vocational interests and environments, but perhaps the measure most widely used is Holland's Self-Directed Search (SDS) (Brown & Lent, 2005). A group of activities created to assist with any of the steps related to career planning and delivered by computer can be referred to as computer-assisted career guidance systems (CACGS) and include an interest inventory. Two such CACGS, Discover's UNIACT assessment tool (ACT, 2006) and MyRoad's Personality Profiler (CollegeBoard.com, 2005) include such components.

Recognizing Strengths and Abilities

In considering other areas in which to increase first-year students' awareness, a key component is realizing one's abilities and strengths. The exploration of one's skills and abilities to perform specific tasks can contribute to future job performance and satisfaction (Krane & Tirre, 2005). Abilities include both innate strengths and those that have been developed through educational and first-hand experiences. Abilities assessment can help students expand or narrow career options, confirm career decisions, and increase eventual job satisfaction (Brown & Lent, 2005). Such assessment can assist in researching realistic career options for which one has the skills or in identifying whether the necessary skills are attainable. Often, course assignments that require students to write about or interview someone in a position they are interested in can help students realize their degree of interest, or lack thereof, for particular occupational areas. Once such occupational groups are identified, then they can be further refined by considering interests and work values. An example is a first-year student who was investigating her desire to work in the field of forensics. She lacked any knowledge of or skills in chemistry. She was unsuccessful in the subject in high school, and said how much she disliked the subject. Her exploration of the characteristics needed for success in the forensics area led her to explore more conducive career areas. The student realized her interest in helping others and explored psychology and teaching as possible career fields. She took a few related courses and decided that she wanted to teach. She combined her decision to teach with her strong background in the Spanish language and decided to double major in elementary education and Spanish.

Often, the self-assessment of personal skills requires students to use a self-rating system to identify their strengths and weaknesses. Self-rated skills and abilities measured by objective assessments are fallible and open to error and should be recognized as only one measurement of competency. The results should be combined with other assessment materials in the interpretation and decision making processes (Brown & Lent, 2005).

Assessing Needs and Values

An area of self-assessment that often needs clarification for first-year students is workplace values. Work values are fundamental to choices about work and are related to reasons for working. In addition, assessing values and needs is important for designing educational and career goals because of its correlation with human motivation, career choice, and future workplace behaviors (Rounds & Armstrong, 2005). Assessing work values includes both what people want from work and their expectations about work (Nord, Brief, Atieh, & Doherty, 1990). These thoughts may be more indicative of an individual who has experience in the workforce but warrant consideration by the inexperienced first-year student as well. Often a simple activity such as requiring students to review a list of values, pick 10 that identify their core beliefs, and then narrow their choices to just a few can cause valuable reflection on things that are important to them in a future job.

Values assessment is not as widely researched as other areas of assessment but is worthy of consideration by major and career explorers (Brown & Lent, 2005). Both CACGS and other assessment tools such as the Minnesota Importance Questionnaire (MIQ) (Weiss, Dawis, & Lofquist, 1971, 1975, 1981) are available as measurement tools. The MIQ describes six values: (a) achievement, (b) comfort, (c) status, (d) altruism, (e) safety, and (f) autonomy. Each is described in terms of the work environment and work rewards that can be generally or specifically discussed with advisees and related to the students' individual needs (Rounds, Henly, Dawis, Lofquist, & Weiss, 1981).

Work values and needs are important for reflection by first-year students for realization that a future occupation and subsequent career may be rewarding and successful if it is correlated with core values and satisfies basic needs.

Self-Assessment Resources

There are myriad resources for self-assessment, and they include both formal and informal means. Self-assessment measures related to career counseling can also be categorized as objective, qualitative, and clinical. Clinical assessments, resulting in a clinical diagnosis, combine data from various sources to make a prediction. Objective or formal assessments have standardized instructions for administration and scoring procedures (Brown, 2003). Objective instruments can be labeled tests or inventories, with the former measuring highest performance resulting from achieving the right answers and the latter assessing typical performance where there are no right or wrong answers (see Table 1). Qualitative assessments, or informal assessments, can be administered anywhere and do not have rigid standards for administration. They can include card sorts, job shadowing, volunteering in a work setting related to career goals, co-op and field experiences, structured interviews, and observations (Brown; Niles & Harris-Bowlsbey, 2005).

Self-assessment resources span the spectrum from printed tools to Internet-accessible CACGS. Some interest inventories that are available in print format and can be either self- or machine-scored are the Career Occupational Preference System (COPS), the Self-Directed Search (SDS), and the Strong Interest Inventory (SII). The Career Key, an interest assessment by Lawrence K. Jones, is available online as a free public service and yields Holland scale scores. Some popular personality inventories are the Myers-Briggs Type Indicator (MBTI) and the Sixteen P. F. Personal Career Development Profile (16PFQ) (Table 1).

Many self-knowledge tools are now located on the Internet. They vary in comprehensiveness from administering and interpreting a single inventory to activities for all steps related to self and major exploration as well as job search strategies and training. CACGS can perform many of the jobs related to interest, value, and skills assessment useful in advising and career counseling with the exception of developing the human relationship (Isaacson & Brown, 2000).

Controversy exists about the use of CACGS for self-assessment due to a concern for reliability, validity, and cultural and ethical issues. There is also concern that students have Internet access and, if they have access, whether they have sufficient computer skills to use the self-assessment instrument and whether their skill level may affect assessment results (Brown, 2003). All of these concerns must be explored when advisors consider using a particular tool before recommending its use to an advisee.

Which instrument is selected by an advisor or advisee depends on many variables. Consideration must be given to the specific purpose for use, the characteristics of the advisee, reliability and validity of data, opinions from reviews and colleagues, cost, scoring, and results (Niles & Harris-Bowlsbey, 2005). The particular assessment instrument suggested by advisors and/or chosen by first-year students may be based on students' choice and willingness to complete, the cost, the reading level, and the advisor's and department's preferences.

Advisors have a large responsibility to recommend appropriate tools for advisees. They must be knowledgeable about self-exploration tools, how to interpret them, and appropriate choices for each individual student.

Table 1
*A Partial Listing of Self-Assessment Resources**

Instrument	Publisher/Author	Components Assessed
Campbell Interest and Skill Survey (CISS)	National Computer Systems, Inc. http://www.pearsonassessments.com/tests/ciss.htm	Interests and skills
Career Occupational Preference System (COPS)	EDITS/Educational & Industrial Testing Service http://www.edits.net/career.html	Interests, values, abilities
Discover's UNIACT	Discover by American College Testing (ACT) http://www.act.org/discover/	Interests, values, abilities
Minnesota Importance Questionnaire (MIQ)	Weiss, Dawis, & Lofquist, 1971, 1975, 1981 http://www.psych.umn.edu/psylabs/vpr/miqinf.htm	Work values and needs
Myers-Briggs Type Indicator (MBTI)	Consulting Psychologists Press http://www.cpp.com/products/mbti/index.asp	Personality
MyRoad's Personality Profiler	MyRoad.com (College and Career Planning) http://www.myroad.com	Interests, values, abilities
O'NET Interest Profiler (IP)	U.S. Department of Labor www.onetcenter.org	Interests
Self-Directed Search (SDS)	Psychological Assessment Resources, Inc. http://www.self-directed-search.com/	Interests
Sixteen P. F. Personal Career Development Profile (16PFQ)	Pearson Assessments http://www.pearsonassessments.com/tests/sixtpf_5.htm	Interests, strengths, and personal growth
Strong Interest Inventory (SII)	Consulting Psychologists Press http://www.cpp.com/products/strong/index.asp	Interests
The Career Key	Career Key, Inc. http://www.careerkey.org	Interests

* Web addresses subject to change.

Interpreting Results

Interpretation is an explanation of the results of self-assessment measures and, ideally, should be done individually with the student (Brown, 2003). An interactive advising session allows the advisor to observe how students receive the interpretative information and assists advisees in using assessment results to make informed decisions. Assessment results are beneficial in developing self-concept, selecting appropriate and exploratory courses, directing future exploration, choosing majors, designing campus involvement, and guiding informed career choices.

Interpretation includes looking at objective data and inferring meaning. Assessment data should be considered with other information about the advisee to be effective. Since this is a very subjective process, the advisor needs to consider the advisee's abilities, interests, values, lifestyle, future exploration, and practicality of suggested options (Niles & Harris-Bowlsbey, 2005). Advisors have an ethical responsibility to be trained in combining data from various sources to provide accurate feedback. Therefore, advisors must be prepared to administer and interpret any assessments and/or inventories that are used by advisees.

Once an instrument is chosen by the advisee, the advisor gives instructions on how to complete it. In addition, the counselor should explain the type and extent of information that will be received as part of the interpretation. Many interest, value, and ability inventories provide a list of career clusters to which the advisee is well-matched based on inventory results. Such a list can be used by the advisee for further exploration of related majors and career options. This narrowing of options is extremely beneficial to the novice explorer. Further investigation of career clusters can provide characteristics of the job and job seeker against which students can compare their own thoughts as part of their exploration. There are numerous resources for further investigation by the advisee including Vocational Biographies, available in print and Internet versions (http://www.vocbio.com/) and various career libraries that include titles such as "Careers for Biology Majors." These resources, often available in campus career centers, should be reviewed by the advisor so that advisees are prepared for the next steps in the exploration process. In summary, overall test interpretation should include preparation by the counselor, preparation of the advisee to receive the information, delivery of the data, review of available resources, and any suggested follow-up sessions (Niles & Harris-Bowlsbey, 2005; Tinsley & Bradley, 1986).

Conclusions

There is much to be said for self-assessment in the first college year. It is not only beneficial but necessary for first-year students and needs to be incorporated in the advising process. Self-exploration for increased self-knowledge and informed educational and career decision making must be an integral part of first-year advising procedures and all advisor training. To facilitate self-assessment as part of the advising process, advisors should seek the necessary training and remain abreast of current instruments and inventories. Advisors must be knowledgeable about appropriate tools to meet the needs and developmental levels of advisees. Careful selection of appropriate instruments should be based on advisors' expertise and the willingness of the advisee to complete the intervention. Interpretation of self-assessment results should be delivered to students using positive terms that are easily understood.

Self-assessment cannot be left to chance nor should it be offered solely in career counseling and advising sessions. It needs to be integrated in advising sessions, college curriculum, and college programming such as in first-year seminar courses and be combined with other self-exploration activities such as learning preference assessments. It is recommended that colleges consider administering self-assessment instruments as part of first-year student orientation, which provides a tremendous opportunity for students to learn more about themselves and to explore how increased self-awareness can contribute to intentional learning and informed decisions. Any introduction during orientation can be followed up with programming and seminar course work and should be designed to fit the individual needs of a campus and its student population.

The value of self-assessment in the first year cannot be underestimated. The more that our campuses incorporate self-assessment into the first-year experience, the greater relevance it will have for students and their academic success and goal attainment.

References

ACT, Inc. (2006). DISCOVER, 2006. Retrieved August 8, 2005, from http://www.act.org/DISCOVER.

America's Career Resource Network. (n.d.). *National career development guidelines.* Retrieved August 8, 2005, from http://www.acrnetwork.org/ncdg.htm

Brown, D. (2003). *Career information, career counseling, and career development.* Boston: Pearson Education.

Brown, S. D., & Lent, R. W. (2005). *Career development and counseling: Putting theory and research to work.* Hoboken, NJ: John Wiley & Sons.

Chickering, A.W., & Reiser, L. (1993). *Education and identity.* (2nd ed.) San Francisco: Jossey-Bass.

CollegeBoard.com. (2005). *MyRoad.* Retrieved August, 8, 2005, from http://www.collegeboard.com/student/testing/psat/about/myroad.html

Creamer, E. G., & Scott, D. W. (2000). Assessing individual advisor effectiveness. In V. N. Gordon, W. R. Habley, & Associates (Eds.), *Academic advising: A comprehensive handbook* (pp. 339-348). San Francisco: Jossey-Bass.

Crookston, B. B. (1972). A developmental view of academic advising as teaching. *Journal of College Student Personnel, 13*(1), 12-17.

Damminger, J. K. (2004). *Transformative learning and leading through a comprehensive learning community experience for undeclared freshmen.* Unpublished doctoral dissertation, Rowan University, Glassboro, New Jersey.

Frost, S. H. (2000). Historical and philosophical foundations for academic advising. In V. N. Gordon, W. R. Habley, & Associates (Eds.), *Academic advising: A comprehensive handbook* (pp. 3-17). San Francisco: Jossey-Bass.

Hansen, J. C. (2005). Assessment of interests. In S. D. Brown & R. W. Lent (Eds.), *Career development and counseling: Putting theory and research to work* (pp. 281-304). Hoboken, NJ: John Wiley & Sons.

Herr, E. L., Cramer, S. H., & Niles, S. G. (2004). *Career guidance and counseling through the lifespan: Systematic approaches.* Boston: Pearson Education.

Isaacson, L. E., & Brown, D. (2000). *Career information, career counseling, and career development.* Boston: Allyn and Bacon.

Jeschke, M. P., Johnson, K. E., & Williams, J. R. (2001). A comparison of intrusive and prescriptive advising of psychology majors at an urban comprehensive university. *NACADA Journal, 21*(1 & 2), 46-58.

Keeling, R. (Ed.). (2004). *Learning reconsidered: A campus-wide focus on the student experience.* Washington, DC: American College Personnel Association, National Association of Student Personnel Administrators.

Krane, N. E. R., & Tirre W. C. (2005). Ability assessment in career counseling. In S. D. Brown, & R. W. Lent (Eds.), *Career development and counseling: Putting theory and research to work* (pp. 330-352). Hoboken, NJ: John Wiley & Sons.

Light, R. J. (2001). *Making the most of college: Students speak their mind.* Cambridge, MA: Harvard University Press.

National Occupational Information Coordinating Committee. (1989). *The national career development guidelines: Local handbook for postsecondary institutions.* Washington, DC: Author.

Niles, S. G., & Harris-Bowlsbey, J. (2005). *Career development interventions in the 21st century* (2nd ed.) Upper Saddle River, NJ: Pearson Merrill Prentice Hall.

Nord, W. R., Brief, A., Atieh, J. M., & Doherty, E. M. (1990). Studying meaning of work: The case of work values. In A. P. Brief & W. R. Nord (Eds.), *Meanings of occupational work* (pp. 21-64). Lexington, MA: Lexington Books.

O'Banion, T. (1972). An academic advising model. *Junior College Journal, 42*(6), 62-69.

O'Banion, T. (1994). Retrospect and prospect. *NACADA Journal, 14*(2), 117-119.

Rounds, J. B., Henly, G. A., Dawis, R. V., Lofquist, L. H., & Weiss, D. J. (1981). *Manual for the Minnesota Importance Questionnaire: A measure of vocational needs and values.* Minneapolis: University of Minnesota, Department of Psychology.

Rounds, J. B., & Armstrong, P. I. (2005). Assessment of needs and values. In S. D. Brown & R. W. Lent (Eds.), *Career development and counseling: Putting theory and research to work* (pp. 305-329). Hoboken, NJ: John Wiley & Sons.

Rowan University. (2005a). *Career development program.* Retrieved August 8, 2005, from http://www.rowan.edu/president/senate/files/CareerDev2006.pdf

Rowan University. (2005b). *Visions of the future learning community for undeclared students.* Retrieved August 8, 2005, from http://www.rowan.edu/open/budgetplanning/PDF/Strategic%20Objectives%2005-10%20plan%20-%20final.pdf

Sandeen, A. (2004, May/June). Educating the whole student: The growing academic importance of student affairs. *Change,* 28-33.

Tinsley, H. E. A., & Bradley, R. W. (1986). Test interpretation. *Journal of Counseling and Development, 64*(7), 462-466.

Weiss, D. J., Dawis, R. V., & Lofquist, L. H. (1971, 1975, 1981). *Minnesota Importance Questionnaire.* Minneapolis, MN: University of Minnesota, Vocational Psychology Research.

Chapter Five

Using Technology to Enhance the Advising Experience

Wesley P. Lipschultz and Michael J. Leonard

It is important to recognize that there can be no substitute for a committed, energetic, and knowledgeable "in-the-flesh" teacher. Such a person, using no technology, still offers superior instruction compared to someone adept at using the tools of technology, but who lacks concern for students, subject matter expertise, and integrity of education. Technology's educational power depends entirely on how it is used. (Mingle, 1997)

This chapter will examine how the current and future uses of technology can enhance the advising/teaching connection and raise the level of discourse between first-year students and academic advisors. It will present a summary of learning theories as they relate to technology and will address concerns about the digital divide and fears that technology may replace academic advisors. This chapter will also include descriptions of exemplary uses of technology that support the teaching function in the advising of first-year students.

Over the past 20 years, nothing has changed the way students learn, instructors teach, and advisors advise more than technology. Twenty years ago, the use of personal computers in academe was fairly rare; now PCs are ubiquitous. The World Wide Web was arcane; now virtually every student, faculty member, and academic advisor uses it. PDAs and the iPod did not exist; now they are being distributed to first-year students at some institutions as learning tools.

Today's first-year students come to college with the expectation that programs and services, academic information and processes, advising, and even advisors themselves will be available through technology. Today's students routinely use the web to do research for class assignments, to locate academic information, and even to receive academic advice without the direct intervention of an advisor. Advisors use the web to manage their advising rosters, review the academic progress of their advisees, and record advising notes. Both students and advisors use the web to access degree audits, calculate grade-point averages, and learn about academic policies and procedures. They communicate with each other often, though asynchronously, through e-mail and listservs. And, sometimes, they even use technology to communicate with each other synchronously through Instant Messaging or chat rooms.

According to a national survey on technology in academic advising (Leonard, 2004), 97% of respondents indicated that they use e-mail on a regular basis in their advising role, 91% regularly use the web, and 89% use word-processing software; 95% said they felt very comfortable or fairly comfortable using technology in their work. In the same survey, 91% reported that their institution's catalog was available online, 84% indicated that students could access their grades online, and 77% indicated that students could register for their courses online.

Because so much academic information is readily available on the web, many advisors now find that first-year students come to advising appointments better educated, better prepared, and with more in-depth questions than advisees of the past who often made advising appointments solely to ask for basic academic information. The use of technology has, in many ways, raised the level of advising discourse.

Technology's Impact on Teaching and Advising

Although I was initially apprehensive about advising technology, I realize that it is coming and will play an integral role in future advising. With this is mind, I feel it is my obligation to my students and my profession to learn and try to use this technology to the best of my ability. (A respondent to the 2002 NACADA technology survey)

Learning Theories

To appreciate the scope of the impact of technology on the advising/teaching of first-year students, advisors must realize the extent to which living with technology has shaped the formative years of those beginning to attend institutions of higher education. In the early 20th century, two linguists, Edward Sapir and Bejamin Whorf, introduced the hypothesis that language influences thoughts and behaviors (Bohannan & Glazer, 1988). In this view, our native language fundamentally both reflects and impacts how we perceive and interact with those around us. Much like a language, technology is a pervasive environmental factor in which first-year students of today have been immersed for most, if not all, of their lives. In fact, Prensky (2001a) indirectly extends the Sapir-Whorf hypothesis from language to technology by calling such students "Digital Natives." He says that "students today are all 'native speakers' of the digital language of computers, video games, and the Internet" (p. 1). He also calls those who did not grow up with technology "Digital Immigrants" (p. 2). As advisors, we thus face the very real possibility that students entering our institutions today tend to process information in ways systematically different than our own (Prensky, 2001b) because we were raised learning different languages (see Table 1).

Indeed, how many of us shake our heads when we pass a student whose consciousness is divided between a cell phone, a newspaper, an iPod, and homework; and then silently make assumptions that this student has problems focusing and will not make it? Prensky might contend that we misinterpret a Digital Native's craving for frequent interactivity, ability to multi-task, and skill at parallel processing as a short attention span.

Think about the fact that many Digital Natives have quite literally grown up with the ability to conduct rich, independent research at a moment's notice on any topic of interest to them. Take, for example, the question, "Why is the sky blue?" For Digital Immigrants, their parents may or may not have known the answer, but most likely Immigrants would have had to hold this question in their minds for a long time until it could be answered at school in the appropriate class, most likely in lecture format. For Digital Natives, to simply Google "why is the sky blue" yields a long list of web sites, the first of which talks about the atmosphere differentially

Table 1

Differences Between Digital Natives and Digital Immigrants

Digital Natives	**Digital Immigrants**
Are accustomed to receiving information at high speeds	Receive information slowly and carefully
Process information simultaneously and/or in parallel	Process information step-by-step
Tend to multi-task	Like to work on one thing at a time
Prefer random (i.e. non-linear) access to information	Prefer linear access to information
Crave frequent interactivity	Are accustomed to lectures

Adapted from Prensky, 2001a.

reflecting and absorbing light waves based on their wavelengths (Science Made Simple, 1997). Digital Natives are rewarded often and fairly accurately for inquisitiveness. Rather than fomenting a short attention span, this dynamic is an extremely powerful force for nurturing lifelong learning (Kassop, 2003).

While technology may foster lifelong learning, has it actually changed the essence of what the Natives will want to learn from us, and what we think they should learn? At face value, it seems pretty clear that first-year students still will want to know what classes they need to take, whether or not their intended areas of study will lead to good jobs, and which classes are "good" ones. Academic advisors, on the other hand, will still want to teach them about how education fosters critical thinking, about matching their interests and abilities with academic options, and about making their education as meaningful as possible. Technology, then, has not changed the essence of what students will want to know or should know, but rather *how* they come to know it. Thus, the impact of technology on advising first-year students is far richer and more interesting than simply declaring that we should use technology for convenience, to be paperless, and to reach a wider audience. Advising new students involves engaging these new students in their education. To engage them, we must learn to speak their language, and that changes everything—our publications, our face-to-face interactions, and even when and how we should use technology.

While a Digital Native-Digital Immigrant lexicon may not yet exist, well-established educational theories on how students learn can help us bridge the language barrier. Theories on how people learn and how to teach to vastly different styles of learning have been around for decades, and emerging technologies have only served to enhance the value and scope of many of these theories. Constructivist theory, which "represents one of the big ideas in education" (Hoover, 1996, p. 1), is a foundational section of this lexicon. Not only does constructivism accommodate and, therefore, legitimize Digital Natives' learning styles, but it also offers guidance on how to incorporate technology into the teaching/learning equation.

Constructivism is based on the long-established work of Piaget, Bruner, Vygotsky, and others both within and outside the field of education (Chen, n.d.). (For more information on constructivism, see chapter 1.) At the core is the belief that learning is "student centered," meaning that learners are not receptacles into which knowledge is placed, but rather agents who build knowledge based on their experiences with the world. One can, therefore, argue that because new students grew up with technology, it is a foundational part of how they have experienced the world and an integral part of how they build knowledge. In general, the constructivist view on how students learn manifests itself in the teaching/learning environment in terms of the following assumptions and prescriptions put forth by Jonassen (Chen):

The learning environment:

◇ Is always situated in a context (real world and/or case study); is thus fuzzy, inexact, and holistic
◇ Should be relevant/meaningful to the learner
◇ Should be self-directed and open (i.e. non-linear)
◇ Should provide multiple representations of that which is to be learned
◇ Fosters construction of knowledge through negotiation with others in the learning environment rather than through competition
◇ Should nurture learning through "reflection on experience"

These tenets should resonate with Digital Immigrants regardless of the existence of technology. Advising at its best is contextualized, holistic, relevant to the life of the learner, negotiated, and reflective. At the same time, these ideas accommodate Digital Natives' learning styles, which have been shaped by technology. Natives crave interactivity; constructivism suggests knowledge negotiation. Natives process information in a non-linear fashion; constructivism encourages self-directed learning. Natives multi-task and prefer processing multiple sources of information simultaneously; constructivism purports multiple representations of information. Thus, constructivist theory is good news for all advisors, whether Luddite, technophile, or somewhere in between. For Luddites, constructivism puts technology in its place, which is to be regulated, explained, and guided by academic advisors' purpose, theories, and philosophies as educators. For technophiles, constructivism can be a muse that inspires new ways of using technology to engage advisees and enrich and revitalize advisors' relationships with them. In either case, as Digital Immigrants with a lexicon to guide them, advisors should be excited about learning the language of the Digital Natives.

When one learns a new language, one discovers ideas and terms that are unique to that language. There is no direct translation from Digital Native to Digital Immigrant, for example, for what "hypertext" means. The *American Heritage Dictionary of the English Language* (2000) defines it as "a computer-based text retrieval system that enables a user to access particular locations in web pages or other electronic documents by clicking on links within specific web pages or documents." Digital Immigrants may think of hypertext in terms of putting a document online and, if one clicks on it, it opens up. Hypertext is being able to access a book, article, or paper online. This Immigrant definition fails to capture the full definition of hypertext. Digital Natives, on the other hand, understand the real definition, but they may not be able to offer a translation in words; for them, hypertext just is, because they live in it authentically. They grew up being able to Google something, read about it, notice an ad for a movie in the background of what they are reading and use it to see what movies are playing, then watch a trailer for the movie, listen to a new song using the same program they used to watch the trailer, then send an Instant Message to a friend telling them about the song. Hypertext just is.

As part of our lexicon, constructivism gives advisors the means to understand hypertext in the Digital Native tongue and use it to engage new first-year students in their education. If we wish to introduce new students to what a baccalaureate degree is, we could make an Immigrant document—a paper catalog that lists each degree and what its requirements are. On the other hand, we could use the principles of constructivism and decide to represent a baccalaureate degree in terms of text, visual metaphors, video, and student testimony, all linked together but in such a way that students could choose which of these resources they want to look at and how deeply they want to delve into each. Each concept would connect with others related to it in a non-linear, almost map-like fashion that more accurately reflects how these concepts are related in reality (see "sample baccalaureate degree" at http://www.psu.edu/ftcap/tutorial/psy.htm or a better visual example of hypertext in service of a constructivist learning environment at http://viking.coe.uh.edu/~ichen/ebook/et-it/cover.htm). Hypertext affords this capability in the form of a web site. An online tutorial given to new Penn State students (Penn State University, 2005d) as part of the beginning of their advising experience offers an example of a web site designed using constructivist ideas and capitalizing on the unique advantages of hypertext. In particular, the representation of a sample baccalaureate degree given on this web site demonstrates how to represent concepts in a non-linear fashion (Penn State University, 2005e).

Other theories can be used to understand the potential of technology and how to use it to engage first-year students. Constructivism is just the first chapter in our primer on speaking Digital Native. More chapters already exist (Penn State University, 2005a) for other theories applied to technology in advising, and some remain to be written. Theories can and should guide the use of technology in the advising of first-year students.

E-mail

Things get more complicated, however, when we look at another realm in which both Digital Native students and Digital Immigrant advisors do have a lifetime of experience, one of primary importance in first-year advising: one-on-one communication. Technology has spawned new communication modalities that are unique, such as e-mail, and how new students grew up using these communication tools may be very different than how Immigrant advisors have reacted to them and begun to use them. Research on the use of e-mail in advising and examining students' and advisors' perceptions of e-mail (Lipschultz, 1999; Lipschultz & Merson, 2000; Woolston & Lipschultz, 1997, 1998) suggests that advisors believe that e-mail should be responded to in a day or two and that they believe e-mail is a good tool to use to disseminate information. Advisors also appear to believe that, if complex thought and/or decision making is involved, students should interact face-to-face with an advisor because e-mail interactions are inherently less rich than personal meetings since nonverbal cues are lost.

However, a survey of more than 1,200 students, including 900 first-year students (Lipschultz & Merson, 2000) revealed some Native views of e-mail that do not necessarily match with those of Immigrant advisors. Students were willing to wait three days or more for a response to some issues; they did not feel uncomfortable talking about serious issues via e-mail; they had varied perceptions about what was appropriate and inappropriate to discuss over e-mail. This discrepancy between students' and advisors' perceptions of e-mail suggests another possible language barrier that could hamper attempts to engage our first-year students in the advising process. Again, with the idea in mind that theory is the foundation of our Native-Immigrant lexicon, Immigrants can examine communication and linguistic theories to reflect on the nature of one-on-one interactions and learn to use e-mail to its fullest potential.

E-mail is a relatively unique communication modality because it can be a one-on-one communication method fostering a dialogue, yet it is asynchronous and place independent (Harasim, 1993). In essence, it affords the opportunity to have a conversation outside of time and space, and written text is used to hold this conversation. In addition, e-mail has been found to be less formal on average than other types of written text, it encourages personal disclosure, and it "helps develop a level conversational playing field" (Baron, 1998, p. 147). Finally, assumptions that something is lost in an e-mail interaction may not be true. Baron suggests that "experienced users of the medium usually deny that it obstructs human contact. It turns out that many ordinary individuals possess a compensatory literary capability to project their personality into writing destined for the computer screen" (p. 145).

In an attempt to better understand its nature, Baron (1998) conducted a linguistic analysis of e-mail by matching it against the well-established communication modalities of speech and writing along dimensions synthesized from a variety of linguistic models/perspectives. Among these dimensions were levels of formality, humor, and emotion; whether or not those involved in the communication were known or anonymous; whether or not what was communicated was perceived as recorded (i.e., written text) or ephemeral (i.e., spoken conversation); and the complexity of vocabulary. Baron concluded that e-mail is at times more like writing, at other times more like speech, and sometimes different from either.

Furthermore, e-mail is new enough to still be "creolizing" (Baron, p. 164), meaning that protocols for its use are evolving and being negotiated by its users in practice. This means that how e-mail will evolve as a communications medium is more a function of the social decisions of those using it than of technology. This is great news for advisors working with first-year students. Advisors can capitalize on the best that e-mail has to offer. It is informal and can help advisors establish bonds with their new advisees. Because conversations can be had outside space and time, students can express questions and concerns when they think of them rather than waiting for a meeting. Finally, while e-mail is often thought of as a conversation, it is text and, therefore, can be documented. At the same time, because e-mail has no formally established social guidelines accepted by all, advisors can explicitly establish protocols with their advisees when first meeting them by stating expectations for e-mail correspondences up-front. For example, issues of response time, what advisors can handle discussing through e-mail and what they cannot, and how comfortable advisors feel with personal disclosure through e-mail. All of these can be shared with new students when first meeting them and can vary from advisor to advisor.

Conversely, advisors should consider asking their advisees about their comfort level with e-mail. If there is a discrepancy between the expectations of advisor and advisee in terms of use of e-mail in the advising relationship, then the opportunity exists both for a teachable moment ("No, John, I cannot add you to a class right away if you e-mail me with a request to do so at three in the morning") and for the advisor to rise to the challenge and meet students halfway ("Jane, I realize that you work during the day, so perhaps we could have a few e-mail conversations about the classes you plan to take next semester").

Instant Messaging, Widgets, and Other New Technologies

E-mail is not the only technology new enough to be lacking a well-established protocol. Many exciting technologies are on the rise and offer great potential for facilitating student learning in the advisor-advisee relationship, but they have as yet no well-established place within that relationship. Instant Messaging (IM) is at the forefront of these technologies. While some institutions have already begun to use it in an advising capacity, its use in advising is far from ubiquitous. IM is similar to e-mail in that it is independent of place. However, unlike e-mail, IM is designed to be used in real time, just like a true conversation. Unlike a face-to-face conversation, however, it is also designed to occupy only a portion of a person's consciousness, i.e., a student can be doing other things (e.g., homework, research) while in an IM session with one or more people. IM's power is in its widespread use among Digital Natives in the social realm. One of our brightest and most organized students, for example, said she plans her life around

IM. Since it is possible that IM use among new students is far more common than even e-mail, it is certainly worth considering as a potential advising tool.

Another new technology with advising potential is the widget. Much as a web browser (such as Internet Explorer or Firefox) is software that allows people to view web pages, widget software allows people to run many different kinds of programs (called "widgets") on their computer desktops. Widgets are usually visual in nature, but can also sometimes involve sound. They can be a clock, a weather forecasting tool, a to-do list, a calendar, a dictionary, RSS feed readers ("Really Simple Syndication" is a format that web sites and blogs can use to send updated headlines to services like My Yahoo!), or anything a widget designer can dream up. One example of such software is Yahoo! Widgets (Yahoo!, 2006). Potential uses of widgets in advising could include a widget that is a calendar of institution-specific events, always visible to students on the desktops of their computers. Another widget could be a glossary of institution-specific terms, and yet another could be a course finder.

IM and widgets are just two new technologies among many. Others include databases for storing student contacts or keeping track of transfer credit articulation, podcasts (e.g., digital audio and/or video recordings of lectures, seminars, radio shows, that can be played back on a player), blogs (i.e., online diaries/journals), and e-portfolios (i.e., online multimedia compilations of and reflections on one's academic work and skills). This list will be ever-changing. So, rather than review these new technologies exhaustively, they are brought up again in the idea of using theories as a lexicon, as a guide to incorporate technology into the relationship between new advisee and advisor. When advisors have knowledge of this lexicon and knowledge of these theories, questions naturally arise that are both academically interesting and pragmatically relevant within the context of advising first-year students.

For example, is IM, linguistically speaking, more like speech or text? Is there an established protocol among Digital Natives for its use, or can advisors establish a protocol? Can a widget be viewed as a viable tool to integrate into a constructivist learning environment? Can widgets afford multiple representations of educational concepts? Can they be interactive? Thinking about and answering these questions before acting will determine whether or not advisors use technology or are used by it.

A Digital Divide?

After having made a case for how to approach the use of technology in the advising of new students, it is perhaps also necessary to address the concerns of some advisors as to whether or not technology should be used at all in advising. This debate revolves around two main concerns: first, that there is a digital divide among students, and second, that heavy use of technology in advising contexts will result in technology replacing advisors. Regarding the digital divide, an article in the May 2, 2003 issue of the *Chronicle of Higher Education* (Survey of College-Bound Students Finds No Digital Divide Among Them) states that there are no significant differences based on race in terms of access and use of technology among high school students bound for four-year colleges. This was based on a sample of 500 college-bound high school students of different races. However, the market research company that conducted the study also said that there probably was still a divide among students not bound for four-year colleges. A more recent article in the *Chronicle of Higher Education* (Farrell, 2005) suggests that perhaps the divide does spill over into college-bound students. The findings were based on the fall 2004 administration of the CIRP Freshman Survey conducted by researchers at the University of California at Los Angeles. The article frames the divide solely in terms of computer use in high school and suggests that it is a reality for Hispanic/Latino and African American students and growing for African American students. Still another source (Mossberger, Tolbert, & Stansbury, 2003) states that the access divide is shrinking but certainly not gone. This study did not specifically examine whether there is a divide among college-bound students; rather, it concluded that college graduates were significantly more likely to have Internet access.

Regardless of whether an access and/or use gap still exists for new students entering our institutions, minimizing use of technology at our institutions is certainly not a reasonable strategy to restore equality for potentially disadvantaged groups. For Mossberger et al. (2003), minimizing use of technology would imply that it is a luxury that we can do without. While they do acknowledge a digital divide, Mossberger et al. also describe technology as representative of "opportunity and democracy" and as a means of "participation in the economy and the political arena" (p. 5).

In other words, use of technology is not a luxury but has become so much a part of Western society that access to it is now more akin to the right to an education or the right to vote, and the digital divide needs to be redefined "beyond the confines of the access issue" (p. 4). In fact, Mossberger et al. (2003) begin to redefine the divide in terms like "information literacy" (p. 12) and "technical competencies" (p. 38). There may be disparities in terms of how able some students are to figure out a new piece of software, for example, or if the Internet is being used by new students to research majors and careers. There may be differences in students' experience with finding keywords for a search, evaluating credibility of a resource, and quoting a source properly as opposed to cutting-and-pasting its contents into a paper. Even Digital Natives, who are fluent in the use of technology, may not have been taught to use it as a tool in the service of thinking critically. As unfortunate as this newly redefined digital divide is, it only underscores the need for us to incorporate technology into advising in order to reduce the divide.

If You Build It, They Will Not Come (Anymore)

Finally, regarding the concern about technology replacing advisors, an initial response is that the legitimacy of this fear depends upon how one defines the advising relationship. If advising is defined as little more than reviewing checklists to make sure requirements are met and dispensing facts about one's institution, then these fears may be legitimate. If, on the other hand, advising is defined in the terms described earlier in this chapter—fostering independent learning and decision making and being interactive, reflective, and negotiated—then technology can only ever be a piece of this model rather than the whole pie. In any case, it should become evident in the following sections of this chapter (dealing with exemplary practices in advising and adapting classroom technologies to advising) that technology has only served to elevate the level of interactions advisors are having with their advisees.

Exemplary Practices

Exemplary practices in the use of technology to advance the teaching/advising connection for first-year students are evident across a variety of higher education institutions. Several specific examples are described below in some detail, and lists of additional related resources are provided.

Online Academic Orientation Programs for First-Year Students

Many institutions have had for years various types of summer orientation programs for their new first-year students. Traditionally, students travel to campus to participate in daylong (or longer) programs that may include placement testing and/or interpretation of placement test results; academic advising sessions; student affairs presentations; contact with faculty, advisors, and other staff members; and first-term course registration.

Georgia Perimeter College's (GPC) Online Orientation offers first-year students an online alternative to the traditional on-campus orientation to college. Through a step-by-step web site that includes links to supplemental material, the Online Orientation introduces students to the academic calendar, the college catalog, academic requirements, general education, degrees and certificate programs, the grading system, types of classes (e.g., traditional lecture, honors, college prep), and the schedule of classes. Part one of the orientation also addresses issues such as how to determine an appropriate course load. Part two provides links to a variety of academic resources (e.g., faculty advisors, tutoring, study abroad) and student services (e.g., advising and counseling services, disability services, enrollment and registration). Part three addresses questions about syllabi, academic honesty, academic success, and seeing an academic advisor. Each section concludes with an instant-feedback quiz that tests students' knowledge and recall of the material presented in the section.

GPC also provides customized paths through the online orientation for various types of students, such as recent high school graduates, nontraditional students, transfer students, and international students, and for various campus locations within the system. GPC estimates that it takes most students about 45 minutes to complete its online orientation program. In effect, Online Orientation offers much of the same material as an advisor does. Online Orientation was a 2003 winner of the National Academic Advising Association's Advising Technology Innovation Award (Georgia Perimeter College, 2005; see also chapter appendix).

Web-Based Student Information Systems

Many institutions have created web sites that provide access to student records for both students and academic advisors. The central features of these systems tend to be course registration, degree audits, grade reporting, and sometimes grade-point average calculations. Although these features do support academic advising, they typically do not actually provide academic advice to students. One exception is Penn State's eLion.

eLion is a web-based interactive advising system for Penn State students, faculty, and advisors. Students can use eLion to check their academic records (e.g., grades, semester schedule, degree audit) and process academic actions (e.g., course registration, entrance to major, late course drop, withdrawal). Advisors can use eLion to view rosters of their assigned advisees, request degree audits, communicate directly with their advisees, and record advising contacts. Faculty can use eLion to view class lists, submit final grades, and provide a link to course syllabi.

One of the most innovative teaching/advising features of eLion is the Late Course Drop module. Students can use this module to receive expert, individualized advice about whether or not to late drop a course from their schedule. When a student logs in to eLion and selects the Late Course Drop module from the menu, he or she is first given the definition of a late course drop. The student's current schedule is then displayed, and the student is asked to select the course to be late dropped. Because eLion interfaces with the university's student information system, it "knows" who the student is (e.g., it accesses data about the student's major, late drop credits already used and remaining, special status as a student-athlete, honors student, international student) and uses this information to advise the student about specific outcomes should the student choose to late drop that specific course. The student is asked to indicate the reason(s) he or she is considering late dropping this course and is then given specific advice about possible ways to resolve the issues surrounding that reason. Students are asked a number of other questions, and their responses are used to provide additional information and advice.

In some cases, students are advised not to late drop a course, but to pursue alternatives instead. In cases where a student would become part-time by late dropping a course, appropriate warnings are given and referrals are made to specific offices as appropriate (e.g., financial aid, support center for student-athletes, office of international students).

The eLion late course drop module is an example of using technology to teach students, especially first-year students who may be more academically naïve than upper-division students, about the policies and procedures concerning a university process and to provide specific advice to the student regarding his or her particular situation. Other advising-related modules in eLion teach students about the policies, procedures, pros, cons, and alternatives related to withdrawing from the university; how to calculate semester and cumulative grade-point averages based on projected grades in current courses; how to calculate the grades needed to reach a target grade-point average; how to prepare for an advising appointment with their assigned advisor; and more.

Since this approach fits well with Digital Natives' way of processing information, first-year students can come to advising appointments already armed with facts. What they then want is the opportunity to discuss, in more nuanced ways, what these facts mean to them, how to weigh the pros and cons, and how to make informed decisions in complex situations. The advisor is no longer just a purveyor of information and facts; the advisor becomes an educator engaged in discussions that must occur at a much higher level of sophistication and discernment. eLion, was a 1998 certificate of merit winner of the National Academic Advising Association's Advising Technology Innovation Award (Penn State University, 2005c; see also chapter appendix).

Web-Based Programs for First-Year Students

The DUS Navigator is a web-based program designed to provide a systematic way for undecided/exploratory first-year students to navigate their first two semesters in college. A winner of the 1998 National Academic Advising Association and ACT Outstanding Institutional Advising Program Award (see also chapter appendix), *The DUS Navigator* was developed by Penn State's Division of Undergraduate Studies (DUS). The overarching goal of the program is to help new, first-year students in making informed educational decisions. It also provides a framework that new advisors can use to understand the process of major exploration and how to advise first-year students who are faced with not only the traditional adjustments to college but also the process of deciding on a major. According to its web site (Penn State University, 2005b)

> *The DUS Navigator*, a series of guides distributed to students at critical times during their first year, includes time lines, related worksheets, and supplemental information. Students use these guides to gain an understanding of the objectives of the educational planning process, to learn how and when to initiate important steps in this process, and to acquire information that is critical for academic success. The *Navigator* enables students to take an active role in their educational planning and to work more productively with advisors to make informed decisions.

The development of the *DUS Navigator* advising program was guided by the following goals:

◇ To teach students to become better planners and decision makers
◇ To encourage students to behave in ways that demonstrate an active and thoughtful approach to problem solving

◇ To assist students to determine what information and/or educational planning activities would be helpful to them as they develop and refine their educational plans
◇ To help students prepare to have more productive interactions with academic advisors
◇ To deliver information to students at critical times during their first year of enrollment to avoid overwhelming them with large amounts of complex information all at once

The DUS Navigator has been adapted by other institutions for their students. Westminster College's version is called the Pathfinder (Westminster College, 2006). According to the *Pathfinder* Advising Program's web site, students will receive guides and information delivered to their campus e-mail addresses throughout the first college years. These guides include information on

◇ How to add or drop courses
◇ How to handle being on a wait-list
◇ Grades, credit/no credit, midterm reports, academic probation
◇ How to conduct academic self-evaluations
◇ Important approaching deadlines
◇ Major and career exploration
◇ How to design your academic plan
◇ Campus resources
◇ The importance of academic advising appointments

Each *Navigator* or *Pathfinder* guide is introduced by a series of learning objectives. Some of the guides are related to the exploration of educational opportunities, while other guides relate to assessing academic performance, deciding whether or not to late drop a course, using degree audits, registering for classes for the upcoming semester, reassessing course schedules, and learning about important academic policies and procedures. Students are expected to complete the worksheets and other activities in the guides and to bring these materials with them to appointments with their assigned advisor.

Although neither the *Navigator* nor the *Pathfinder* is a formal course, both are structured as such in the sense that they incorporate a curriculum and syllabus, lessons, supplemental readings, assignments, and assessments. The students' academic advisor is the de facto instructor. The most significant difference is that students do not earn course credit or a grade; instead, they learn about themselves, the characteristics of academic programs, the fit between their personal characteristics and the program, important academic policies and procedures, and the value and variety of educational opportunities available to them.

The *Navigator* is an example of the use of technology (in this case, the web and hypertext) as an educational tool to apply what we as advisor/educators know about student development, learning theories, and learning styles in the process of helping first-year students (Digital Natives) make a successful transition to higher education.

Course management software (CMS)—such as Blackboard (http://www.blackboard.com), Moodle (http://moodle.org/) or ANGEL (http://cyberlearninglabs.com/)—is a technology that was designed to supplement traditional classroom instruction. It is also used to create and manage courses that are offered completely online, often (but not solely) for distance education programs. CMS allows instructors to create web-based materials for their courses without having to know how to create web pages. CMS may also include functions such as online quizzes, chat (Instant Messaging between a student and the instructor or among students and the instructor), lesson submission, e-mail, calendars, grade books, automatic creation of student teams, and similar kinds of tools. The software allows an instructor to control all of these functions for a given course from a single access point (i.e., one CMS web site). It allows students who are enrolled in multiple courses whose instructors are all using the same CMS to view course materials and participate in class activities all from a single access point (web page) as well.

Although CMS was designed primarily as a tool for instructors and students affiliated with a specific course, it can also be used to instruct other groups of individuals who share a common bond, such as all first-year students assigned to a particular advisor. By creating instructional groups (courses), advisors (teachers) can use CMS to provide instruction to their advisees (learners). Advisors can also conduct chat sessions with their advisees, create self-scoring quizzes to test their advisees' knowledge of key academic policies and procedures, e-mail their advisees as a group, and use other CMS functions in much the same way that a traditional classroom instructor would use these functions. According to the results of a national survey on technology in academic advising (Leonard, 2004), 21% of the respondents were already using CMS on a regular basis in their role as advisors, and 27% were interested in learning more about it.

At Providence College, ANGEL (A New Global Environment for Learning) is a CMS that is being used not only in traditional classroom instruction for hundreds of courses but also to support academic advising (Providence College, 2005). Advising "groups" (similar to courses, but without requiring official course registration) have been created (a) by academic advisors for special subpopulations of advisees (e.g., first-year students, undeclared major students, premedical science students), (b) as resources for faculty advisors, and (c) to administer pre-orientation placement exams in mathematics and Spanish to incoming first-year students. The intention is not to replace one-on-one advising contacts between students and advisors but rather to supplement these contacts.

The use of course-management software at Providence changes the nature of the personal student contacts from "bookkeeping to advising" (Crafts and Haberle, 2004). This is the same outcome that was experienced with the introduction of advising modules in Penn State's eLion and the introduction of telephone registration at many institutions. Students continue to need and want individual contact with academic advisors, but the level of the discourse between students and advisors is raised to a higher level because advisors are no longer seen as the primary source for basic academic information. Students can and do obtain their information from a variety of web resources that are available almost continuously, while most advisors are available only for a limited number of hours each week (see chapter appendix). Given the information that has been presented in this chapter about learning theories as they relate to technology, about the types of technology that can be used in academic advising, and about notable examples of how technologies are being used to support the teaching/advising connection, how should academic advisors and their institutions approach technology in advising first-year students?

Recommendations

Technology divorced from humanity is worse than no technology at all. (Harvey Mudd College, 2000)

1. Keep in mind that first-year students (as Digital Natives) may view technology in very different ways than academic advisors (as Digital Immigrants) but that both can learn to speak a common language.
2. Do not be afraid to use technology just because you are uncomfortable with it; learn to use it as you would any other teaching tool or skill.

3. Do not use technology just because it is there! (see point #4)
4. Use theories and what you know as an educator to guide the use of technology in advising.
5. Make every effort to define advising at your institution at a level beyond bookkeeping and checklists, so that it becomes clear in your environment that technology does not replace advising but rather elevates the level of discourse.
6. Use ideas from the exemplary web sites in this chapter if it will help your institution develop technology in advising.

The Future?

Many of the types of technologies that have been discussed in this chapter have undergone and will continue to undergo rapid changes. Laptops, which are already replacing desktop computers, are in turn being replaced by handheld computers; wireless is replacing wired; cellular technology is replacing landlines; iPods are replacing CD players; and cell phones are becoming "smarter" (i.e. providing additional functions such as e-mail and web browsing). It is likely that we will see further convergence of existing (and emerging) technologies into a sort of überdigital Swiss army knife that could include all of the following functions (and probably more) in devices no larger than today's cell phones: telephone, e-mail, e-text (i.e., books, newspapers, blogs, dictionaries, encyclopedias, class notes), instant messaging, television, radio, satellite, music, video, web surfing, digital photography and videography, games, GPS (global positioning systems), personal information management (i.e., calendars, address books, or "to do" lists), word processing, spreadsheets, and databases.

All of these technologies currently exist in handheld devices (though not as yet in a single device) and even newer technologies and uses for those technologies are under development. It is possible that higher education in general and academic advising in particular may be slow to adopt or even adapt to these new technologies. If, however, higher education acts with foresight, it will, rather than merely adapting to the changes, anticipate and take advantage of those changes. As students begin to do more with personal technologies, they will also expect education to do more for them with those technologies, whether through instructors or through academic advisors. Just as lectures, for example, can be provided in a variety of digital formats (e.g., streaming or downloadable audio and/or video), some academic advising information and functions could be made available through various technologies as well.

Advisors, then, would be well-advised to anticipate, plan for, understand, adapt to, and appropriately adopt those technologies that will used by their first-year students in the coming years.

References

American Heritage Dictionary of the English Language. (2000). Retrieved November 30, 2005, from http://www.bartleby.com/61/7/H0360700.html

Baron, N. (1998). Letters by phone or speech by other means: The linguistics of email. *Language & Communication, 18*, 133-170.

Bohannan, P., & Glazer, M. (Eds.). (1988). *High points in anthropology* (2nd ed.). New York: McGraw-Hill.

Chen, I. (n.d.). *Constructivism.* Retrieved November 30, 2005, from http://viking.coe.uh.edu/~ichen/ebook/et-it/constr.htm

Crafts, C. B., & Haberle, C. (2004). *Building bridges between teaching & advising with course management software.* Retrieved October 31, 2005, from http://72.14.207.104/u/nacada?q=cache:zOQ4GWA2fegJ:www.nacada.ksu.edu/nationalconf/2004/handouts/S060H1.ppt+cms&hl=en&ie=UTF-8

Farrell, E. F. (2005, February 4). Among freshman, a growing digital divide. *The Chronicle of Higher Education*, p. A32.

Georgia Perimeter College. (2005). *Online registration.* Retrieved November 30, 2005, from http://www.gpc.edu/orientation

Harasim, L. M. (Ed.). (1993). *Global networks: Computers and international communication.* Cambridge, MA: MIT Press.

Harvey Mudd College. (2000). *Introduction: A message to prospective Harvey Mudd College students.* Retrieved October 31, 2005, from http://www.hmc.edu/admin/colrel/catalogue/2000-2001/Introduction.html

Hoover, W.A. (1996, August). *The practice implications of constructivism. SEDL Letter, IX(3).* Retrieved November 30, 2005, from http://www.sedl.org/pubs/sedl-letter/welcome.html

Kassop, M. (2003, May/June). Ten ways online education matches, or surpasses, face-to-face learning. *The Technology Source Archives.* Retrieved November 30, 2005, from http://technologysource.org/

Leonard, M. J. (2004). Results of a national survey on technology in academic advising. *NACADA Journal, 24*(1 & 2), 24–33.

Lipschultz, W. (1999). What can and should we do with e-mail? An outline for a systematic approach. *The Mentor: An Academic Advising Journal, 1*(1). Retrieved November 30, 2005, from http://www.psu.edu/dus/mentor/

Lipschultz, W., & Merson, D. (2000, October). *Students' and advisors' perceptions of appropriate e-mail use.* Paper presented at the 24th Annual National Conference, National Academic Advising Association, Orlando, FL.

Mingle, J. R. (1997). *Technology 2000: Recommendations on the utilization of information technology in the Oklahoma higher education system.* Retrieved October 31, 2005, from http://www.okhighered.org/pdf/oktechno.pdf

Mossberger, K., Tolbert, C. J., & Stansbury, M. (2003). *Virtual inequality: Beyond the digital divide.* Washington, DC: Georgetown University Press.

Penn State University. (2005a). *Basic concepts from select educational theories and their suggested application to advising web sites.* Retrieved November 30, 2005, from http://www.psu.edu/dus/technology/theories/advising.pdf

Penn State University. (2005b). *The DUS Navigator.* Retrieved November 30, 2005, from http://www.psu.edu/dus/navigate/

Penn State University. (2005c). *eLion.* Retrieved November 30, 2005, from https://elion.oas.psu.edu/

Penn State University. (2005d). *First-year testing, counseling, and advising program.* Retrieved November 30, 2005, from http://www.psu.edu/ftcap/tutorial/

Penn State University. (2005e). *Psychology.* Retrieved November 30, 2005, from http://www.psu.edu/ftcap/tutorial/psy.htm

Prensky, M. (2001a, October). Digital natives, digital immigrants. *On the horizon, 9*(5). Retrieved November 30, 2005, from http://www.marcprensky.com/writing/

Prensky, M. (2001b, December). Digital natives, digital immigrants, part II: Do they really think differently? *On the Horizon, 9*(6). Retrieved November 30, 2005, from http://www.marcprensky.com/writing/

Providence College. (2005). *Angel*. Retrieved November 30, 2005, from http://angel.providence. edu/frames.aspx

Science Made Simple. (1997). *Why is the sky blue?* Retrieved November 30, 2005, from http:// www.sciencemadesimple.com/sky_blue.html

Survey of college-bound students finds no digital divide among them. (2003, May 2). *The Chronicle of Higher Education*, p. A37.

Westminster College. (2006). *Welcome to the Pathfinder advising program: A program of exploration - designed for first year students*. Retrieved April 24, 2006, from http://www.westminstercollege.edu/start_center/index.cfm?parent=373&detail=3031

Woolston, D., & Lipschultz, W. (1997, October). *E-mail advising: Art, science, or waste of time?* Paper presented at the 21st Annual National Conference, National Academic Advising Association, Kansas City, MO.

Woolston, D., & Lipschultz, W. (1998, October). *Using e-mail effectively in academic advising*. Pre-conference workshop conducted at the 22nd Annual National Conference, National Academic Advising Association, San Diego, CA.

Yahoo! (2006). *Yahoo!Widgets. Keep the stuff that you love right at your fingertips*. Retrieved April 24, 2006, from http://widgets.yahoo.com/

Appendix

Selected Online Orientation Web Sites

First-Year Advising (Florida Gulf Coast University)
    http://enrollment.fgcu.edu/advising/

First-Year Testing, Counseling and Advising Program (Penn State)
    http://www.psu.edu/ftcap/tutorial/

iCAN Integrated Counseling and Advisement Network (Central Piedmont Community College)
    http://www1.cpcc.edu/ican/orientation/default.htm

New Student Advising Session (Harper College)
    http://www.harpercollege.edu/services/newstu/orientation/advising1.htm

New Student Orientation (Del Mar College)
    http://www.delmar.edu/orientation/

Online Orientation (Cypress College)
    http://www.cypresscollege.edu/%7Ecounseling/orientation/

Preview Prep (University of Florida)
    http://www.preview.ufl.edu/prep/

Virtual Orientation (Carroll Community College)
    http://www.carrollcc.edu/studentlife/orientation/default.asp

Selected Student Information System Web Sites

iCAN Integrated Counseling and Advisement Network (Central Piedmont Community College)
    http://www.cpcc.edu/ican/

My Online Services (Bellevue Community College)
    http://www.bcc.ctc.edu/services/

MyISU Portal (Indiana State University)
    http://myisu.indstate.edu/cp/home/loginf

MyUCLA (University of California at Los Angeles)
    http://my.ucla.edu/
PAWS (Lousiana State University)
    http://paws001.lsu.edu/paws000.nsf

Selected Web Sites for/About Advising and First-Year Students

First-Year Advising Services Handbook (Florida Gulf Coast University)
    http://enrollment.fgcu.edu/advising/fashandbook/
Freshman Year Advising (National Academic Advising Association)
    http://www.nacada.ksu.edu/Awards/archive/fya.htm
The FYI Program at Beloit College (Beloit College)
    http://www.beloit.edu/~fyi/
National Resource Center for the First-Year Experience & Students in Transition
    http://www.sc.edu/fye/
Policy Center on the First Year of College (Brevard College)
    http://www.firstyear.org

Selected Course-Management Resources

Chastain, M. (2002). *Online academic advising.* Retrieved October 31, 2005, from http://conference.wcet.info/2002/presentations/documents/Chastain_000.ppt

Donnelly, N., & Bucey, B. (2003). *Online academic advising using Blackboard.* (University of Cincinnati). Retrieved October 31, 2005, from http://www.oln.org/conferences/OLN2003/papers/Online_Academic_Advising_Using_Blackboard.pdf

Woods, R. G. (2004). Creating a virtual advising center: Student services in an online environment. *The Mentor: An Academic Advising Journal.* Retrieved October 31, 2005, from http://www.psu.edu/dus/mentor

Chapter Six

Advising First-Year Students Before Enrollment

Jim Black

In U.S. higher education, references to the importance of academic advising can be traced to the early work of Newman (1872, 1873). More recently, the research of Light (2001) reaffirmed that "good advising may be the single most underestimated characteristic of a successful college experience" (p. 81). There are many, sometimes discrete, components that combine to make academic advising effective. The concepts of course scheduling, mentoring, and academic advising are all grounded in the "two historical aims of undergraduate education: to involve students with the content of their learning and to involve them with the teacher" (Frost, 2000, p. 3). When decoupled and applied early in the student's college experience, the impact of mentoring and course scheduling, two critical components of academic advising on student success, is significant.

At no time in the college student's experience is the connection with an academic advisor more important than during and before his or her first semester. Students tend to be more vulnerable, disoriented, and consequently more receptive to receiving advice at the beginning of their postsecondary academic career. Many researchers and educators have recognized that students' pre-enrollment characteristics such as their cultural background, prior academic experience, gender, and socioeconomic status may have a greater impact on college success than the campus environment and the educational experience (Newcomb, 1966; Astin, 1977, 1993; Tinto, 1987, 1993; Upcraft, Gardner, & Associates, 1989). These findings complement Light's (2001) conclusion that "the best advising is tailored to each undergraduate's unique situation—his or her particular background, strengths, areas that need improvement, and hopes and dreams" (p. 85). Understanding the pre-enrollment characteristics and corresponding developmental and educational needs of entering students is the foundation for this chapter.

An underlying premise central to this chapter is that effective academic advising, before enrollment, is paramount to influencing a positive academic outcome for entering students. Mentoring and scheduling are two academic advising strategies that impact both short- and long-term academic outcomes, match student developmental needs with course offerings, and protect the students' first-semester schedules from high-risk courses or high-risk combinations of courses.

Mentoring is critical as students make the transition to college. Meaningful advisor/advisee relationships not only contribute to student success but also have residual benefits for the institution: student and alumni loyalty, future financial donations, positive word-of-mouth testimonials about the educational experience, and, tangentially, institutional image.

A second component of advising, course scheduling, requires different methodology and strategies. Advisor skills, training, knowledge, personality, and advisee interactions vary depending on the desired outcome. Treating course scheduling and mentoring as discrete, but connected, entities of academic advising allows for a targeted selection, training, and evaluation of advisors and the implementation of creative strategies for engaging students with faculty and staff prior to enrollment.

Though separating course scheduling and mentoring components of academic advising may be preferable from an internal management perspective, integrating the pre-enrollment experience is preferable from the students' perspective. This chapter explores integration through coordination of communication flow; streamlining of enrollment processes such as admissions, placement testing, advising, and orientation; and a blend of high-touch and high-tech advising services. Regarding the latter, technology, in this context, is not intended to replace personal contact but rather to foster and enhance human interactions. In addition, advising models that are illustrative of these integration principals are described in chapter 5.

The Advisor's Conceptual Framework

Generational differences often lead to incongruence between advisor and advisee expectations—resulting in a less than satisfying advising experience. Gordon and Steele (2005) speak to generational differences among advisors and how those differences affect advising styles. Traditionalist advisors (born between 1922 and 1943) are likely to value fairness, avoid conflict, and be uncomfortable with change. They have strong work ethics and expect others to as well. Viewing interactions with advisees through their experiences as an undergraduate is common among all generational types but because of the age gap, differences between the Traditionalist advisor's collegiate experiences and the real world of his or her students may be acutely pronounced. For example, Millennial students are more likely to view issues of fairness as absolutes that are either right or wrong, while the traditionalist advisor may have many interpretations of fairness depending on circumstances, precedence, institutional politics, or personal experiences. Another significant difference is how these two groups tend to view the world in relation to change. The Traditionalist advisor tends to avoid change at all costs while most Millennials embrace it.

According to Gordon and Steele (2005), Baby Boomer advisors (born between 1943 and 1960) are often service-oriented, accommodating team players, sensitive to student and peer needs. They tend to be good problem solvers; therefore, they can effectively assist their advisees with some of their more difficult issues. Because many of them went to college in 1960s and 70s, a time of activism and self- enlightenment on college campuses, they expect their students to be actively engaged in socially relevant campus life experiences and, consequently, in their academic advising sessions.

Generation X advisors (born between 1960 and 1980) are adaptable and independent (Gordon & Steele, 2005). They dislike the bureaucracy common to higher education policies and procedures and, as such, are able to empathize with their frustrated advisees. Often, they will seek out unconventional methods for working with their advisees—granting exceptions, advocating for a student's unique circumstance over institutional policies and practices, and recommending seemingly unorthodox strategies and solutions to academic challenges.

Developmental Needs of First-Year Students

While the advisor's conceptual framework is important to understand, it is imperative to respond to the developmental needs of prospective students. Since the vast majority of college students are Millennials or Gen-Xers, the needs of both populations are described in detail in this chapter. To put into perspective, 10.4 million college students in the United States are between the ages of 18 and 24 (Millennials), 3.6 million are between the ages of 25 and 34 (Gen-Xers), and only 2.8 million are age 35 or older—many of whom are also Gen-Xers (U.S. Department of Education, 2005).

Gen-Xers

Today's Generation X student is most often a returning adult who has prior higher education experience. Nonetheless, it should not be assumed prior experience equates to awareness of educational options and corresponding self-directed action. Indeed, many returning adults are in transition: changing careers, looking for job security or mobility, facing life challenges such as divorce, the loss of a loved one, or an empty nest. Such change can be unsettling at this stage in their lives, so many are eager for advice from an advisor while others who are incredibly busy balancing family, work, and community obligations may view the pre-enrollment advising experience as an unnecessary burden.

They bring to the advising session a wide variety of attributes (i.e., different educational backgrounds, diverse life experiences, fears of the new technologies of instruction and the classroom) and needs (i.e., for remedial programs, strategies to pay off previously accumulated student loan debt, feelings of intellectual inadequacy, and becoming a member of a community). They also expect prompt and reliable service and perceive the faculty as performing a service they have purchased (Lindsey, 2003). For the advisor, the typical Gen-Xer's pre-enrollment attributes and needs require a customized approach delivered by an individual with considerable skill and knowledge.

Millennials

According to Howe and Strauss (2000, 2003), Millennials are confident, optimistic, team-oriented, rule-driven, achievement-focused, engaged, technologically sophisticated, consumer-savvy, and civic-minded. Millennials may, however, rely too heavily on their parents (labeled somewhat pejoratively by the media as "helicopter parents" because of their tendency to hover over their children and be involved in every aspect of their lives). They often are not concerned about how colleges and universities are organized and will make only minimal efforts to understand the current nomenclature, policies, and procedures of higher education. Even more so than Gen-X peers, the Millennials may have zero tolerance for delays. Frand (2000) describes them as a culture of immediacy. They expect their inquiries to be answered immediately. They also expect rapid turnaround of admissions decisions, financial aid awards, transfer credit evaluations, and housing assignments.

Astute Millennials anticipate being assigned an advisor soon after being admitted and expect the advisor to contact them even before orientation. They may expect the advisor they meet at orientation to remain their advisor throughout at least their first year. Contrary to our desire to have them assume responsibility for their own educational future, most first-year students are content with having courses pre-selected for them. Like the Gen-Xers, the attributes and experiences Millennials bring to pre-enrollment advising can shape the outcome and dictate advising strategies.

Components of Academic Advising: Course Scheduling and Mentoring

The course scheduling and mentoring functions are distinctly different—requiring different advising skills and advisor/student roles and actions. Furthermore, by focusing on course scheduling and mentoring as separate functions, advisor and advisee interactions are no longer confined to the narrow advising window during new student orientation or prior to the beginning of each subsequent registration period. Though scheduling is limited to specific time frames, mentoring should occur throughout the academic year.

Course Scheduling

Course scheduling is not the sum total of academic advising; but in the rush to meet student and institutional needs (i.e., to assure that students leave their preenrollment advising experience with a first-semester schedule), course scheduling often takes precedence over the more nuanced aspects of advising, thus sending the "wrong message" to students about the nature and purposes of academic advising. By educating students more fully during their pre-enrollment phase to the goals of academic advising, students can then come to appreciate and more fully use their subsequent contacts with advisors to go beyond the mechanical process of scheduling. In fact, course scheduling as an outcome of academic advising has now become one of the most technologically enhanced activities on our campuses. Hopefully, by introducing students to the true purposes of academic advising, students will be able to separate this course scheduling function from the educative purposes and learning outcomes of academic advising.

Mentoring

Mentoring can be defined in many ways, yet it is best described as a one-to-one learning relationship (Lester & Johnson, 1981) between an advisor and advisee. How and when this relationship is first initiated and then cultivated determines its impact on recruitment, advising, and retention outcomes. Pre-enrollment advising may take many forms. Kramer (2000) presents a model for viewing the difference between prescriptive learning and developmental teaching (Table 1). A developmental model is preferred at the pre-enrollment stage because it is designed to view students holistically while meeting them where they are developmentally. The model also requires students to become active participants in the process—exploring their interests, setting goals, and assuming shared responsibility with their advisor for achieving identified goals. Furthermore, developmental learning has accountability built into the process. As students continue their academic career, these skills will serve them well.

One emerging approach to academic advising begins with contacts at the point of admission. Advisors engage in outreach through phone, e-mail, or face-to-face meetings. The purpose of the first contact is to create a profile of the student that expands beyond the academic information captured at the point of application (e.g., interests, preferred learning styles, and educational and career goals). Profiles are used throughout the advising experience to customize the interactions. The second contact more thoroughly explores life and educational goals and associates identified goals with specific action plans. As the learning relationship strengthens, advisors provide periodic reality checks to ensure the student's action plan is still aligned with related goals. By the third interaction, advisors begin to encourage their advisees to accept more personal responsibility for the achievement of their goals. Other subsequent advising sessions involve teaching the student how to access institutional resources and checking the student's progress toward goals. With each interaction, the advisor and advisee engage in a series of reflections often followed by adaptations either to the advisor's approach or the student's action plan.

Table 1

Difference Between Prescriptive and Developmental Teaching

Prescriptive Learning	Developmental Teaching
Advisor has primary responsibility.	Advisor and student share responsibility.
Focus is on limitations.	Focus is on potentialities.
Effort is problem oriented.	Effort is growth oriented.
Relationship is based on status.	Relationship is based on trust and respect.
Relationship is based on the giving of advice.	Relationship is based on equal and shared problem solving.
Evaluation is done by the advisor.	Evaluation is a shared process.

Source. Adapted from Kramer, 2005, p. 85. Reprinted with permission.

A specific example of such a model can be found in Johnson County Community College (JCCC) Lifelines. The JCCC model begins with life, education, and career planning followed by investigation through assessment (Burnett & Oblinger, 2003). From exploration of goals and related assessment, skilled advisors guide prospective students through the development of an educational plan and discuss options for integrating the plan into their present life. The advising session ends with a discussion of enrollment options that are flexible enough to fit within a student's busy lifestyle yet substantial enough to move him or her forward in a timely completion of an educational plan.

Course Scheduling in the Context of Academic Advising

Course scheduling is essentially a prelude to formal registration. This process typically occurs during an orientation program before the start of a semester. However, an increasing number of institutions are participating in block scheduling—providing enrolling students with a prepackaged set of courses based on their intended area of study, the institution's general education requirements, or linked learning experiences.

Regardless of how pre-enrollment advising is implemented, the same fundamental tenets designed to enhance student success should be followed. First, advisors should make every effort to match student goals and abilities with course offerings. Completing unnecessary courses and failing to successfully complete a course result in delayed time-to-degree. Second, advisors should protect first-semester schedules, if possible, from high-risk courses (i.e., courses with high percentages of D, F, and W grades). Taking fewer than 13 and more than 18 hours (in a semester configuration) can also place a student at risk unnecessarily. For some students, it may be prudent to limit the number of large lecture classes, as well. Third, good advising may mean intervening when students alter the original schedule, placing them at risk. Automated notifications of schedule changes can alert advisors that an intervention is needed.

Integration of the Pre-enrollment Advising Experience

Students desire a streamlined enrollment process leading up to and following the advising experience. To consistently deliver timely, relevant information in an organized fashion, it is important to have an integrated communication flow, carefully engineered processes, and sophisticated technological support.

Communications Flow

Too often, prospective students receive disconnected communications from their institution. The Admissions Office sends recruitment materials, the Financial Aid Office sends a request for verification, Residence Life mails out housing assignments, the Orientation Office invites students to participate in a pre-enrollment activity, and Student Accounts sends the bill. Though these communications each have a distinct and necessary purpose, seldom are they coordinated to ensure a message of consistency. Nor are these communications always sequenced in a manner that is natural to the student recipients. Rarely does one office even know that the other has communicated with prospective students. Regrettably, institutions can appear disorganized to students.

Addressing this disconnect requires creating a campus-wide communication plan. Every contact must be included in a master calendar of communications, follow the institution's design template, incorporate the core message, and be shared broadly on campus. Regarding the latter, sample communications should be placed on an intranet, network folder, or a student's electronic file with one-click access. The goal is that when students contact any office on campus to inquire about a communication they have received, an informed employee will be able to help them.

Process Engineering

There are many processes that interface with or impact the new student academic advising experience. Four will be discussed here: (a) admissions, (b) placement testing, (c) orientation, and (d) summer bridge programs. The first three prepare students for the advising experience, while summer bridge programs often incorporate advising components.

Communication throughout the *admissions cycle* is about influencing choice and providing useful information. As it relates to advising, admissions communication should focus on establishing and managing expectations along with cultivating a relationship with the prospective student. A description of the steps in the advising process should be included in the letter of admission or an enclosed enrollment handbook. Ideally, this written communication would be followed by phone or e-mail contact from the assigned advisor to answer any questions about the advising process, delineate expectations for the role of the student and the role of the advisor in this newly forged partnership, and begin a dialogue about the student's goals. While there are transactional elements to this communication, it is primarily relational by design. Relationships, not transactions, influence the college decision making process. For the advisor/advisee partnership to succeed, it must be grounded in mutual respect and trust, hence, it is critical to build a relationship between the advisor and student early in the pre-enrollment process.

Private colleges and universities and some public institutions are quite adept at connecting students with advisors before enrollment. For the institutions that engage in such practices, the potential benefit could be a higher yield from admit-to-enroll, increased first-year persistence, improved academic success in the first-year, and enhanced student satisfaction. Various models exist for creating advisor/advisee connections. Some are as simple as advisor phone-a-thons, automated e-mail campaigns or direct mail, and events such as open houses and area receptions where face-to-face interactions can occur. More sophisticated models involve ongoing communication usually through multiple channels such as those described above as well as web-based portals designed around students' preferences and characteristics as they relate to their life with the institution (e.g., major, classification, residency status); virtual, self-paced advising modules to gain mastery of some specific content; web chats or blogs (web journals) with advisors and peers in an advising group; and podcasts (digitized audio broadcasts), vodcasts (digitized video broadcasts), or webinars (seminars delivered on the web) with content about the advising process, curriculum options, and degree requirements. Technology provides a means to engage students with people and content as early and as often as deemed necessary to ensure the antecedents for success have been well established. (For more information on technology, see chapter 5.) Such antecedents might include assessing interests, defining student goals, understanding degree requirements, developing an academic plan, and identifying strategies for successfully completing the first semester (e.g., time management, note-taking, understanding professors, transitioning from high school to college, and embracing new responsibilities).

Cultivating relationships typically requires less technical and more human interaction. At many institutions, advisors assume a mentoring role, while others have developed programs where a student has both an academic advisor and a mentor. For example, the University of North Carolina at Greensboro has 42 mentors who each adopt a cohort of up to 25 high school seniors. Though these mentors are not the students' advisor of record, they begin interacting with these students in the fall of their senior year and continue this mentoring relationship until the end of the first month of the students' first year at the university or until students opt out of the program. They begin interactions with these new students by exploring life, career, and educational goals followed by assistance in creating an educational map including a tentative schedule of courses. The mentor program concludes with two early intervention contacts within the first four weeks of class. Along the way, mentors direct students to campus resources, provide reality checks, and challenge students to take responsibility for their academic pursuits.

Another exemplary program is at Arkansas State University. New students are assigned a mentor who also is their instructor for the first-year transition course. The continuity and frequency of interaction fostered through this model allows for strong bonding to occur. In addition to the assigned mentor, students have a separate advisor from their program of study.

Placement Tests

Placement-test results are used to gain a heightened understanding of a student's academic needs beyond what can be gleaned from a college application, high school transcripts, and standardized test scores (Astin 1971, 1984; Carranza & Ender, 2003). Cumulative information gathered to create a student profile is used by advisors to provide guidance about appropriate course levels (particularly in English, mathematics, foreign languages, and some sciences), identify the need for tutorial assistance in a specific academic area, connect a student's interests to the academic curriculum, and suggest related cocurricular activities (Kramer & Spencer, 1989).

Unfortunately, placement testing on some campuses is viewed as a "necessary evil" and crammed into a busy orientation schedule. Some campuses have decoupled placement testing from orientation and, thus, require students to come on site at a different time to complete the testing. One-stop models such as those at Capital Community College and Indiana University-Purdue University Indianapolis ease the burden on students by allowing them to complete multiple "business" transactions during a single visit. A growing number of institutions have placement exams offsite or online to make them more accessible to students. Others use scores from the SAT or ACT to make initial course placements.

Regardless of the mode of delivery, placement tests must be valid predictors of student readiness to be useful. Furthermore, advisors must know how to interpret placement test results to make appropriate course selection. It is critical that institutions validate their instruments and assess their use in academic advising.

Orientation

Orientation has evolved from being the much maligned "fun and games" approach to (a) encompassing such topics as health and wellness, career exploration, student conduct, and academic integrity; (b) disseminating practical information about financial aid, housing, and commuter life; (c) facilitating enrollment processes and business transactions such as placement testing, advising, registration, bill payment, student ID cards, parking permits, book orders, and even immunization; (d) underscoring institutional values such as respecting diversity and appreciating global issues; and (e) instilling a sense of pride in the institution (Jacobs, 2003). In other words, orientation has become the vehicle for conveying everything the institution wants a student to absorb as well as the single point in the enrollment process to capture every transaction a student has to complete before the start of classes.

Schuh (2003) states that orientation planners need to link program activities with functions such as academic advising. From the student's perspective, orientation is an extension of all prior and future interactions with the institution, not a stand-alone program. It needs to be fully integrated with the prospective student experience, including but not limited to (a) the coordination of communications with other areas on campus, (b) the integration of the placement testing, academic advising, registration, and payment processes, (c) a symbolic hand-off between the Admissions Office and the rest of campus, and (d) the launch of a new academic experience and membership in a community of learners.

As Perigo and Upcraft (1989) write: "Orientation is any effort to help freshmen make the transition from their previous environment to the collegiate environment and enhance their success" (p. 82). For the student participant, there are two fundamental objectives: (a) to connect with faculty, staff, and other students and (b) to depart with an appropriate schedule of courses.

On the first day of orientation at University of Vermont, orientation groups listen to a presentation regarding course options, the course selection process, and degree requirements. Adequate time is provided following the presentation to process the information and draft a tentative schedule with course numbers. The student orientation leader is available to students who need assistance. A separate presentation features the mechanics of the online registration process. On the second day, students meet with their advisors at scheduled appointment times. Advising sessions occur in small groups of two to three students to one advisor. Throughout the registration process, the advisor is available to help students navigate the registration system, find courses, resolve scheduling conflicts, and answer questions. Each session lasts approximately 15 minutes and concludes with the student printing a schedule. Students are advised of the option to alter schedules throughout the summer via remote access to the registration system.

Although *summer bridge programs* are not for all students, they do present an intense academic advising opportunity for those who participate. Summer bridge programs typically include components such as academic skills assessment, instruction in two or more courses (e.g., English composition, math, and a transitions course), an orientation to higher education, and a residence experience (Cuseo, 2003). Small class sizes and frequent interactions with faculty and staff outside of class, common to most summer bridge programs, make such programs conducive to advising. Extensive assessment of academic preparedness and learning styles along with observations of intangibles such as motivation and self-discipline enhance the existing profile of each student and provide advisors with insights that can refine the nature of academic advising.

Bridge programs like the one at Vincennes University engage students in the exploration of career options and expose them to campus resources. The programs at Sonoma State University and the University of South Florida have their own orientation to the university, academic advising, and registration. Academic advising is an integral part of the bridge program at the University of South Florida as well as at California State University Northridge. These institutions represent emerging models of summer bridge programs that integrate aspects of advising in a bridge program.

Using Technology

Prospective students, particularly Millennials, are comfortable interacting with any organization through multiple media. Often, their choice of medium is driven by convenience and comfort level. We should not assume that every Millennial prefers electronic communications or that every Gen-Xer fears technology and, therefore, prefers person-to-person interactions. Preference varies by individual as well as by specific need. For instance, the person who needs to schedule an appointment with an advisor may prefer to do so online, while the actual meeting to discuss conflicting work and class schedules occurs in person.

Online systems such as the University of California (UC) Gateways or the College Foundation of North Carolina (CFNC) offer excellent examples of blending various technologies. In both cases, these systems are designed to reach out to middle-school students to begin the college planning process. Students create a multidimensional portfolio representing their academic work, extracurricular activities, along with their career and college interests (Burnett & Oblinger, 2003). In the UC Gateways model, student participants are assigned a UC staff member to their "Success Team"—a person from whom they can seek guidance. The CFNC model provides a hotline staffed primarily by graduate students in the counselor education program at one of the system's campuses. Students using either system can find much of what they need online, but when they need or want to interact with a person, they can.

Some colleges and universities have created their own online tools. Valencia Community College pioneered the concept of "Life Maps." The college offers online modules for each transition stage of the students' experience, counting the initial entry transition. Included in the "Postsecondary Transition" are success indicators and campus resources designed to increase student contact with these resources. Similarly, the University of North Carolina at Greensboro has developed a competency-based virtual academic advising system that allows students to engage in web chats with trained advisors when questions arise.

Regardless of the electronic tools and strategies deployed, blended advising systems must have relevant content—where possible using data in the student information system to customize content. The first-year student has specific academic advising needs. The system should be designed to learn through every encounter with a student much like Amazon.com knows the genre of books preferred based on an initial purchase. With online advising systems, students need decision making tools such as degree audits and change of major simulations. They also need mechanisms to transact business with the institution, not designed around the existing organizational structures but around seamless processes they understand (i.e., paying for college, ordering books, and/or requesting a transcript). Finally, students need opportunities to connect with peers, staff, and faculty via phone, e-mail, web chat, and online communities.

Conclusion: Compelling Outcomes

By investing in the approaches described in this chapter, institutions may find an increased yield of admitted students, reduced academic probations or suspensions of first-year students, improved first-year retention, as well as enhanced student satisfaction and loyalty. These benefits are direct by-products of satisfying relationships between advisors and students. More important, quality academic advising assists students in making the transition from dependent to independent learners. Students learn to set goals, understand the nature of a chosen curriculum, develop plans to achieve their goals, seek constructive feedback that they use to improve their approach or alter a course of action, solve problems, take responsibility for their own future, and ultimately enhance their own educations. Perhaps, there is nothing more meaningful we can impart to our new students than these life skills.

References

Astin, A. W. (1971). *Predicting academic performance in college: Selectivity data for 2300 American colleges.* New York: Free Press.

Astin, A. W. (1977). *Four critical years.* San Francisco: Jossey-Bass.

Astin, A. W. (1984). A look at pluralism in the contemporary student population. *NASPA Journal, 21*(3), 2-11.

Astin, A. W. (1993). *What matters in college: Four critical years revisited.* San Francisco: Jossey-Bass.

Burnett, D., & Oblinger, D. (2003). Student academic services: Models, current practices, and trends. In G. L. Kramer & Associates (Eds.), *Student academic services* (pp. 27-52). San Francisco: Jossey-Bass.

Carranza, C., & Ender, S. C. (2003). Responding to students' needs. In G. L. Kramer & Associates (Eds.), *Student academic services* (pp. 311-332). San Francisco: Jossey-Bass.

Cuseo, J. B. (2003). Comprehensive academic support for students during the first year of college. In G. L. Kramer & Associates (Eds.), *Student academic services* (pp. 271-310). San Francisco: Jossey-Bass.

Frand, J. (2000, September/October). The information age mindset: Changes in students and implications for higher education. *EDUCAUSE Review, 35*(5), 15-24.

Frost, S. H. (2000). Historical and philosophical foundations for academic advising. In V. N. Gordon, W. R. Habley, & Associates (Eds.), *Academic advising: A comprehensive handbook* (pp. 3-17). San Francisco: Jossey-Bass.

Gordon, V. N., & Steele, M. J. (2005, Spring). The advising workplace: Generational differences and challenges. *NACADA Journal, 25*(1), 26-30.

Howe, N., & Strauss, W. (2000). *Millennials rising: The next great generation.* New York: Vintage Books.

Howe, N., & Strauss, W. (2003). *Millennials go to college.* Washington, DC: American Association of Collegiate Registrars and Admissions Officers.

Jacobs, B. C. (2003). New student orientation in the twenty-first century: Individualized, dynamic, and diverse. In G. L. Kramer & Associates (Ed.), *Student academic services* (pp.127-146). San Francisco: Jossey-Bass.

Kramer, G. L. (2000). Advising students at different educational levels. In V. N. Gordon, W. R. Habley, & Associates (Eds.), *Academic advising: A comprehensive handbook* (pp. 84-104). San Francisco: Jossey-Bass.

Kramer, G. L., & Spencer R.W. (1989). Academic advising. In M. L. Upcraft, J. N. Gardner, & Associates (Eds.), *The freshman year experience: Helping students survive and succeed in college* (pp. 95-107). San Francisco: Jossey-Bass.

Lester, V., & Johnson, C. S. (1981). The learning dialogue: Mentoring. In J. Fried (Ed.), *Education for student development* (New Directions for Student Services, No. 15, pp. 49-56). San Francisco: Jossey-Bass.

Light, R. J. (2001). *Making the most of college: Students speak their minds.* Cambridge, MA: Harvard University Press.

Lindsey, P. (2003). Needs and expectations of Gen-Xers. In J. Black (Ed.), *Gen-Xers return to college: Enrollment strategies for a maturing population* (pp. 53-67). Washington, DC: American Association of Collegiate Registrars and Admissions Officers.

Newcomb, T. M. (1966). The nature of peer group influence. In T. M. Newcomb & E. K. Wilson (Eds.), *College peer groups.* Hawthorne, NY: Aldine.

Newman, J. H. (1872). *Historical sketches.* London: Basil Montagu Pickering.

Newman, J. H. (1873). *The idea of a university.* London: Basil Montagu Pickering.

Perigo, D. J., & Upcraft, M. L. (1989). Orientation programs. In M. L. Upcraft, J. N. Gardner, & Associates (Eds.), *The freshman year experience: Helping students survive and succeed in college* (pp. 82-94). San Francisco: Jossey-Bass.

Schuh, J. H. (2003). The interrelationship of student academic services. In G. L. Kramer & Associates (Eds.), *Student academic services* (pp. 53-75). San Francisco: Jossey-Bass.

Tinto, V. (1987). *Leaving college: Rethinking the causes and cures of student attrition.* Chicago: The University of Chicago Press.

Tinto, V. (1993). *Leaving college: Rethinking the causes and cures of student attrition* (2nd ed.). Chicago: The University of Chicago Press.

Upcraft, M. L., Gardner, J. N., & Associates (1989). *The freshman year experience: Helping students survive and succeed in college.* San Francisco: Jossey-Bass.

U.S. Department of Education. (2005). *College enrollment profile, 1984-2014 by age bracket.* Retrieved August 8, 2006, from http://www.collegeboard.com/prod_images/prof/highered/res/hel/hel28.gif

Chapter Seven

Collaborations Beyond the Advising Office

Mary Stuart Hunter, Jean Henscheid, and Michelle Mouton

Educators who seriously consider how academic advising takes place on campus will realize that students seek and are provided advice in locations far beyond faculty offices and institutional advising centers. Likewise, we recognize that all students have a first-year experience whether or not we intentionally design it for them. Successful student transitions and effective advising cannot be left to chance. Creating a wide variety of intentional advising initiatives is an important element in shaping a culture where a campus-wide, comprehensive, and collaborative approach to advising will exist. Well-conceived and designed collaborations with academic, curricular, and student support programs can extend the goals of academic advising across campus. First-year seminars, learning communities, and early alert programs provide opportunities for such collaboration among academic advisors, faculty, staff, and students.

This chapter will make a case for the value of extending academic advising beyond the academic advisor's office. It will draw on information gleaned from research conducted as part of the National Learning Communities Project, by the staff of the National Resource Center for The First-Year Experience and Students in Transition, and by this chapter's authors. In addition to providing pertinent information drawn from research results, the chapter will include brief descriptions of model programs as described by advisors and administrators at campuses across the country.

Academic Advising and First-Year Seminars

First-year seminars are not new to American higher education. Reed College offered the first, credit-bearing, extended orientation course for students in 1911 (Fitts & Swift, 1928), although evidence of special advising initiatives for first-year students existed long before that. Almost a century later, first-year seminars have proliferated and morphed into a variety of forms and functions and are found at institutions of all types. At their core, first-year seminars address institutional efforts to ease the transition to college for new students and systematically address unacceptable rates of student attrition. First-year seminars represent an exceptional method for institutions to challenge and support new students.

Types of First-Year Seminars

While first-year seminars vary in structure and organization, common goals of most seminars are to assist students in their academic and social development and in their transition to college. By definition, a seminar is a small discussion-based course in which students and their instructors exchange ideas and information (*The American Heritage College Dictionary*, 1997).

The 1991 National Survey of First-Year Seminar Programming provided a typology and definitions for the most prevalent types of seminars (Barefoot & Fidler, 1992). Basic types and definitions of first-year seminars have changed little over time, even though the content of seminars on any given campus can evolve to reflect current institutional and student needs. For the most part, first-year seminars can be identified as one of five types: (a) extended orientation seminars, (b) academic seminars with generally uniform content across sections, (c) academic seminars on various topics, (d) professional or discipline-linked seminars, or (e) basic study skills seminars. At times, though, seminars combine elements from several of these categories to take a hybrid form. The following information is drawn from the most recent national survey of first-year seminars conducted by the National Resource Center for The First-Year Experience and Students in Transition in 2003 (Tobolowsky, 2005).

Extended Orientation Seminars

Sixty-five percent of institutions (79.8% of two-year institutions and 60% of four-year institutions) reporting first-year seminars indicate offering an extended orientation type, making this the most frequently reported type. These seminars focus on transition issues, student survival, and college success strategies. Content includes introduction to campus resources, time management, academic major and career decision making, study skills development, and issues related to student development.

Academic Seminars

Two types of academic seminars exist, those with uniform content across all sections and those with topics that vary from section to section. As with all types of seminars, they may be either required or offered as an elective and may sometimes be part of an institution's general education or core curriculum.

Academic seminar with generally uniform academic content. These seminars focus primarily on an academic theme common to all sections, but may also address critical academic skills such as writing, reasoning, and critical thinking. They may be interdisciplinary in nature. In total, 27.4% of institutions (18.4% of two-year institutions and 30.6% of four-year institutions) reporting first-year seminars offer an academic seminar with generally uniform academic content.

Academic seminars with variable content. Academic seminars on various topics make up 24.3% of first-year seminars (7.4% of two-year institutions and 30.4% of four-year institutions). These seminars are similar to the first type of academic seminar except that the topics vary from section to section and will most likely cover a wide variety of disciplines and social issues. The topics most often reflect the faculty members' individual areas of academic or social interest and expertise.

Pre-Professional or Discipline-Linked Seminars

Pre-professional or discipline-linked seminars are reported less frequently than other first-year seminar types. They constitute 14.2% (10.4% of two-year institutions and 15.5% of four-year institutions) of reported first-year seminars. Professional and discipline-linked first-year seminars are designed to prepare students for the demands of a specific profession (e.g. medicine, law) or academic discipline.

Basic Study Skills Seminars

Institutions enrolling students underprepared for the rigors of college-level academic work will frequently offer this type of seminar to address these student needs. These seminars focus primarily on basic study skills including note-taking, test-taking, and critical reading skills. Twenty percent of first-year seminars reported can be classified as study skills seminars (37.4% of two-year institutions and 13.8% of four-year institutions).

Other Types of Seminars

At any one institution, more than one type of seminar may exist. Additionally, not all seminars can be easily categorized as purely one type or another with such seminars characterized by elements of two or more types. When responding to the 2003 national survey of first-year seminar programs, 8.2% of institutions (5.5% of two-year institutions and 9.2% of four-year institutions) reporting that they have a first-year seminar indicated that their seminar(s) fell into in this other or hybrid category.

Rationale for Linking Academic Advising With First-Year Seminars

First-year seminars in their most generic form are small classes where students and instructors develop a sense of community and engage in reciprocal teaching and learning. Collegiate transition issues form the basis upon which the seminar experience is built. Interest in facilitating a positive and productive transition experience for students is shared by many educators in the collegiate environment. Both academic advisors and first-year seminar instructors are likely to address the challenges of moving from the high school or pre-college culture to the culture of higher education and its many subtleties that affect student success.

Learning-centered instructors seek opportunities and settings to extend student learning beyond course content and work to create occasions for students to apply their learning. Academic advisors seek more time with their advisees so that they can know them better which, in turn, creates the opportunity for more productive and powerful advising relationships. First-year seminars provide a setting where, when linked with advising, the goals and objectives for both academic advising and first-year seminars can reinforce each other, creating a more potent student learning experience.

Common Goals and Objectives of Academic Advising and First-Year Seminars

First-year seminars and academic advising have much in common. A quick review of the goals of academic advising and the objectives and topics taught in first-year seminars in the literature demonstrates their similarities.

Goals of Academic Advising

The landmark 2000 publication by Gordon, Habley, and Associates, *Academic Advising: A Comprehensive Handbook*, identified eight goals for academic advising: (a) assisting students in self-understanding and self-acceptance; (b) assisting students in considering their life goals by relating their interests, skills, abilities, and values to careers, the world of work, and the nature and purpose of higher education; (c) assisting students in developing an educational plan consistent with their life goals and objectives; (d) assisting students in developing decision making skills; (e) providing accurate information about institutional policies, procedures, resources, and programs; (f) referring students to other institutional or community support services; (g) assisting students in evaluation or reevaluation of progress toward established goals and educational plans; and, (h) providing information about students to the institution, college, academic departments, or some combination thereof.

Objectives and Topics Taught in First-Year Seminars

First-year seminars vary tremendously from campus to campus depending on the culture of the institution and the needs and characteristics of the students. Thus, a common set of goals for first-year seminars does not exist. There are, however, objectives and topics that are found in many, if not most, first-year seminars. The 2003 national survey of first-year seminar programs addressed issues related to academic advising in several of the survey questions (Tobolowsky, 2005). Course objectives, course topics, and course instruction have clear links to advising goals, organization, and content.

Course objectives. Respondents were asked to "select three of the most important course objectives" for their seminar. Of the eight optional items on the survey, three items are directly linked to advising goals: (a) encourage self-exploration/personal development; (b) provide orientation to campus resources; and (c) introduce a discipline. Of the two-year campuses responding to the survey and indicating that they have a first-year seminar, 55.8% identified "encourage self-exploration/personal development," 71.8% identified "provide orientation to campus resources," and 4.3% identified "introduce a discipline" as one of their three top course goals. For the four-year institutions indicating that they have a first-year seminar, responses were lower for the first two objectives with 34.1% identifying "encourage self-exploration/personal development," 55.2% identifying "provide orientation to campus resources," and higher for the third objective, 8.3% identifying "introduce a discipline" as one of their three top course goals.

Course topics. Survey respondents who indicated the existence of a first-year seminar on their campus were asked to "select five of the most important topics that comprise the content of this first-year seminar" (Tobolowsky, 2005, p. 104). Of the 11 options on the survey instrument, five items are directly linked to advising goals: (a) campus resources, (b) academic planning/advising, (c) career exploration/preparation, (d) college policies and procedures, and (e) specific disciplinary topic. Of the two-year campuses responding, 71.2% indicated campus resources; 64.4% indicated academic planning/advising; 47.2% indicated career exploration/preparation; 39.3% indicated college policies and procedures; and 5.5% indicated specific disciplinary topic. The four-year campus responses for topics were lower than the two-year campus responses with 58.1% indicating campus resources; 55.9% academic planning/advising; 30.6% career exploration/preparation; and 28.6% college policies and procedures. A significantly larger number of the four-year campuses, 25.3%, indicated specific disciplinary topic as an important course topic.

Connecting Academic Advising and First-Year Seminars

The 2003 national survey of first-year seminar programs also queried campuses about the connection of academic advising and first-year seminars (Tobolowsky, 2005). Less than one third (30.4%) of the institutions responding indicated that students were intentionally placed in first-year seminar sections taught by their academic advisors. Connecting these two activities is more prevalent in private schools (36.1% vs. 24.7%) and in highly selective schools (44.6% vs. 29.0%).

In April 2005, survey respondents answering yes to this question were contacted in an attempt to gather additional information about the rationale and motivations for placing students in seminar sections with their academic advisors and to determine if outcomes of doing so were being measured. Responses from 39 institutions yielded rich information in support of such a link. In general, all eight goals of academic advising are addressed in the seminars at a variety of institutions. Assisting students in developing decision making skills was the academic advising goal most frequently mentioned by the survey respondents contacted in 2005.

Factors That Lead to the Inclusion of Academic Advising in the First-Year Seminar

For some institutions, linking advising with first-year seminars is not new; it has been a characteristic of these institutions' seminars since their inception. For many others, however, it is new, and various reasons were given for moving to this model. Some respondents cited research on the importance of student involvement and the creation of community and saw embedding academic advising in the first-year seminar as a way to put that theory into practice. Some institutions surveyed students and learned that students did not know their advisors well, but knew their professors. Others reported that advising relationships were awkward and lacked meaning; their meetings were sporadic and shallow. Students on many campuses reported a general dissatisfaction with advising. Other campuses indicated unacceptable rates of student attrition and low levels of achievement. Some saw many of the same issues and topics being dealt with in advisor offices and seminar classrooms and thought that intentionally linking the two would benefit both.

Outcomes Measured

Assessment of the intersection between first-year seminars and academic advising is under development. While many institutions rigorously assess these two initiatives independently, measuring outcomes of advising embedded in first-year seminars is a complex undertaking. Few institutions surveyed indicate that they have completed such assessments. Most who have conducted any assessment at all report that they have studied such measures as course satisfaction, advisor satisfaction, academic achievement, academic progress, retention, and advising effectiveness. Many institutions conduct informal assessments that point to higher levels of satisfaction and retention. Some report higher levels of persistence among their more troubled or academically disadvantaged students. Clearly, this is an area ripe for further research and assessment.

The Importance of Including Academic Advising in the First-Year Seminar

Advantages to combining advising and seminar instruction exist for institutions, students, and advisors. When advising is embedded in the curriculum, it emphasizes its importance to the entire campus community. It states that, first and foremost, academic advising is teaching.

When college students are taught by their advisor in a first-year seminar, strong connections develop from the first day of the term. Relationship building is important because first-year students need such connections on campus. Students receive attention early in the term, and advising expectations can be communicated in a timely manner. Students are less likely to fall through institutional cracks when their seminar instructor is also their advisor. One possible caveat, however, is that advisors teaching their advisees may find the relationship with those students changed by the power differential inherent in the professor-student relationship as professors are in the position of assigning course grades to their advisees.

For advisors, when they see students several times a week in a classroom setting, they get to know them as students and as advisees. Frequent contact with students builds closer, richer connections between advisors and students. Intentional interactions at least twice a week offer faculty first-hand experience with the students' adjustments to college. A genuinely closer connection can develop, and informal interactions can be encouraged. Furthermore, time in the classroom allows for greater opportunities to conduct first-year student advising, a more complex task than many think. These students have many questions, and in a classroom setting, there is efficiency inherent in answering at one time common questions many students typically have.

Appropriateness of the First-Year Seminar as a Place to Address Academic Advising

Linking academic advising with first-year seminars teaches students the importance of communicating with faculty on several levels. Seminar faculty can be seen by their students in multiple roles—as instructors, as advisors, and as caring educators and representatives of the institution.

Connecting advising and first-year seminars also brings two facets of college life—social and academic—together. Advising the whole student becomes possible. The first-year seminar is an appropriate setting for exploration of values, goals, and interests. Knowledge of students' learning styles and study skills is also helpful for advisors as they assist students in career planning, major selection, and course choices. As students explore their academic goals and capabilities, they can discuss these issues with a professor/advisor who knows them well, whom they trust, and who can provide them needed direction.

The beauty of combining advising with the first-year seminar is that it provides a good setting for encouraging academic planning at the early stage in students' academic careers. This is especially appropriate and possible in the pre-professional or discipline-linked type of first-year seminar.

Summary

Because academic advising and first-year seminars share many goals and objectives, linking the two has the potential to produce increased effectiveness and efficiency in each. The possibilities for moving our institutions toward a philosophy of advising as teaching has no more fertile ground than within the first-year seminar. Student transition to the collegiate culture offers many opportunities for learning-centered educators to collaborate in addressing student needs, institutional systems, and educational outcomes. One way to achieve a comprehensive approach to student transition issues, student success strategies, academic orientation to the institution, career exploration, and decision making strategies may well be through linking these two important initiatives. By developing opportunities for cross-campus conversations, institutions can begin to address the satisfaction, productivity, and learning of all involved in these important academic endeavors.

Learning Communities and Academic Advising

The curricular reform movement known as learning communities is fundamentally about bringing every member of the campus community into the teaching and learning process. Since their inception nearly 100 years ago, about the time of first-year seminars, collegiate learning communities in North America have attempted to remedy what Alexander Meikeljohn characterized as unhealthy specialization and social and intellectual fragmentation of the academy (Orrill, 1995, 1997). In seeking a cure for personal and institutional disunion, learning communities share the mission of academic advising to connect what is too often disconnected in the personal and intellectual lives of students, faculty, and staff. Described here are the myriad ways academic advisors shape campus-wide policy and counsel and teach individuals and groups of students as part of their critical work in learning communities.

Types of Learning Communities

Multiple Models

Learning communities in higher education assume a variety of forms that share in common the linking of two or more courses and other student experiences, typically around a central theme or problem. Cohorts of students are enrolled in these links or clusters of courses and are often also housed together in the same residence hall. Connecting student experiences in this manner extends the amount of time available to build community among students, faculty, staff, and academic disciplines and to offer richer learning experiences than typically available through traditional scheduling practices. Most learning communities are offered to students in their first college year and involve general education courses, courses for underprepared or honors students, or beginning courses in the major.

Learning communities in large courses. Learning communities within larger classes represent the bulk of these programs, with the largest number of this type found at research extensive institutions (Barefoot, 2002). In these learning communities, a student subset of a large course's enrollment is also enrolled in at least one other large course plus, typically, a small seminar that either integrates content across these courses or offers augmenting first-year seminar experiences as described above. A lengthier discussion of the role of these seminars in learning communities, often instructed or co-instructed by academic advisors, is offered in Henscheid (2004).

Learning communities of linked courses or course clusters. In course clusters, learning-community students comprise the entire enrollment of each of the linked courses, which allows for a more intense relationship between the content and process of the linked courses. Instructors teach the courses separately but pre-plan linkages between their courses to foster social and intellectual connections in and outside the classroom.

Team-taught learning communities. This most integrated form of learning communities brings together the equivalent of up to four classes into an interdisciplinary, team-taught whole. The instructors work together to adapt content and processes to create a single syllabus organized around projects or themes.

Rationale for Linking Advising and Learning Communities

Today's learning communities are founded in the thinking of progressive educators, chiefly John Dewey, who believed that traditional education, as a disjointed process of "formation from without" ignores the rich experiences each student brings to the learning enterprise. Dewey (1938) advocated a "development from within" (p. 17) approach that requires educators to work together to understand and appreciate their students as individuals and to experiment with personally relevant active forms of instruction that engage students intellectually and socially. This philosophy, fundamental to modern learning-community work, shares a close kinship to that underpinning the academic advising process described previously in this monograph (chapter 1).

Administrators in successful learning communities learn early on that an active role, or multiple roles, for academic advisors is absolutely critical to their effort to understand and develop students as individuals. As members of the same philosophical family, academic advisors and learning-community practitioners can be a powerful force for merging the individual needs and purposes of students and education into a unified, discipline-specific knowledge conveyance.

Roles for Advisors in Learning Communities

The Many Roles of Academic Advisors

From the initial conversation about instituting learning communities to assessment and retooling, academic advisors on campuses where these programs are successfully sustained work closely with instructional faculty, administrators, and other campus staff members. Augsburg College, for example, is a small Lutheran-affiliated institution in Minneapolis, which uses its linked AugSem first-year seminar to integrate advising functions into its learning communities. Typical advising functions, such as goal clarification and personal interest assessment, are built into the course syllabi and are integrated into course assignments throughout the academic term. At LaGuardia Community College (City University of New York), learning communities have, since the 1970s, relied heavily on the integration of traditional advising methods into linked basic skills courses. LaGuardia's New Student House and the newer First-Year Academies are designed to build the confidence and academic skills of first-year students from more than 140 countries as they enter the campus community. Through these programs, students are involved in learning communities that closely tie acquisition of academic content to development of the kind of skills needed for students to move more easily into their academic major courses. The Center for Academic Support and Achievement at Tacoma Community College recently reworked its college success class, which is now taught by academic advisors and offered as stand-alone courses and as links in learning communities. At Indiana University-Purdue University of Indianapolis (IUPUI), a large, open-admission institution, each learning community is team-designed and taught by a faculty member, student peer mentor, academic advisor, and librarian. At Washington State University in Pullman, the Student Advising and Learning Center, the new student's first academic advising stop, co-administers that institution's various learning-community programs with the offices of the Vice Provost for Academic Affairs, General Education, and Residence Life. These and other roles for academic advisors in learning communities are further described below.

Advisors as members of advisory and steering committees. A first order of business in launching a learning-community program is the creation of a collaborative leadership team comprised of individuals from key offices (Smith, MacGregor, Matthews, & Gabelnick, 2004). Academic advisors generally top the list of members of these important groups along with instructional faculty, faculty development professionals, student recruiters, librarians, space and scheduling staff, residence life, marketing and assessment and evaluation experts, and other policy makers and administrative support personnel. These groups are responsible for a wide array of policy decisions and administrative functions. At Harper College, the steering committee reviews program proposals, recruits and supports faculty and staff learning-community teams, and offers general program advice. At Iowa State University, the committee attempts to bring coherence to multiple learning-community programs that exist in departments and colleges throughout campus. As members of these learning-community leadership groups, academic advisors serve as student advocates and experts on the curriculum and cocurriculum.

Advisors as administrative partners. While there is no single most appropriate place to administratively house a learning-community program, situating it where academic advisors can play a central role in its development and ongoing operation is a common choice. Choosing an administrative home is a decision dependent on the program's goals, the individual campus' formal and informal culture, its administrative structure, and budgetary considerations. On many campuses, such as Iowa State, Washington State, and the University of Missouri at Columbia, this coordination is a shared responsibility between academic and student affairs. While co-administration has its drawbacks, one advantage is the opportunity for student advocates, including academic advisors, to sit at the table with instructional faculty and others to design and support the rich student learning and development experiences that distinguish learning communities.

Advisors as front-line promoters of learning communities. A recent in-depth review of practices at 12 institutions revealed that most students learn about learning communities through personal contact, often through the academic advisor (Smith et al., 2004). Even as institutions spend time and resources on slick brochures and colorful, interactive web sites for their learning communities, effort is generally best expended on developing individual academic advisor's understanding of and support for these programs. Advisors understand better than most the primary concerns of students, including the need to move efficiently toward graduation, the need to achieve academic goals, and the need for intellectual as well as personal and social development. Advisor support has been central to the success of learning-community programs such as those at large institutions including the University of Oregon, California State University-Hayward, Arizona State University, Temple University, the University of Washington, and the University of Missouri at Columbia. Effective learning-community web sites, including those at De Anza College, Lane Community College, New Century College at George Mason University, the University of Oregon, and the University of California-Los Angeles, explicitly address the primary concerns and questions typically shared by academic advisors and students.

Advisors as learning-community instructors. The most direct means for academic advisors to work with students in learning communities is through service as instructors in the programs. Many campuses have identified advising as a central goal of their learning-community work, including Arizona State University, Augsburg College, Florida International University, IUPUI, Kutztown University of Pennsylvania, Louisiana State University, Loyola College of Maryland, Moorpark College, the State University of New York at Potsdam, University of Illinois-Urbana-Champaign, University of Northern Colorado, University of Southern Maine, University of Wisconsin-Madison, Wagner College, and Western Washington University. Some of these, and many other campuses, tap academic advisors to work as learning-community curriculum designers and instructors.

When not serving in these capacities, academic advisors are still often brought into learning-community classrooms at various points throughout the academic term to link the students' current activities to larger academic and personal goals and to offer general advice.

Summary

As heirs to Dewey's notion that student identity is inextricably linked with the capacity to learn, feminist theorists opened the possibility that learning is deeply entwined with gender. That belief has now been extended to identity as defined by race, ethnicity, sexual orientation, and other individual contexts (Zaytoun, 2005). With so much to know about how individual students learn, institutions have developed learning communities to expand the amount of time available for students to discover how their identities shape their learning and have invited many members of the larger campus community into the work of helping students in this discovery process. When academic advisors are brought into learning communities, as steering committee members, administrators, promoters, curriculum designers, and instructors, they join other educators who share their passion for understanding, appreciating, and developing students as individuals. Academic advising and teaching in learning communities are, in essence, the same work.

Early Alert Programs and Academic Advising

First-year students face a number of challenges in their first semester of college. Academic advisors can serve as strong support systems for these students in many ways as discussed throughout this monograph. Early alert programs can provide essential information to first-year students about their progress early in the semester and offer students suggestions for improvement. Academic advisors collaborate with faculty in the use of early alert programs to provide extra support for at-risk or struggling students.

Early alert programs are a collaborative effort between instructors of undergraduate students and the advising staff of an institution. Sometimes called early advantage referral, early warning, or red flag programs, early alert systems identify students who are academically at risk in a course. In most early alert programs, around midterm, instructors identify students in their courses who are not performing at their potential. The names of these students are then sent to the advising office along with a description of the instructor's rationale for the referral, such as poor test grades, too many absences, and lack of basic skills (Pfleging, 2002). These referred students are then contacted, usually by mail or e-mail, followed by a phone call. The initial contact indicates to the student that he or she has been referred by the instructor and outlines some of the resources available to the student to help improve performance (Eimers, 2000). In the letter, many institutions request that the student schedule an appointment with his or her advisor. The advisors can then follow up with the student throughout the semester (Rudmann, 1992). Early alert programs vary across campuses, but follow this common system of contacting students who are struggling academically mid-semester in order to help them become aware of services and other options available to them. Although helpful for all students, early alert programs can especially help first-year students as they adjust to the rigors of college work and learn about available campus resources.

Rationale Behind Early Alert Programs

Early alert programs are important in helping first-year students succeed in their academic courses. However, additional reasons for instituting such a program include improving retention rates and serving at-risk populations such as low-income students. Institutions with high attrition rates, especially those of first-year students, may find that early alert programs keep students enrolled (Pfleging, 2002). The early alert program not only serves as a reality check for students on their academic progress, it helps them establish a personal connection with an academic advisor and encourages them to succeed in the course. Additionally, institutions serving large populations of low-income or under-prepared students may find that early alert programs provide the students with greater opportunities for success (Muraskin, Lee, Wilner, & Swail, 2004). Some institutions, which have been successful in retaining low-income students, engage in intensive advising and early alert programs to make sure that these students complete their education requirements (Muraskin et al.).

The majority of students who typically receive these early alert referrals are first-year students, aged 18-19 (Cartnal & Hagan, 1999; Geltner, 2001). Therefore, programs like these can be especially beneficial and effective for first-semester students as they begin their college careers. Assessment studies of early alert programs reveal that faculty members correctly identify students who are genuinely at risk. That is, most of the students who receive early alert referrals have lower grade point averages and complete courses at lower rates than other students (Pfleging, 2002). Surprisingly, students are not as accurate as their faculty members in identifying themselves as struggling in a course. For example, in an assessment of the early alert program at Antelope Valley College in California, only 11% of early alert students self-reported that they were doing poorly in a course, but 37% actually failed the course (Lewallen, 1993). Similar findings of students' inaccurate perceptions of their academic success are found in other institutions (Pfleging). Thus, early alert systems, which allow faculty members to assist students in realizing their skill level and helping them find ways to improve, can be of great value to these students.

Aspects of Successful Early Alert Programs

Timing of the alert. Timing the first contact in an early alert is a crucial aspect of the program (Rudmann, 1992). The alert needs to happen after enough time has passed in the semester to determine a student's level of success, but it should also occur early enough to allow the student to drop the course or seek help to improve their progress.

At New Mexico State University-Carlsbad (NMSU-Carlsbad), the academic alerts are timed prior to midterm. No later than the sixth week of class, faculty members report their concerns about attendance or academic performance on an academic alert form. This deadline is two weeks before the date to withdraw from classes, which allows students time to take the necessary actions without it affecting their course grade. The academic alert form (see chapter appendix) offers a list of reasons for concern from which faculty may choose in evaluating the student. Statements such as "poor or sporadic attendance" or "has not submitted assignments" allow faculty members to easily and accurately describe their concerns about the students. At NMSU-Carlsbad, special attention is paid to first-semester students at this stage. In addition to a letter each student receives indicating the kind of concern the faculty member expressed about class performance and providing options for academic support, each first-semester student receives a phone call from the advising office and is encouraged to meet individually with an advisor. This specialized process for first-semester students allows the university to establish a stronger connection with the student and gives the first-year student ample opportunity to find helpful resources and to be successful in the course.

Keep it positive and supportive. Desired learning outcomes of the early alert process are important to consider when implementing such a program. Students should feel that instructors and advisors are reaching out in a helpful way. The initial contact is important in establishing the tone of this relationship. Eimers (2000) notes that some early alert referral letters may scare students, especially first-year students, and cause them to drop the course or panic. Additionally, for first-year students who may already be struggling with their confidence and who are unsure of their ability to succeed, a strongly worded letter can lower their self-esteem (Eimers). Therefore, it is important that these letters or e-mails to students be positive and encouraging. These letters should be supportive and informative, giving the students honest information and listing a variety of options and resources. This initial contact should also compliment the students on what they are doing well. Additionally, a phone call could be used to follow up with non-responsive students in order to highlight the institution's level of concern.

The action students will be asked to take when receiving the letter should also be considered at program implementation. In analysis of early alert programs, students' actions were, in some instances, not what the institution would likely recommend (Eimers, 2000). For example, rather than talking to their instructors or advisors, students spoke with friends or parents about their situation. Although this likely provided them with some comfort, these contacts were not able to give them the kind of assistance needed to be successful in the course, and as a result, the students' habits did not improve (Eimers). Advisors working with an early alert program should listen to their students to alleviate their most pressing concerns. Contact made through early alert letters or phone calls needs to demonstrate receptivity to student concerns and should list the specific steps necessary for that student to succeed. For example, encouraging meetings with advisors or instructors, recommending tutoring or study sessions for the specific subject(s) the student is struggling with, or simply giving the student a reminder that someone on campus is interested in their success can help the student take the correct steps to address the challenges they face. This approach also helps students learn how to be successful on their own in the future.

At Abilene Christian University, the Office of Career and Academic Development facilitates an early alert program called Save Our Students (SOS). The SOS system provides a structured way for faculty, staff, parents, and students themselves to create a supportive environment for struggling students, especially first-semester students. This support system offers students a strong network to rely on, with students, faculty, and staff trained to provide academic and personal support. Parents may also contact the office for information on supporting their student through this transitional period.

Involve faculty from the beginning. Other important aspects of the success of an early alert program are making the system easy to use and understand and involving faculty in the system from the start (Rudmann, 1992). At the Community College of Baltimore County, a core group of faculty members, called the Intervention Project Faculty Participants, are directly involved in the process and function of the early alert program. Faculty members have access to a database and are responsible for the input of early alert notices and contact records. This direct involvement allows them to play a part in the overall process and become more invested in the purpose of the alerts. At the University of North Florida, faculty members are invited to e-mail alerts to an advisor contact in the Academic Center for Excellence, which houses first-year and sophomore student advising. The advisor is then able to contact the student and initiate the advising process. A paper system is also available for faculty who are more comfortable with that option than with electronic alerts. This process is user-friendly for faculty members and encourages a high rate of participation from this constituency. Both the Community College of Baltimore County and the University of North Florida offer systems that encourage faculty participation and provide a simple way for instructors to communicate with the advising office.

Summary

Early alert systems provide students with an academic progress report that enables them to make adjustments in their habits and efforts in school in order to improve their chances for achievement. By doing this, the institution also benefits by increasing student success and improving retention rates and student progress toward graduation. In order for early alert systems to be effective, contacts should be continuous and involve personal meetings, progress checks, and support from other campus services. The process should be encouraging and positive and allow the student to learn how to be academically successful. By taking time to build relationships across campus and working with various offices to coordinate an early alert program, advisors can help institutions retain first-year students, increase student confidence, and improve student opportunities for a successful college experience.

Conclusion

Just as teaching and learning occur throughout the campus, academic advising takes place in a variety of locations beyond the advising office. By intentionally including first-year seminars, learning communities, or early alert programs in campus-wide advising outreach efforts to first-year students, institutions can help to make the first year of college more meaningful and purposeful for its students. As discussed throughout this monograph, when viewed as an act of teaching and learning, academic advising provides an opportunity for students to learn about themselves and make better choices regarding their academic futures. As advisors reach out, become involved, and extend their teaching in these programs, they will have a greater impact and foster further learning and development in their students.

References

The American heritage college dictionary (3rd ed.). (1997). Boston, MA: Houghton Mifflin.

Barefoot, B. O. (2002). *Second national survey of first-year academic practices.* Brevard, NC: Policy Center on the First Year of College, Brevard College. Retrieved May 18, 2005, from http://www.brevard.edu/fyc/Survey2002/index.htm

Barefoot, B. O., & Fidler, P. P. (1992). *The 1991 national survey of freshman seminar programming; Helping first-year college students climb the academic ladder* (Monograph No. 10) Columbia, SC: University of South Carolina, National Resource Center for The Freshman Year Experience.

Cartnal, R. & Hagan, P. F. (1999). *Evaluation of the early alert program, spring 1999.* (Research Report No.98/99-06). San Luis Obispo, CA: Cuesta College. (ERIC Document Reproduction Services No. ED 441 541)

Dewey, J. (1938). *Experience and education.* Old Tappan, NY: Macmillan.

Eimers, M. T. (2000). *Assessing the impact of the early alert program.* Paper presented at the annual meeting of the Association of Institutional Research, Cincinnati, OH.

Fitts, C. T., & Swift, F. H. (1928). The construction of orientation courses for college freshmen. *University of California Publications in Education, 1897-1929, 2*(3), 145-250.

Geltner, P. (2001). *The characteristics of early alert students, fall 2000.* (Research Report No. 2001.6.1.0). Santa Monica, CA: Santa Monica College. (ERIC Document Reproduction Services No. ED 463 013)

Gordon, V., Habley, W., & Associates. (2000). *Academic advising: A comprehensive handbook.* San Francisco: Jossey-Bass.

Henscheid, J. M. (Ed.). (2004). *Integrating the first-year experience: The role of first-year seminars in learning communities* (Monograph No. 39). Columbia, SC: University of South Carolina, National Resource Center for The First-Year Experience and Students in Transition.

Lewallen, W. C. (1993). *Early alert: A report on two pilot projects at Antelope Valley College.* Lancaster, CA: Antelope Valley College. (ERIC Document Reproduction Services No. ED 369 452)

Muraskin, L., Lee, J., Wilner, A., & Swail, W. S. (2004). *Raising the graduation rates of low-income students*. Washington, DC: The Pell Institute for the Study of Opportunity in Higher Education.

Orrill, R. (Ed.). (1995). *The condition of American liberal education: Pragmatism and a changing tradition*. New York: College Board.

Orrill, R. (Ed.). (1997). *Education and democracy: Reimagining liberal education in America*. New York: College Board.

Pfleging, E. (2002). *An evaluation of the early alert program at Columbia College*. Unpublished master's thesis, California State University at Stanislaus.

Rudmann, J. (1992). *An evaluation of several early alert strategies for helping first semester freshmen at the community college and a description of the newly developed Early Alert Retention System (EARS) software*. Irvine, CA: Irvine Valley College. (ERIC Document Reproduction Services No. ED 349 055)

Smith, B. L., MacGregor, J., Matthews, R. S., & Gabelnick, F. (2004). *Learning communities: Reforming undergraduate education*. San Francisco: Jossey-Bass.

Tobolowsky, B. F. (2005) *The 2003 national survey on first-year seminars: Continuing innovations in the collegiate curriculum* (Monograph No. 41). Columbia, SC: University of South Carolina, National Resource Center for The First-Year Experience and Students in Transition.

Zaytoun, K. D. (2005, January/February). Identity and learning: The inextricable link. *About Campus, 9*(6), 8-21.

Appendix

Academic Alert Form From New Mexico State University-Carlsbad

ACADEMIC ALERT FORM
Please return to Karla Thompson, Counseling & Student Development (234-9265)

Date: _____

Class/Sec.: _____Instructor: _____Phone: _____

Instructions: For each student, write his/her name, social security number and place a check mark in all columns that apply, whether your concerns are about attendance, academics, or both. Add any notes in the "Comments" section. Thank you!

Name, SSN	Attendance		Academics		Office Use Only		
	Has never attended	Poor or sporadic attendance	Low class average	Has not submitted assignments	1st semester frosh	Academic warning or probation	Financial aid
1.							
Comments:							
2.							
Comments:							
3.							
Comments:							
4.							
Comments:							
5.							
Comments:							
6.							
Comments:							
7.							
Comments:							
8.							
Comments:							
9.							
Comments:							
10.							
Comments:							

Chapter Eight

Assessment of Advising: Measuring Teaching and Learning Outcomes Outside the Classroom

Victoria McGillin and Charlie Nutt

Assessment of first-year advising is the critical process of documenting student learning outcomes from encounters with their first-year academic advising programs. Embedded within this statement are several key assumptions. First, this takes as given the premise that advising is teaching and that academic advisors engage students in critical and reflective learning encounters whereby those students come to understand themselves, their institutions, their curricula, and the meaning of the academic and life choices they are making. Second, this statement presumes that this series of lessons about self and academia serve as the intended student learning outcomes from advising. Finally, this statement makes clear that to assess means to document those learning outcomes as clearly and as carefully as one can.

This chapter explores the critical components of the assessment process, from mission through measurement, and what to do once the results are known. This chapter will cover where and how to begin the assessment process, as well as direct the reader to resources available for those preparing to document the learning outcomes of advising first-year students. Ultimately, whether novice or expert in the field of first-year student advising, this chapter will explain why it is critical to assess the outcomes of advising and how to engage the campus community in documenting and responding to those outcomes.

Definitions

Advising: Teaching and Learning

Academic advising, particularly in the first year, directly shapes students' primary encounters with and understanding of our curricula, and most specifically the general or liberal educational components that shape the foundations of the first year(s) of study. First-year advising offers students what is often their sole opportunity to understand, appreciate, and gain value from this foundation to the curriculum, too often dismissed by students as merely "requirements to get rid of…" while they are engaged in the process of completing their degree in a specialized field. According to the American Association of Colleges and Universities (AAC&U, 2005), foundational study in liberal education "…aims to empower individuals, liberate the mind from ignorance, and cultivate social responsibility. Characterized by challenging encounters with important issues, a liberal education prepares graduates both for socially valued work and for civic leadership in their society" (p. 1). Given degree audits, students can certainly pick their way through institutional general education requirements, but if they are to also achieve the learning goals intended by those who designed their core curriculum and as significant as those detailed by AAC&U, students will not only require guidance on their choices but also instruction about the meaning of the choices and the opportunity to reflect upon the learning embedded within those choices. First-year advising often offers the sole opportunity for such an academic dialogue. The growing understanding of the critical teaching and learning outcomes possible through academic advising have contributed to a paradigm shift in both advising and in first-year programming.

A second critical area of teaching/learning occurs in first-year advising as students explore the disciplines. While many students arrive on our campuses with a major area "declared," they may not arrive with a commitment to that discipline. Advising relationships offer a teaching/learning opportunity for students to learn about the disciplines, to explore related areas of study, and to reflect on the match between the primary teaching styles in the disciplines and student's preferred learning styles.

Assessment: Documenting Learning Outcomes

According to Palomba and Banta (1999), "Assessment is a process that focuses on student learning, a process that involves reviewing and reflecting on practice as academics have always done, but in a more planned and careful way" (p. 1). This simple quotation encompasses several important points. Assessment is, first and foremost, our effort to "…determine how well our students are learning" (Pellegrino, Chudowsky, & Glaser, 2001, p. 4). Second, Palomba and Banta's definition tells us that assessment is not episodic; it is a process. It is the systematic, ongoing exploration of learning outcomes. Once results of the assessment of your first-year advising programs are analyzed, changes in that program will be implemented based upon those results. After these changes are introduced, first-year program administrators must then reassess their program to determine whether that change proved effective. As a consequence, assessment will never be "over." Programs and students never stay the same; each change prompts the need for a new assessment cycle to determine the consequences and responses to those changes.

Third, this definition of assessment makes clear that assessment is not just measurement and numbers. For example, while first-year advising programs are often discussed in relation to the numbers of students retained, such numbers do not adequately capture the maturation process and learning that may underlie that retention. Assessment is about "review" and "reflection." The effective inclusion of both quantitative (numerical) and qualitative (descriptive) methodologies enables administrators of first-year programs to better capture what is often considered unmeasurable. Effective assessment efforts incorporate multiple forms of information collection, the better to meaningfully document the learning that is taking place.

Fourth, Palomba and Banta's (1999) definition of assessment clarifies that assessment is not performance evaluation. While advisor evaluations have their place and might be incorporated as part of an assessment of the advising process, individual evaluations should not be confused with student learning outcomes assessment. The goal of individual, performance evaluation is either to provide formative information (i.e., developmental and skill-enhancing feedback) or summative information (i.e., regular performance measurement designed to support personnel decisions, such as hiring, firing, and promotion). While these are important measures, this information reveals nothing about what students have learned from the process of advising.

Fifth, Palomba and Banta's (1999) definition also conveys that assessment is not just an administrative process of interest only to managers of programs; it is the business of every member of the academy. In the case of first-year advising programs, assessment offers clear feedback on whether advisors or programs actually achieve the learning results that they purport to offer. Assessment should be "…an integral part of the quest for improved education" (Pellegrino et al., 2001, p. 1). Advisors should embrace high-quality assessment as those results can and should inform their work with first-year students on a daily basis, helping them better understand what works best with which students.

Finally, assessment is neither easy nor quick. Good assessment is multi-dimensional and will take time and resources to do, much less to do well. Student satisfaction surveys, while offering valid information, are insufficient measures of what those students have learned. They only reveal that students are satisfied; not why they are satisfied nor what might have helped them better achieve their goals. Alternatively, others might assess specific skills learned, complete an analysis of academic decisions (e.g., major declaration) carried out in a timely manner, and/or interview students or hold focus groups tapping into the meaning and significance of the advising-related learning that has taken place. All are meaningful measures of the same phenomenon, each providing a different, but important, window into the same learning outcomes.

Assessment Process

For many years, assessment in higher education meant documentation of what they, the institutions, provided to students (e.g., numbers of courses offered, majors completed, programs designed). Once the campus assessed those who provided the learning encounters (i.e., number of first-year advisors) and enumerated the number of learning encounters offered (i.e., number of appointments), the institutional accountability needs would have been met. For years, students, families, alumni, boards, and regional accrediting organizations were satisfied when their institutions so documented the efficiency and presumed effectiveness of their programs. It was enough to say that the institution provided X advisors to Y students during their first year. Higher education focused on the teacher and what was taught rather than the learner and what was learned.

The national assessment movement in higher education was part of a national paradigm shift, emerging from the resurgence in focus on teaching/learning encounters. It was no longer sufficient to just document what one offered to students, whether through the curriculum or through a first-year advising process. If it was not possible to document what students had learned as a result of their encounters with the teaching/learning experiences (whether a first-year course or an advisor), the assessment was incomplete. Student learning outcomes' assessment asked what students knew, valued, or did differently as a result of their encounters with first-year academic advising. For example, those who assessed first-year advising learning outcomes might ask how academic advising promoted knowledge, such as cognitive development and increased understanding, among first-year students. Assessment of skills that emerged as outcomes of advising might explore how well students learned to run their own degree audits. An assessment of values could ask questions such as whether or not our new students not only understood but also valued their academic choices, such as their selection of a particular course to meet a certain requirement. These three critical learning outcomes call for a model of assessment vastly different from the model of measurement that has been prevalent in higher education. While advising assessment instruments began to appear in the advising literature 20 years ago (e.g., Academic

Advising Inventory, Winston & Sandor, 1984), most instruments focused on advisor actions. Given this model of assessment, accountability of advisor "inputs" was no longer sufficient; assessment called for the documentation of the learning "outcomes" of advising.

Components of Assessment

Assessment of advising must involve a cycle (Maki, 2004) that runs from the expression of the goals for first-year advising, through the exploration of the values embedded within those goals, the vision or aspirations for this educational process, the mission that forms the roadmap to achieve that vision, and ultimately, the articulation of the necessary learning outcomes for students that emerge from that mission. Once those learning outcomes have been identified, then those responsible for the first-year student advising programs must identify where and when that learning actually takes place and, as a consequence, when, where, and how the learning can best be assessed.

This cycle must be embedded within the institutional goals, vision, and mission, and involve all relevant stakeholders from the very first stage in the cycle. Therefore, the crucial prelude to any implementation of an assessment cycle is the assemblage of powerful voices from all those who have a critical stake in those student learning outcomes. The following provides greater detail about each step in this process.

Values to mission. First-year advising programs must reflect the institution of which they are a part. So, too, must their assessment. First-year advising programs must mirror the values, goals, mission, vision, and outcomes of their institution and be responsive to the unique institutional culture. The assessment practices must mirror the same. For example, while it is certainly possible to create an intrusive first-year advising program that retains students by making all the hard decisions for them, if the institutional mission is to graduate self-directed learners, such an advising program might not be compatible with these goals. Similarly, any assessment of advising at that same institution that only measured percent retained and did not evaluate the development of self-directed learning by students who stayed at the institution would be similarly off the mark.

By assembling a significant group of stakeholders, those who have a stake in the success of the first-year advising program, and engaging them in the process of developing learning outcomes based upon the unique institutional values, vision, mission, and goals, the first-year advising program administrators can ensure that the assessment process will meaningfully reflect those institutional goals.

The most important step in this cycle of assessment is to assemble the active and powerful voices from all critical constituencies into an institutional first-year advising assessment committee. Any component of the institution that may find themselves being evaluated (e.g., advisors or first-year students) or participating in the evaluation process (e.g., first-year seminar instructors or orientation group leaders) should be represented so that their voices may be heard in the development stages. Everyone committed to the success of the first-year class also has an important perspective that needs to be considered when developing learning outcomes for first-year advising. Faculty, students, administrators from academic and student affairs, advisors, deans, possibly alumnae, or parents each have differing yet important perspectives on the definition of a successful first-year advising program. What are the values of the institution, and how are they reflected in the values of the advising program? What does the institution aspire to become, and is that also reflected in the aspirations of the first-year advising program? Does the first-year advising program have separate values, vision, and mission statements? In what way do those statements reflect the institutional values, vision, and mission? If the program and institutional missions are aligned, and advisors are prepared to meet the institutional and programmatic goals for first-year advising, the committee should be ready to articulate what the students who emerge from this program should then know, value, and do differently as a result of this experience.

Mission to learning outcomes. Institutional outcomes should define the programmatic outcomes for any first-year advising program, both articulating what the program expects that students will know and do as a result of participation in that program (i.e., student learning outcomes) as well as how the advising program is delivered (i.e., process or delivery outcomes). These institutional and programmatic missions should articulate learning and delivery objectives and allow for the specification of both student learning outcomes and process delivery outcomes.

Student learning outcomes can be divided among cognitive, affective, and psychomotor areas. The cognitive area encompasses the knowledge and information that first-year students should have acquired as a result of engagement with the first-year advising program. What kind or level of complexity of knowledge would be expected? Using Bloom's taxonomy of the cognitive domain (Bloom, Englehart, Furst, Hill, & Krathwohl, 1956), a stakeholder's group can construct reasonable levels of "knowing" based on the students' levels of development. Bloom's six levels of cognitive complexity begin with the knowledge level, where students could be expected to list, label, or describe the learning that they have encountered in their first-year advising program. For example, at the lowest level, students may be expected to list or identify from a list the components of the general education curriculum. At Bloom's comprehension level, students should be capable of explaining or discussing that learning (e.g., what the requirements actually mean), while at the application level, they could demonstrate or make use of that knowledge (e.g., find and describe exciting courses that might meet the same requirement for different majors). At the analysis level, Bloom's model proposes that students should be able to break this knowledge down into component parts and compare one set of knowledge with another. Using the same example, students might be expected to compare and contrast the writing requirement at their own institution with the comparable requirement at a peer's institution. At the synthesis level, students should be able to reassemble those parts into something creative and new, while, at Bloom's evaluation level, students might be expected to judge the value of and come to conclusions about the knowledge gained. (For more information on Bloom's taxonomy, see chapter 13.)

The second domain of learning outcomes that must be assessed is the psychomotor area. What should students be able to do (i.e., the skills they should have acquired) as a function of engagement with the first-year advising program? Can they initiate self-assessment? Do students practice this on their own? Have they developed a habit of assessment and reflection? Can they map a career path? Assessment of the psychomotor domain should engage students in tasks in which they can demonstrate their new skills and or evaluate their confidence in those skills. Additionally, others in a position to assess those skills, such as advisors, might be asked to do so.

The third student learning outcomes domain, the affective domain, addresses what students have learned to value or believe as a function of the first-year advising program. Have students so integrated the dimensions of the liberal education curriculum via discussions with their first-year advisors that they now believe in the importance of this model for higher education? Not surprisingly, this domain also overlaps Bloom et al.'s (1956) highest level of cognitive complexity (i.e., the evaluation level). The assessment of affective learning outcomes should tap into that evaluation domain.

Mapping the Learning

Once the team of stakeholders has identified the student learning outcomes, then they must identify when and where within the first-year advising program that learning actually takes place and assess that outcome. It is insufficient to confidently assert that an educational value permeates a first-year seminar. If it is not possible to identify where in the curriculum that value is covered, then it becomes very difficult to determine when one might assess that this value has been learned. By tracing backwards, from the learning outcomes to the points (possibly multiple) where the material most likely is covered (e.g., orientation programs, first-year seminars, workshops, mid-semester advising discussions), it becomes possible to identify events and complete the assessment.

Assessment Measures

Standardized versus home-grown measures. What should be evident from the discussion of assessment's ties to mission, vision, goals, and unique learning objectives is that the design of any advising assessment cycle and the selection or development of most advising assessment measures must be shaped by each unique institutional culture. While published standardized measures of advising do exist (see Table 1), the primary challenge of such instruments is that they were not developed in response to individual institutional or programmatic learning objectives or goals. That seriously limits their applicability to specific institutions. Published instruments will usually have established significant validity and reliability (that is, they measure what they purport to measure and they do so consistently over time). This does allow for cross-institutional comparisons of results, but that same broad applicability could limit the "relevance" of that instrument on one's own campus. A review of all instruments referenced in the *Mental Measurement Yearbook* (Buros Institute of Mental Measurement, 2005), the longest established reference source of psychological, educational, and personality measures, found only 10 standardized instruments cited under searches for "advisor," "advisee," or "advising." Of these 10, only the College Student Experiences Questionnaire (CSEQ; Pace & Kuh, 1998) and the National Survey of Student Engagement (NSSE; Kuh et al., 2001) specifically identified student learning outcomes as a primary purpose for the assessment. However, these learning outcomes were only secondarily associated with advising assessment as the NSSE and CSEQ focus on larger, institutional assessments of learning outcomes.

At the same time, the development of "home-grown" instruments is not without risk. Any measure developed "in house" must document reliability and validity before results can be interpreted meaningfully on any campus. That means that the instrument must go through a reasonable development process, including pilot testing for initial item development, testing of the validity of the items against measures with established validity, and testing the reliability of students scores (e.g., do they score the same under similar circumstances?). Active consultation with institutional research staff or faculty members familiar with test construction and instrumentation is strongly advised to ensure that any institutionally developed instruments will produce results that are reliable (i.e., obtaining the same results tomorrow as today and across different student groups) and valid (i.e., actually measuring what you purport to measure, rather than some artifact of testing, such as writing skills, or an entirely different dimension of advising altogether).

Quantitative and qualitative measures. A second consideration is that no single score or questionnaire can capture everything needed for program improvement. There are several reasons for this. As stated in the definition of assessment, learning assessment is both quantitative and qualitative. Many of the learning and process outcomes developed cannot easily be reduced to

Table 1
Published Measures of "Advisors," "Advisees," or "Advising"

Measure	Author(S)	Purpose	Intended User(S)	Review Summary
Academic Advising Inventory	Winston & Sandor, 1984	Assesses the nature of the advising relationship (developmental-prescriptive advising), the frequency of activities that take place (advisor-advisee activity) and student satisfaction with advising.	Intended to provide formative or summative evaluation to advising programs.	Brown (2005a) concluded that more research was needed but modest evidence of reliability and validity was provided. This instrument could serve as the core of an assessment of advising.
ACT Evaluation Survey Service: Advising services subscales	American College Testing, 2002	Assesses six areas of advising services: advising information, academic advising needs, impressions of your advisor, additional advising information, additional questions, comments and suggestions.	Intended to assist institutions to investigate the plans, goals, and impressions of their students.	Belcher (2005) concluded that this instrument was comprehensive and stable. Validity and reliability were not reported for most postsecondary scales. Morner and Belcher (2005) reported the results appear to be stable.
Assessing Motivation to Communicate	Morreale, Hamilton, & Berko, 1994	Assess communication apprehension and willingness to communicate.	Intended for college students for advising, teachers for pedagogic purposes, and administrators for placement or programmatic assessment.	Brown (2005b) and Wright (2005) reported "useful" psychometric properties, but the manual reported no specifics on reliability or validity and a technical manual was needed.
College Student Experiences Questionnaire	Pace & Kuh, 1998	Assesses students' willingness to invest in using undergraduate resources and opportunities, students' perceptions of the campus environment and priorities, and how students' perceptions and efforts relate to personal estimates of progress towards learning outcomes.	Learning outcomes-based results generated for institutions, but can also be generated in individual student advising reports.	Geisinger (2005) and Miller (2005) concurred that this instrument was comprehensive, with established psychometric properties, and extensive norms based on more than 30,000 students.

Table 1 continued p. 122

Table 1 continued

Measure	Author(S)	Purpose	Intended User(S)	Review Summary
College Student Inventory (part of Retention Management System)	Stratil, 1988	Assesses motives and background information related to college success, improved retention, enhanced advising effectiveness.	RMS intended to facilitate communication between advisors and students through interpreting results, identifying resources, and making referrals.	Campbell (2005) found the RMS useful for counseling students and policy decisions or program assessment, but limited for research. Hogan (2005) recommended that the manual be updated.
National Survey of Student Engagement	Kuh et al., 2001	Assess students on five factors of student learning outcomes: academic challenge, active and collaborative learning, student-faculty interaction, enriching educational experiences, and supportive campus environment.	Intended to aid institutional performance to help institutions improve undergraduate education, and inform accountability, accreditation, and benchmarking.	Sauser (2005) and Sheehan (2005) found this instrument to be a theoretically meaningful, thoroughly documented, and psychometrically established measure of student learning and student satisfaction. They concluded that it was well researched, valid, and reliable.
Noncognitive Variables and Questionnaire	Sedlacek, 1998	Assesses non-cognitive variables important for success and for retention of minority students: self-confidence, self-appraisal, dealing with racism, long-range goal preference, supportive other, leadership experience, community, and knowledge in field.	Individual results could guide advisors working with minority students; could be used to assess outcomes in programs serving multicultural students.	The reviewers disagreed. Marchant (2005) reported that this was a useful research instrument, but not sufficiently psychometrically sound for individual admissions decisions, while Smith (2005) reported that it was psychometrically sound for use in individual admissions decisions and for predicting student success in college.

Table 1 continued

Measure	Author(S)	Purpose	Intended User(S)	Review Summary
Perceptions, Expectations, Emotions, and Knowledge About College	Weinstein, Palmer, & Hanson, 1995	Assesses prospective students' social, academic, and personal expectations about college to identify realistic versus unrealistic expectations based upon comparisons with site-specific norms developed at own institution.	Implication that this could be given to advisors and students to assess their expectations, identify unrealistic gaps between expectations and reality, and identify "at risk" groups.	Gillespie (2005) concluded that this instrument could be used by individual advisors to help individual students make realistic decisions but lacked psychometric data to interpret the results. Yazak (2005) concurred that predictive accuracy was not possible.
Student Developmental Task and Lifestyle Inventory	Winston, Miller, & Prince, 1987	Assist student in understanding own development, establish own goals and plans for future. Based on Chickering's (1969) model.	Primary consumers intended to be counselors, advisors, and student life staff.	Henning-Stout (2005) and Porterfield (2005) found the instrument to be psychometrically sound, useful for research and program development but limited by middle-class, male bias in Chickering's model.
Student Goals Exploration	Stark, Lowther, Shaw, & Sossen, 1991	To understand goals of groups of students and changes in those goals over a period of time and to measure goals as a mediating variable between intended outcomes and actual outcomes.	Student and faculty versions, pre- and post-versions allow assessment of changes in student goals (primarily academic). Not intended for individual advising purposes.	Brown (2005c) concluded this instrument was psychometrically sound for research on student goals and to stimulate discussion. Shaw and Benson (2005) concurred that this instrument was useful for program assessment of large groups of students, but not for individual assessment. Reliability and validity were not established.

Note. Indexed in the *Mental Measurements Yearbook* (Buros, 2005).

one point on a Likert-type scale (e.g., "On a scale of 1 to 5, how thoughtful and transforming have your advising reflections on life and the curriculum become?"). Some life experiences are best reflected in narrative form, as life stories, not as quantitative data.

Quantitative measures are most useful when the program seeks to measure something (e.g., amount of cognitive growth achieved) or describe (e.g., percent retained) a phenomenon. They are called for when you seek to test a hypothesis and fit best when you work within a predetermined evaluation design (e.g., comparing those in a first-year seminar with those not in a seminar) that could be replicated on other campuses. Quantitative measures can be employed with large (and representative) samples of students. Questions designed to gather quantitative data would most likely be closed-ended (e.g., select one of four specified answers in response to a question), given the large sample size needed. Evaluators employing quantitative assessment measures might use surveys, questionnaires, or other numerical counts (e.g., percent of requirements completed by the end of the first-year) as they can easily be submitted to an objective method of data analysis.

In contrast, qualitative methods seek to understand or derive deeper meaning from a phenomenon. The qualitative methods of data collection flexibly respond to the answers given and, as they probe further and explore a question, may differ for each first-year student (e.g., in an interview with a first-year student, those with a positive advising encounter might receive a different follow-up question from those who reported a less positive advising encounter). Those employing qualitative measures most often use open-ended questions that allow the respondent to generate their own, unique response. These responses must then be codified through a content analysis of the responses. This rich, detailed analysis can only be carried out with a small (and probably not representative) sample of students. Through content analysis of the responses, for example, one can use participants' own words to describe the experience, interpret the phenomenon, and understand that experience. Examples might include written responses to open-ended questions, interviews, content analyses of advising manuals, or focus groups of first-year students. Qualitative data is rich in detail, capable of telling complex narratives about the advising learning outcomes; however, because of this complexity, the conclusions that can be drawn may be limited to the immediate student population. Moreover, it may not be possible to generalize to other samples of students (e.g., to next year's class, to older students, to men).

Multiples measures. Because the student is not the only source of information on student learning outcomes, multiple assessments including data from multiple sources (e.g., from students, advisors, parents, or employers) are necessary. Each data source brings an important perspective to the total understanding of student learning outcomes. For example, cognitive growth is a complex process that is not necessarily transparent to the individual student as she or he engages in reflective discussions with their academic advisors. However, that cognitive growth may be assessed by a more sophisticated observer over multiple encounters (e.g., a trained observer). Second, student learning outcomes are not necessarily obvious immediately after an advising encounter. Some of the most important advising encounters can involve challenges and difficult feedback from one's advisor. Students often need to reflect, at length, upon such an encounter to best make sense of such feedback and to incorporate that into one's revised self-assessment. Multiple assessments (even into the students' lives as alumnae) may be called for to best document the learning outcomes of such encounters.

Direct and indirect measures. In addition to thinking about assessment in terms of the inclusion of quantitative and qualitative measures, multiple sources of data, and potentially multiple points for assessment, it is also important to consider both direct and indirect methods of data collection. Direct assessment reveals what students know and can do (e.g., projects, portfolios) while indirect measures provide explanations for why that performance might be above or below expectations (e.g., exit interviews, surveys) (Palomba & Banta, 1999). Direct measures may be qualitative or quantitative but share in common the direct assessment of student learning. If first-year advising promotes reflection by students, a direct (qualitative) measure of this could be a reflective essay written by the student while an indirect measure might be the advisor's or the student's own perception of reflective skills in the advisee. Alternatively, if knowledge of the curriculum is one goal, a direct (quantitative) measure might be a true-false test of a list of curricular requirements, while an indirect measure could involve interviews with students about their confidence in their curricular understanding. The strongest assessment of learning outcomes will always consider several different measures of an outcome, wherever possible (e.g., quantitative, qualitative, direct, indirect, using multiple sources), as each contributes unique dimensions to the full understanding of the impact of advising in a first-year advising program.

Using the Data

The most unfortunate outcome of any assessment cycle may be the pile of assessment reports that can be found collecting dust on the shelves of institutions across the United States. This dusty outcome most typically arises from three sources: (a) the failure to keep the intended audience in mind when writing the final report, (b) the failure to understand that assessment is inherently about change and, as a result, (c) the failure to understand that the cycle of assessment is ongoing, with new questions emerging from each set of results.

Depending on the instruments used, those leading the assessment process may need consultations concerning the coding and thematic or statistical analysis from their institutional research office, research colleagues, or research assistants. That assistance may also prove helpful through the process of interpreting the results. The raw data need to be summarized, and those summary findings then need to be meaningfully interpreted for others. The results need to be shared with the stakeholders for a full discussion of what the findings mean and what the implications are for first-year programs. While some preliminary interpretations of the results may be possible when presenting the data to the stakeholders, it is often best to leave final interpretations open until they have all had the opportunity to share their multiple perspectives on the results. They, then, can also be in the best position to share ideas for change; either changes in the first-year programs or needed change in the assessments.

While stakeholders may be comfortable (and indeed, may require) reviewing multiple tables and charts, institutional officers and decision makers (e.g., presidents, chancellors, vice presidents, deans, associate deans, directors) have neither the time nor the inclination to wade through massive amounts of data in comprehensive assessment reports with multiple tables and charts. Adding them in an appendix will satisfy the needs of those who want to examine data closely and those who will not have the time to do so. Assessment reports that are acted upon are those that have been condensed to a one- to two-page "executive summary" with the primary findings pulled out as "bullets" and with a separate set of "action items" or "budget items" pulled out for clear decision making. While this report structure might not allow for the richness of the assessment information discussed previously, it does ensure that the report will be read and acted upon. It is here that the "cultural" conflict may emerge between the assessment specialist who is passionate about the explicit reporting of his or her data, and the institutional decision maker, who needs just enough information to act decisively.

This leads directly to the second critical reason reports may gather dust: the failure to understand that assessment is inherently about change. Failure to secure the endorsement of institutional leadership and first-year stakeholders at the very onset of the assessment cycle can leave directors of first-year programs with identified areas in need of change but with no mandate to make change happen. As stated at the beginning of this chapter, this is why assembling stakeholders is critical.

The third and most critical issue about understanding the final report and its role in the assessment cycle is the importance of understanding that this is only one stage in an ongoing cycle. The results of a first cycle of assessment of first-year advising should lead the stakeholders to identify a second or third set of learning outcomes that they now need or want to assess. Alternatively, the first assessment cycle may have indicated weaknesses in the first-year program that called for adjustments in the program. That adjustment then would call for a re-assessment in the following year, to determine if the adjustment had successfully addressed the weakness. Alternatively, a first assessment cycle may have identified weaknesses in the assessment instruments or process, itself, leading to the need for further refinement of that process. Finally, just as students change, the goals of first-year programs and first-year advising may also change, thus creating the need for changes in the assessment of those programs as well. Assessment is never over.

Resources for Those Assessing Advising Learning Outcomes

It is useful to consult the Council for the Advancement of Standards (CAS) set of standards for academic advising programs, which articulate student learning and student development expectations for the advising process (e.g., intellectual growth, clarified values) and assumptions concerning the personal, legal, and fiscal expectations for advising programs (Appendix C in this monograph). An alternative source to consider when developing process outcomes would be the NACADA Core Values, which specify advisors' responsibilities to students, their peers, their institution, and the community (Appendix B in this monograph). Some excellent examples of instruments can be found at the NACADA Assessment of Advising Commission Resources web site (http://www.nacada.ksu.edu/Commissions/C32/C32-AdvisingAssessmentTools.htm).

Published instruments identified as measures of advisors, advisees, or advising are reflected in Table 1. These measures include assessments of what students (or, presumably, advisors) bring into the advising encounter (advising "inputs"), assessments of their interactions (advising "process"), and assessments of the impact of advising (advising "outcomes"). Part 1 of the Academic Advising Inventory (Winston & Sandor, 1984) evaluates student perceptions of advisor philosophy (developmental or prescriptive advising), while the Student Goals Exploration (Stark et al., 1991) allows for the assessment of students' academic goals. Such assessments can be valuable in formative or summative evaluations of advisors or to provide a pre-advising "baseline" of what students knew prior to an advising encounter. Behavioral measures of "input" might include numbers of appointments available or frequency with which students keep their appointments.

The College Student Experiences Questionnaire (Pace & Kuh, 1998) has scales that target faculty-student interaction as well as student measures of their own learning outside the classroom. Part 3 of the Academic Advising Inventory (Winston & Sandor, 1984) includes a five-item assessment of student satisfaction with advising. An alternative measure of outcome might be the Student Developmental Task and Lifestyle Inventory (Winston, Miller, & Prince, 1987), which assess students' understanding of their own developmental outcomes, including Academic Autonomy. Behavioral measures of outcome might include timely graduation or successful registration for appropriate courses.

Summary and Conclusions

Academic advising during the first year of a college student's higher education experience is key to his or her success academically, personally, and developmentally. It is through the academic advising experience that students learn the key issues regarding the institution, their curricula, and how making decisions concerning their life and academic career can affect their success and their persistence in college. Further, it is through the first-year academic advising experiences that students should begin that reflective learning that leads to self-discovery, self-reflection, and self-realization. Last, it is during this first year that advisors can provide instruction and learning experiences from which students gain an understanding and value for the general education curriculum. However, in order to clearly measure the impact on students and the effectiveness of the first-year advising experiences, it is essential that institutions have clearly outlined and implemented an assessment process for the advising experiences. An institution must develop strategies for measuring the achievement of the mission and outcomes and for making changes as needed to more effectively make the stated achievements. It is clear the assessment of learning at all stages of students' higher educational experiences is essential. However, as the first year is critical to continued success, focusing on this assessment as outlined in this chapter can greatly enhance the first-year programs on any campus.

References

American Association of Colleges and Universities (AAC&U). (2005). *Advocacy*. Retrieved August 3, 2006, from http://www.aacu.org/advocacy/what_is_liberal_education.cfm

American College Testing,Inc. (2002). *The ACT Evaluation Survey Service*. Iowa City, IA: ACT, Inc.

Belcher, M. (2005). Review of the ACT Evaluation Survey Service. In *The 16th mental measurements yearbook*. Retrieved November 30, 2005, from EBSCO Mental Measurements Yearbook database.

Bloom, B., Englehart, M., Furst, E., Hill, W., & Krathwohl, D. (1956). *Taxonomy of educational objectives: The classification of educational goals. Handbook I: Cognitive domain*. New York: Longmans, Green.

Brown, R. (2005a). Review of the Academic Advising Inventory. In *The 16th mental measurements yearbook*. Retrieved November 30, 2005, from EBSCO Mental Measurements Yearbook database.

Brown, R. (2005b). Review of Assessing Motivation to Communicate. In *The 16th mental measurements yearbook*. Retrieved November 30, 2005, from EBSCO Mental Measurements Yearbook database.

Brown R. (2005c). Review of the Student Goals Exploration. In *The 16th mental measurements yearbook*. Retrieved November 30, 2005, from EBSCO Mental Measurements Yearbook database.

Buros Institute of Mental Measurement. (2005). *The 16th mental measurements yearbook*. Retrieved November 30, 2005, from EBSCO Mental Measurements Yearbook database.

Campbell, M. (2005). Review of the College Student Inventory. In *The 16th mental measurements yearbook*. Retrieved November 30, 2005, from EBSCO Mental Measurements Yearbook database.

Geisinger, K. (2005). Review of the College Student Experiences Questionnaire. In *The 16th mental measurements yearbook*. Retrieved November 30, 2005, from EBSCO Mental Measurements Yearbook database.

Gillespie, (2005). Review of Perceptions, Expectations, Emotions and Knowledge About College Questionnaire. In *The 16th mental measurements yearbook*. Retrieved November 30, 2005, from EBSCO Mental Measurements Yearbook database.

Henning-Stout, M. (2005). Review of Student Developmental Task and Lifestyle Inventory. In *The 16th mental measurements yearbook*. Retrieved November 30, 2005, from EBSCO Mental Measurements Yearbook database.

Hogan, T. (2005). Review of College Student Inventory. In *The 16th mental measurements yearbook*. Retrieved November 30, 2005, from EBSCO Mental Measurements Yearbook database.

Kuh, G., Hayek, J., Carini, R., Oimet, J., Gonyea, R., & Kennedy, J. (2001). *NSSE 2000 Norms*. Bloomington, IN: Indiana University Center for Postsecondary Research.

Maki, P. (2004). *Assessing for learning: Building a sustainable commitment across the institution*. Sterling, VA: Stylus Publications.

Marchant, G. (2005). Review of Noncognitive Variables and Questionnaire. In *The 16th mental measurements yearbook*. Retrieved November 30, 2005, from EBSCO Mental Measurements Yearbook database.

Miller, M. (2005). Review of the College Student Experiences Questionnaire. In *The 16th mental measurements yearbook*. Retrieved November 30, 2005, from EBSCO Mental Measurements Yearbook database.

Morner, C., & Belcher, M. J. (2005). Review of the ACT Evaluation Survey Service. In *The 16th mental measurements yearbook*. Retrieved January 12, 2007, from EBSCO Mental Measurements Yearbook database.

Morreale, S., Hamilton, R. & Berko, R. (Eds.). (1994). *Assessing motivation to communicate*. Washington, DC: National Communication Association.

Pace, C. R., & Kuh, G. D. (1998). *College student experiences questionnaire* (4th ed.). Bloomington, IN: Indiana University.

Palomba, C. A., & Banta, T. W. (1999). *Assessment essentials: Planning, implementing, and improving assessment in higher education*. San Francisco: Jossey-Bass.

Pellegrino, J. W., Chudowsky, N., & Glaser, R. (2001). *Knowing what students know: The science and design of educational assessment*. Washington, DC: National Research Council.

Porterfield, W. M. (2005). Review of Student Developmental Task and Lifestyle Inventory. In *The 16th mental measurements yearbook*. Retrieved November 30, 2005, from EBSCO Mental Measurements Yearbook database.

Sauser, W. (2005). Review of National Survey of Student Engagement. In *The 16th mental measurements yearbook*. Retrieved November 30, 2005, from EBSCO Mental Measurements Yearbook database.

Sedlacek, W. E. (1998). Admissions in higher education: Measuring cognitive and noncognitive variables. In D. J. Wilds & R. Wilson (Eds.), *Minorities in higher education 1997-98: Sixteenth annual status report* (pp. 47-71). Washington, DC: American Council on Education.

Shaw, S. N., & Benson, M. (2005). Review of Student Goals Exploration. In *The 16th mental measurements yearbook*. Retrieved November 30, 2005, from EBSCO Mental Measurements Yearbook database.

Sheehan, E. (2005). Review of National Survey of Student Engagement. In *The 16th mental measurements yearbook*. Retrieved November 30, 2005, from EBSCO Mental Measurements Yearbook database.

Smith, C. (2005). Review of Noncognitive Variables and Questionnaire. In *The 16th mental measurements yearbook*. Retrieved November 30, 2005, from EBSCO Mental Measurements Yearbook database.

Stark, J., Lowther, M., Shaw, K., & Sossen, P. (1991). The Student Goals Exploration: Reliability and concurrent validity. *Educational and Psychological Measurement, 51*, 413-422.

Stratil, M. (1988). *College Student Inventory*. Iowa City, IA: Noel Levitz.

Weinstein, C., Palmer, D. & Hanson, G. (1995). *Perceptions, Expectations, Emotions, and Knowledge About College*. Clearwater, FL: H & H Publishing Co.

Winston, R., & Sandor, J. (1984). *Academic Advising Inventory*. Athens, GA: Student Development Associates.

Winston, R. B., Jr., Miller, T. K., & Prince, J. S. (1987). *Student Developmental Task and Lifestyle Inventory*. Athens, GA: Student Development Associates.

Wright, C. (2005). Review of the Assessing Motivation to Communicate Survey. In *The 16th mental measurements yearbook*. Retrieved November 30, 2005, from EBSCO Mental Measurements Yearbook database.

Yazak, D. (2005). Review of Perceptions, Expectations, Emotions, and Knowledge About College Questionnaire. In *The 16th mental measurements yearbook*. Retrieved November 30, from EBSCO Mental Measurements Yearbook database.

Section Three

Critical Issues and Strategies for Advising Diverse Populations of First-Year Students

Chapter Nine

Academic Advising
of First-Year Adult Students

Penny J. Rice and Sharon Paterson McGuire

The image of the traditional-aged college student who is 18 to 22-years-old, lives on campus, is financially dependent on his or her parents, is full-time, and entered postsecondary education directly following graduation from high school (Birkenholz, 1999) applies to an ever decreasing percentage of students enrolled in postsecondary education today. The U.S. Department of Education estimates that more than 9 million adult students are enrolled in postsecondary institutions (NCES, ...). In fact, the Department of Education predicts that by the year 2014, 50% of the students enrolled in postsecondary education will be 25 years of age and older (NCES, 2005). With this increase in the number of adult students on our campuses, it is vital that we understand their unique needs so that we can provide appropriate supports.

Adult Student Characteristics

Adult learners comprise the fastest growing segment of the college student population today. Usually, they are financially independent from their parents, not entering postsecondary education directly from high school, and, perhaps, arriving on campus with a partner/spouse and/or dependents. Adults come to campus with a wide array of life experiences and multiple personal and professional responsibilities and priorities, which make them very different from traditional-aged students (Graham, Donaldson, Kasworm, & Dirkx, 2000; Kasworm, 2003).

Even though the number of adult learners is eclipsing that of other students, most student services are geared to the traditional-aged student (Sissel, Hansman, & Kasworm, 2001). A quick review of many higher educational institutions' recruitment materials, schedule of classes, and office hours reflects that traditional-aged students are seen as their primary clients.

To enhance student success over the past few decades, colleges and universities have focused on developing supports for traditional first-year students (Upcraft & Gardner, 1989). However, the concept of the first year is useful when looking at adult learners as well. It is important to recognize that the definition of "first year" for many older students may be both the chronological first year when the adult student enrolls in higher education for the first time and the subsequent "first year" when they choose to return to campus after a hiatus from academia. While most traditional-aged students experience a transition during the first year because they are newly on their own for the first time in their lives, adult students may continue to feel new each time they return to higher education. Many adults dropping into and out of higher education due to finances, family composition, and employment status may cause them to experience a perpetual first year (Kerka, 1995). In contrast, relationships for traditional-aged students can more easily continue without breaks because of time and proximity for continual, uninterrupted interactions.

Academic advisors play an important role in adult learning. First-year advisees may be thought of as learners and the advisor as the instructor. Certainly, the role of an advisor includes curriculum guidance, institutional policy dissemination, and enforcement. However, increasingly attention must be paid to advisors' role in learning, retention, and the overall quality of life for students (Light, 2001).

Knowles (1984), a pioneer in adult learning, suggests adult students are:

◇ Self-directed and autonomous when grasping new knowledge
◇ More likely to draw on life experiences and knowledge in new learning situations
◇ Goal- and relevancy-oriented in their learning activities and experiences
◇ More responsive to a learning process built on mutual respect

Analysis of responses to the College Student Experience Questionnaire from 20,000 students attending 20 institutions during 1998-1999 suggests that factors related to learning for traditional students are different from students who are more than 23 years old (Lundberg, 2003). Peer relationships are not so significant to adult student learning. This is good news since adult students are less likely to have social or academic relationships with peers. However, an area of opportunity to enhance learning and retention is the adult students' relationships with administrators and faculty, because the quality of these relationships affects them more than traditional-aged students (Lundberg). The more positive the relationship, the more adult students are motivated and invested in their studies. A positive relationship with an academic advisor could be the catalyst that keeps adult students directed toward their goals.

Adult Students' Challenges and Needs

Adult students are enrolled in postsecondary education for a multitude of reasons. At this time in their lives, they may have a change in career, family relationships, employment status, and/or a lessening of parenting responsibility that has made it an opportune time to pursue their academic dreams. Successfully transitioning through all the multiple changes in adult students' lives will require time, attention, and patience.

Clearly, adult students face unique challenges. To begin with, first-year students who are over the age of 25 may doubt their academic abilities to sustain academic standards and cannot imagine completing their undergraduate degrees (Cross, 1981). "The feeling of being too old to learn increases steadily with age until it becomes a common barrier to education for older people" (Cross, p. 57). Complicating this challenge, adult students may find connecting to campus and classmates more difficult because of off-campus commitments. Some are parenting with a partner or alone, others are caring for their elder parents, and some are caring for the children of a relative with or without children of their own (Kasworm, 2003). These life commitments challenge adult students to persist toward meeting their educational goals.

Working full-time, part-time, sporadically, or seasonally can lead to finances being the first priority and the one over which students feel the least amount of control. Each increase in fees and tuition ripples out into every aspect of the adult students' finances. If the institution needs

$25 more in fees each semester, this could be the breaking point for the adult student's budget. This may lead some adult learners to choose to stop-out for a time to earn a full-time salary and catch up on expenses before continuing.

In addition to the general transition experiences of being a first-year student, adult students also must balance commitments to family and employers and the demands of coursework. Moreover, these students and their family members are making many sacrifices for little or unknown returns. Kent and Gimmestad (2004) studied how adult student persisters, those who continue to degree attainment, and adult non-persisters, those who leave before degree attainment in postsecondary education, differed in the level they felt they mattered to their institution. One of the five environmental areas examined in this study was academic advising. The researchers (Kent & Gimmestad) found that while persisters and non-persisters felt the same about their interactions with advisors, the adult students who persisted felt they mattered more to the institution than was reported in the other variables measured (i.e., administration, interaction with peers, and multiple roles). Therefore, this finding suggests that academic advisors can play a key role in how an adult student feels about the level of value they bring to the campus.

Thus, it is imperative to examine what academic advisors can do to increase the sense of mattering (Schlossberg, 1989). Feeling marginalized is "a sense of not fitting in [that] could lead to self-consciousness, irritability, and depression" (Evans, Forney, & Guido-DiBrito, 1998, p. 27). Mattering is "our belief, whether right or wrong, that we matter to someone else" (Schlossberg, p. 9). Depending on the class size and teaching load, faculty may not interact one-on-one with adult students. Ideally, adult students will perceive that they matter during their interactions with advisors since academic advisors may be the sole person to interact one-on-one with adult students continuously. The academic advisor's input into an adult student's future (e.g., class schedule, majors, and career) can cause the student to feel cared about and noticed, key aspects of a sense of mattering (Rosenberg & McCullough, 1981). What might seem like a simple interaction to the academic advisor may be a critical conversation to the adult student (Fairchild, 2003).

Adult students are more likely to be academically successful and attain a degree with the support and encouragement of friends and family members (Lundberg, 2003). However, the single greatest barrier to a students' success are the people in their lives: parents, children, spouses, and partners (Rosenthal, 1997; Wlodkowski, Mauldin, & Campbell, 2002). If students do not have a strong support system off campus, it is important that they have strong support systems and encouragement on campus from student services and other students (Rosenthal). Academic advisors might make suggestions about which student service offices provide support to adult students, where adult students might meet other students, or even how adult students can organize a support group (Donaldson, Graham, Martindill, Long, & Bradley, 1999).

Strategies for Advising

The adult student's needs are complex and can be overwhelming at times to both the student and advisor. However, advisors can best begin to understand the needs of first-year adult students by gaining an understanding of the developmental and personal challenges of this group of students and of each specific student they advise. Gaining this understanding will take time, but is well worth the investment.

Similar to traditional-aged students, some adult students will arrive completely prepared for the first advising appointment. They may have a suggested schedule completed and simply need to be reassured that their plan fits the major and ensures a degree. Other adult students, like traditional-aged students, will approach postsecondary education without a sense of what steps to take or what questions need to be asked and will rely heavily on their academic advisors for guidance, direction, and resources.

The adult student with a pre-established plan would benefit from knowing that the plan is flexible. If interests outside the degree develop, it is acceptable to explore other options while enrolled in higher education. In addition, pointing out that students strictly adhere to the plan with which they entered postsecondary education is important, as is assuring the student that, if they continue to show up each day and do the things they need to, there will be progress over time. The uncertain student will need guidance on how to narrow their choices, where to go for career exploration advice and assessments, and personal assurance that they can be successful.

Academic advisors should remind these students that the institution would not permit them to enter if they did not think the students would be successful. Academic advisors can also address these doubts by referring adult students to offices on campus that assist with developing study skills, access to tutors, and support groups (Graham et al., 2000). Advisors can help adult students visualize where they want to be employed and what opportunities the degree will give them. Advisors should provide opportunities for students to dream and verbalize their wishes. If the end result feels real to the students, they are more likely to persist (Kasworm, 2003).

Many adult students have a wealth of life experiences that can be used to help them find examples of personal success that can be transferred to the academic enterprise. For example, adult students who owned and managed a business already know a great deal about financial and time management. Advisors who point out the multiple successes in adult students' lives will be planting seeds for future self-advocacy in their advisees. These experiences and perspectives will be valuable to the student and their academic advisor as students face new and perhaps even more challenging experiences. As the advisor and students engage in academic planning together, the advisor would be wise to learn more about the students, their responsibilities, their life and career goals, and any potential challenges to success that might be present. Advisors of first-year adult students will need to provide accurate information, show concern for their advisee, and develop rapport and more in order to become a credible source of information and support. The adult student must see the advisor as an authority in his or her area of study as well as an authority on campus resources and information (Fields & Barrett, 1996). Again, this may take more time than the advisor might give to traditional-aged, first-year students; however, being able to provide help at the level needed by each individual student is what makes an academic advisor outstanding. Remember, time invested early in the advising relationship will pay off later when adults begin to understand the system and are able to advocate for and find answers for themselves.

Given the characteristics of adult learners, a variety of strategies should be employed when advising adult students. A general interview is needed to understand the interconnected, multifaceted context of the postsecondary experience for adult students. While holistic interviews are important for all students, this process is essential for adult students because their lives can be more complex and benefit more from long-range planning. Some questions could include:

◇ What are your long-term academic, career, and personal aspirations?
◇ How are you involved with family, work, community, and on campus?
◇ What are potential obstacles to achieving your academic and personal goals?
◇ What kinds of support systems are in place at home and at work to assist you with school?
◇ What are some of your past experiences, skills, and successes that can be applied to working on your degree?
◇ What support systems on campus can help you reach your academic and personal goals?

◇ What responsibilities do you have in your life that you anticipate changing and what contingency plans have been developed if needed?

◇ What are your greatest fears in going to/going back to college?

◇ What else can I, as your academic advisor, do to help you?

Invaluable knowledge can be gained from a holistic interview. In addition, advisors should offer significant amounts of resource information because the adult students may not know what they do not know. For example, adult students are less likely to apply for financial aid and may underestimate their ability to pay for postsecondary education (Hatfield, 2003). Information about resources and contacts in financial aid can reduce significant barriers. For example, Rowan University established the Adult Intern Program to assist adult students who have some specific financial challenges in paying for their college tuition. In exchange for a tuition waiver, students work a predetermined number of hours each week in one of the offices at the University. The goal of this work component is, where possible, to provide meaningful work experiences that will assist students in meeting their academic and career goals. Both full-time and part-time students may apply. The Pennsylvania State University (Penn State) has a number of scholarships that are targeted specifically for adult students, in some cases only for adult students who are attending part time. In addition, the Commission for Adult Learners at Penn State sponsors the Returning Adult Student Scholarship. Part-time women adult students are eligible for the Suzanne Seamans Memorial Scholarship.

Outcomes of Advising

From an advising standpoint, the desired outcome for adult students as a result of the advising relationship is similar to that for traditional-aged students. The desire is that students narrow their focus of what they wish to learn, recognize and remove barriers to learning, have knowledge of resources and services, develop and implement plans to achieve goals, and feel connected and supported along the way. Based on the information presented in this chapter, the process to achieve these desired outcomes is multidimensional due to the complexities of adult student lives.

In addition to these outcomes, which are similar to desired outcomes for all students, there are societal outcomes of advising adult students. Many communities are experiencing economic transitions, so there is a need to retrain potential employees from a manufacturing-based economy to service- or computing-based economy. Similarly, communities are becoming more ethnically or racially diverse, so there is a need for increased cultural knowledge, sensitivity, and fluency in other languages. Employers need to hear positive stories about adult student experiences that may come from advisors, so that employers see the positive aspects of supporting employee education.

To make generational changes through education, a positive advising relationship can lead to adult students "catching the education bug" such that the student continues to graduate or pursue professional degrees. Another outcome is positive referrals to friends, coworkers, family, and neighbors regarding a useful contact person (advisor) at an institution, which enhances enrollment and impacts the community in which the adult student lives and works. Finally, interactions with adult students through an advising relationship has unanticipated outcomes, such as advisors learning more about themselves, their institution, and adult students. The adult student helps reframe and refresh the frame of reference academic advisors have of their campus, community, and society.

References

Birkenholz, R. J. (1999). *Effective adult learning.* Danville, IL: Interstate.

Cross, K. P. (1981). *Adults as learners: Increasing participation and facilitating learning.* San Francisco: Jossey-Bass.

Donaldson, J. F., Graham, S. W., Martindill, W., Long, S., & Bradley, S. (1999). *Adult undergraduate students: How do they define success?* (Report No. HE 032-114). Montreal, Quebec, Canada: American Educational Research Association. (ERIC Document Reproduction Services No. ED 431 351)

Evans, N. J., Forney, D. S., & Guido-DiBrito, F. (1998). *Student development in college: Theory, research, and practice.* San Francisco: Jossey-Bass.

Fairchild, E. E. (2003). Multiple roles of adult learners. In D. Kilgore & P. J. Rice (Eds.), *Meeting the special needs of adult students* (New Directions for Student Services, No. 102, pp. 11-16). San Francisco: Jossey-Bass.

Fields, H. R., & Barrett, A. (1996). *Improving and developing the academic advising process at Grambling State University to enhance students' academic success.* (Report No. HE 033-889). Nova Southeastern University: Practicum Papers. (ERIC Document Reproduction Services No. ED 451 761)

Graham, S. W., Donaldson, J. F., Kasworm, C. E., & Dirkx, J. (2000). *The experiences of adult undergraduate students: What shapes their learning?* (Report No. CE 080 040). New Orleans, LA: American Educational Research Association. (ERIC Document Reproduction Services No. ED 440 275)

Hatfield, K. M. (2003). Funding higher education for adult students. In D. Kilgore, & P. J. Rice (Eds.) *Meeting the special needs of adult students* (New Directions for Student Services, No. 102, pp. 27-34). San Francisco: Jossey-Bass.

Kasworm, C. E. (2003). Setting the stage: Adults in higher education. In D. Kilgore & P. J. Rice (Eds.), *Meeting the special needs of adult students* (New Directions for Student Services, No. 102, pp. 3-16). San Francisco: Jossey-Bass.

Kent, S. E., & Gimmestad, M. J. (2004). *Adult undergraduate student persistence and their perceptions of how they matter to the institution.* Association for the Study of Higher Education Paper Depot Archives. Retrieved November 22, 2005, from http://www.ashe.ws/paperdepot/2004kansascity.htm

Kerka, S. (1995). *Adult learner retention revisited.* ERIC Clearinghouse on Adult Career and Vocational Education, 166. Retrieved May 8, 2006, from http://www.ericdigests.org/1996-3/adult.htm

Knowles, M. S. (1984). *The modern practice of adult education: From pedagogy to andragogy* (2nd ed.). San Francisco: Jossey-Bass.

Light, R. J. (2001). *Making the most of college: Students speak their minds.* Cambridge: Harvard University Press.

Lundberg, C. A. (2003). The influence of time-limitations, faculty, and peer relationships on adult student learning: A causal model. *Journal of Higher Education 74*(6), 665-688.

National Center for Education Statistics (NCES). (2002). *Digest of educational statistics 2001.* NCES 2002-130 (table 213). Washington, DC: Office of Educational Research and Improvement, U.S. Department of Education.

National Center for Education Statistics (NCES). (2005, September). *Projections of education statistic to 2014.* Retrieved December 3, 2005, from http://nces.ed.gov/pubs2005/2005074.pdf

Rosenberg, M., & McCullough, B. C. (1981). Mattering: Inferred significance to parents and mental health among adolescents. In R. Simmons (Ed.), *Research in community and mental health* (Vol. 2, pp. 163-182). Greenwich, CT: JAI.

Rosenthal (Rice), P. J. (1997). *Correlates of persistence for adult women enrolled in college.* Unpublished master's thesis, Minnesota State University, Mankato.

Schlossberg, N. K. (1989). Marginality and mattering: Key issues in building community. In D. C. Roberts (Ed.), *Designing campus activities to foster a sense of community* (New Directions for Student Services, No. 48, pp. 5-15). San Francisco: Jossey-Bass.

Sissel, P. A., Hansman, C. A., & Kasworm, C. E. (2001). The politics of neglect: Adult learners in higher education. In C. A. Hansman & P. A. Sissel (Eds.), *Understanding and negotiating the political landscape of adult education* (New Directions for Adult and Continuing Education, No. 91, pp. 17-27). San Francisco: Jossey-Bass.

Upcraft, M., Gardner, J., & Associates. (1989). *The freshman year experience: Helping students survive and succeed in college.* San Francisco: Jossey-Bass.

Wlodkowski, R. J., Mauldin, J., & Campbell, S. (2002). *Early exit: Understanding adult attrition in accelerated and traditional postsecondary programs.* (Report No. HE 035-095). Indianapolis, IN: Lumina Foundation for Education. (ERIC Document Reproduction Services No. ED 467 088)

Chapter Ten

Creating Vital Students of Color Communities in the First Year With Academic Advising

Evette J. Castillo

My academic advisors were not simply interested in ensuring that I had the appropriate classes, but were interested in my overall success as an African American at a traditionally White institution…academic advisors must understand and embrace the added burden that many of us students of color are first-generation college students. Consequently, my success in college represents a victory for me as well as for my family. (African American student)

My mom wanted me to be a doctor. She couldn't understand why I wanted to be a psychology major. I had to explain to my mom about what being a psychology major was. It's hard because she doesn't know what to tell people exactly what I will do when I graduate; to her, it's not concrete enough of a major for her to explain to others. (Asian American student)

It is very discouraging as a student to have an academic advisor act as if you are insignificant. We need to have some degree of caring when it comes to making decisions about our lives. Remember, not all students are lucky enough to have strong support from family or friends to excel or even succeed in college. (Latina student)

Traditionally, a stigma is attached to dropping out, labeling it as a student failure, but life happens and things change, leading to a reprioritization of your goals and responsibilities. Native American cultures typically put family responsibility first, making school secondary…if we can understand this, perhaps educators should provide a means to integrate the two. (Native American student)

I felt like my advisors didn't know how to help me find a "fit" on campus in reference to my biracial identity. Their sensitivity was whether I wanted to be a part of the White crowd or the Asian crowd. I always wanted to know both sides, not to have to choose…I wish my advisors got to know more about me, my personal life; had asked me more questions about home, friends, things that I want, what I do outside of school, so that they can understand me better. (Biracial student)

As an academic advisor, reading these cogent testimonials from students of color may invoke reflective questions such as, "Do I really take the time to learn about the experiences of students of color that come in for advising? Am I really advising the whole student and offering the necessary tools for learning and success in and out of the classroom? Is there something more that I can do to transform my advising into meaningful learning opportunities for both the student and myself?" These questions and their answers call for academic advisors to recommit to continuous learning in the profession, refine advising skills to be more intentional and purposeful when interacting with students of color in the first year, and rethink the role of advising practitioners as that of "teachers" in a learning, student-centered context.

This chapter focuses on advising African American, Asian and Pacific Islander American, Latino/a, Native American, and multiracial and biracial students. It begins by describing the concept of academic advising as teaching in a learning paradigm, highlighting the status of students of color in higher education, and reviewing the different cultural contexts and critical issues specific to the student populations. The sections that follow offer strategies for actualizing learning communities with students of color, recommend items for action, and conclude with implications for the profession.

Throughout this chapter, the term "students of color" is used to identify students who are (a) members of racial/ethnic groups who have been historically underrepresented and underserved in America's educational system and (b) socially defined as minorities who are most likely to become targets of oppression, prejudice, stereotyping, and discrimination regardless of numerical status and distribution (Rendón, García, & Person, 2004, p. 7). I specifically use the terms African American, Asian and Pacific Islander American, Latino/a, Native American, and Multiracial and Biracial to describe the various groups that comprise "students of color." Let me preface by saying that labeling groups of people is difficult and politically charged and that these labels are "constantly changing given political, economic, and social realities" (Rendón et al., p. 5).

Academic Advisors as Teachers in a Learning Context

We have entered a "learning revolution" (Harvey-Smith, 2005) in higher education where the role of staff and faculty has shifted from providers of information to that of facilitators of student learning. Traditionally, it has been the position of professionals in student affairs to develop and educate the student holistically.

This attention to holistic approaches opens students' minds, engages their study of the college experience, helps them to think critically, and makes them partner with university educators in a creative, collaborative, and participatory way. hooks (2003) asserts that marginalized students have a learned experience of interconnectedness and community prior to entering college. When students experience a disconnect with the campus community, often, the result is attrition and poor academic performance. She further states, "for many high achieving students from backgrounds that are marginalized by race, class, geography, sexual preference, or some combination, college continues to be a place of disconnection" (p. 177).

Pedagogy and learning entail sharing information, embracing dialogue, knowing your students, and exchanging ideas. This relationship and learning context emphasizes that, as partners in education, we are responsible for creating community. Great teaching is to first know, feel, and sense your community and then to draw your students into it (Palmer, 1998). We cannot assume that it is the students' sole responsibility when they first enter our institutions of higher learning to navigate the campus on their own. We have an obligation as educators to create the best climates for learning and we must do so as partners strengthening our community and relationships with our students.

This transformative approach of academic advisors as teachers is progressive education. Institutionalizing a learning-centered approach as well as anchoring it into the campus culture are the biggest challenges in higher education (Harvey-Smith, 2005). Though it is imperative for full institutional commitment to be behind this change, lack of commitment should not stop essential work from being done to successfully maintain and enhance the academic community as partners and co-learners with students of color. Advisors are central in this effort to help students of color during their first-year college experience. We cannot leave their success to chance.

Students of Color College Participation and Degree Attainment

Students of color continue to experience unique challenges and difficulty accessing and succeeding in higher education today despite the growing enrollment numbers, establishment of diversity and outreach programs, multicultural centers, and thriving cultural-based student organizations, clubs, fraternities, and sororities. What we can expect as educators is that as demographics change and as demands for more of an ethnic and racially diverse society increases (Rendón & Hope, 1996), our college student body will undoubtedly be more diverse, dynamic, and complex. We need to be thoughtful about evaluating our teachings, practices, service delivery, views, and approaches. According to Harvey-Smith (2005), in the past 20 years, minorities have made significant progress in higher education, changing the face of the American college-going population, but they trail behind their White counterparts in key areas such as high school achievement, college attendance, retention, and graduation. With the exception of Native American students, whose enrollment numbers remained the same, the percentage distribution of enrollment of 18- to 24-year olds in colleges and universities between 1980 and 2000 shows a larger proportion of students of color attended college in 2000 than in 1980. It is important to be aware of this increase, because it impacts our role as teachers in a learning-centered environment.

Participation

Table 1 shows that Asian, African American, Hispanic, and White students, in fall 2001, are not equally distributed throughout the country's two- and four-year institutions. White, foreign, African American, Asian, and Native American students show higher attendance rates at four-year institutions while Hispanic attendance rates are higher at two-year institutions (57.9%) as compared to four-year institutions (42.1%). African American students on college campuses today comprise the largest student of color population with almost two million students in both two and four-year institutions. However, students of color in aggregate, make up only a fraction of the entire undergraduate enrollment in the nation's college systems with only 11.6% being African American students (participating in two and four-year institutions), 9.8% being Latino/a, 6.4% being Asians, and 1% being Native Americans.

Table 1

Distribution of College Enrollment by Racial and Ethnic Groups, Fall 2001

Race/Ethnic Group	Total Percent Undergraduate Enrollment	Public/Private Four-year (Percent)	Public/Private Two-year (Percent)
All Undergraduate Students		60.8	39.2
Native American	1.0	50.5	49.4
Asian	6.4	59.0	41.0
African American	11.6	57.0	43.0
Latino/a	9.8	42.1	57.9
White	67.6	63.3	36.7
Foreign	3.5	82.4	17.5

Source. Chronicle of Higher Education (Almanac, 2004).

Degree Attainment

Associate and bachelor degrees conferred between 2001-2002 for White, African American, Hispanic, Asian, Native American, and Nonresident Aliens are shown in Table 2. African American students continue to be the largest student of color population earning degrees at both two-year and four-year institutions. White students remain the majority in the attainment of both associate (70.2%) and bachelor (74.2%) degrees across our nation's campuses, while Native Americans' degree attainment is the lowest (1.1% of associate degrees, 0.7% of bachelor's degrees).

Creative and collaborative measures are necessary to address the alarmingly low enrollment of undergraduate students of color across our college campuses. In addition, first-year attrition rates for students of color in public two-year institutions is 54.2% and 30% at four-year

Table 2

Distribution of Degrees Conferred by Colleges and Universities by Racial and Ethnic Groups, 2001-2002

	Total (%)	White (%)	African American (%)	Latino/a (%)	Asian (%)	Native American (%)	Nonresident Alien (%)
Associate Degree	100	70.2	11.3	10.0	5.2	1.1	2.1
Bachelor's Degree	100	74.2	9.0	6.4	6.4	0.7	3.2

Source. Chronicle of Higher Education (Almanac, 2004).

institutions (Carnevale, 1999). As educators, we need to transform and rethink how to offer successful support to students of color, particularly in the first year. As the demographics of our undergraduate student body becomes more diverse, heterogeneous, and complex (Pascarella & Terenzini, 1998), our role as practitioners and educators is even more apparent and timely in furthering our understanding of and competence in how culturally related behaviors intersect with the learning process.

Understanding Cultural Contexts of Students of Color

An academic advisor once indicated that she could not help or advise a student successfully because she was not from that student's ethnic background. Though the advisor actually did possess an adequate knowledge of the student's academic, personal, and cultural background, she still thought her efforts would be unsuccessful because of the racial difference. Sensitivity to the student's culture and background and how that may affect academic achievement are very important for the academic success and retention of first-year students of color. However, a more valuable and empowering skill is an academic advisor's ability to engage in critical dialogue about the students' characteristics and experiences and create positive learning environments (James, 2005; Rendón, 2004). In addition, advisors need to create meaningful relationships, enriched learning environments, and a culture of caring when working with first-year students of color. While it is critical for institutions to be conscientious and active in hiring a critical mass of staff and faculty of color to reflect the student populations they serve, it does not mean that academic advisors whose cultural or racial backgrounds are different from the students cannot provide quality support or service to any student. Academic advisors as teachers and partners in a learning environment do more than provide a service; they are agents who can transform education and contribute to the success of first-year students of color.

To engage in transformational practice, academic advisors should not treat students of color as a homogenous population. To think of them monolithically is a disservice to our profession as teachers and educators. Microculturally, some of these differences may include gender, sexuality, class, generation, language, economics, values, identity, age, religion, disability, academic achievement, and region (Attinasi & Nora, 1996; Rendón et al., 2004). We do more harm to students of color by megagrouping (Anderson, 1995), that is, the tendency to homogenize the diverse characteristics within a group. As a result, the acquired skill, one that merits careful attention from educators and practitioners, is to have the necessary knowledge base of the students' cultural context and upbringing. Simultaneously, it is essential to listen to and understand their individual voices and what makes them unique among their peers within cultural groups.

To effectively meet the advising and counseling needs of students of color, academic advisors, as teachers, should give strong consideration to their students' racial identity and how students perceive themselves as racial beings before making any assumptions about their level of psychosocial development (Pope, 2000). Helms' People of Color Racial Identity Statuses (Helms, 1990, 1995; Helms & Cook, 1999) illustrates the developmental process of a student of color, starting from an implicit acceptance of White standards (conformity) and devaluing one's own racial group (dissonance), progressing to the idealization of one's racial group and dismissing anything perceived as White (immersion). The next state is an affective state of communalism (emersion), which eventually leads to a critical acceptance and commitment toward one's racial group (internalization), and ultimately to embracing work against oppressions shared with other groups (integrated awareness) (McEwen, 2003). Given the many complexities in the backgrounds of students of color, Helms' model provides an important conceptual structure that guides practice, learning, and teaching.

African American Students

The focus on creating a strong and close community of African American students, staff, and faculty is necessary for the retention and success of first-year African American students. Advisors as educators have a shared responsibility in designing quality college experiences for African American students.

African Americans have historical links throughout the world, representing many different countries. The ethnic realities of African American students, generally, are grounded in African culture, with roots not only in Africa but also in the West Indies, the Caribbean, Canada, Central and South America, and the United States (Lee, 2004; Rendón et al., 2004).

African American students who attend predominantly White institutions are more likely to view the campus as alienating, hostile, unjust, and less supportive to their needs (Fleming, 1984; Schmader, Major, & Gramzow, 2002; White, 1998). A study by Wasson (1990) also discovered that African American students perceived the faculty as unresponsive and unwilling to support their academic development. African American students are fully aware of "race" and how it can affect their academic success. Fries-Britt and Turner (2001) reveal that African American students experience the stress of feeling intellectually inferior to their White peers and may question their academic abilities. Compounding the additional stress of facing racial stereotypes, their study indicated that African American students undergo a "proving process" in order to validate their feelings of intellectual competence. If the classroom, work environments, and other professional and academic settings are all examples of domains that matter to African American students, then we, as educators, must create positive learning climates that build confidence, self-esteem, and repair their "academic sense of self" (Fries-Britt & Turner, p. 426).

Much research about African American college students has been in the areas of identity development as an aggregate group, comparing their experiences with other minority groups and what they face on predominantly White campuses. There is limited research on within-group differences among African American students (White, 1998); however, this is an important factor, because it relates to how they view themselves in the context of others within their community, their sense of belonging to the college community, and their overall persistence. White's groundbreaking study on how African American students perceive and interpret themselves and their community identity suggests that (a) African American identity is complex, ever-present, and situationally determined; (b) African American students who have not been around their peer group before college may have different social adjustment issues than students from predominantly African American environments; and (c) African American students have dual social relationships to the campus—their relationship to the campus as a "student" and their relationship to the campus as "a Black student" (p. 95-96). Malveaux (2005) writes that it is challenging to deal with issues of internal diversity in any community and to understand some of the tensions that may impede unity within communities. When educators on college campuses consider designing and implementing programs and services for first-year African American students, they should be mindful of how African American students view themselves within their own cultural community and its affects on identity development and level of academic adjustment and success.

Asian and Pacific Islander American Students

Academic advisors are instrumental in the teaching and learning paradigm specifically addressing outcomes that relate to integration of interpersonal and intrapersonal competence for Asian and Pacific Islander American students. The term Asian and Pacific Islander American applies to a highly diverse population encompassing Americans from East and South Asian backgrounds as well as the Pacific Islands. Asian American (or Asian Pacific American or Asian Pacific Islander) is now a term in common use in institutional data and throughout U.S. society (Hune, 2002). As a culturally diverse population that is rapidly growing, many educators should be mindful of the various microcultures and complex issues faced within the Asian Pacific Islander American community. Asian Americans, however, share enough cultural similarities and common issues that they can be regarded as a unique student population (McEwen, Kodama, Alvarez, Lee, & Liang, 2002), but it is important to note the differences (e.g., socioeconomic status, ethnicity, culture, language proficiency, family size, and immigration patterns) that shape their individual experiences.

Although Asian and Pacific Islander Americans are increasingly attending and graduating from higher education institutions (Suzuki, 2002), they are still invisible on U.S. campuses with respect to campus policies and programs (Hune, 2002). In fact, a more accurate measure of Asian and Pacific Islander Americans' progress can be attained when international students from Asia are excluded from domestic statistics. It is also important to differentiate between the experiences of Asian Pacific Islander Americans that represent a racial minority group (e.g., Pacific Islanders, Lao, Hmong, and Cambodian) from the majority of Asian Pacific Islander Americans. Also, aggregate data may show that Asian and Pacific Islander American college students are "success stories" or "model minorities." This stereotype carries negative consequences for many students and is often challenged by Asian American researchers and educators (Suzuki). Academic success may be hard for first-year Asian Pacific Islander American students to achieve if they are under pressure to perform. Eventually, for some, the pressure becomes such a burden and challenge that they drop out.

Asian Pacific Islander Americans see themselves as individuals but also as an integral part of a family. Conflict may occur as these first-year students are highly focused on community and family, while college campuses focus on individuality and competition (Chew-Ogi & Ogi, 2002). For example, choosing a major may be more of a family decision than an individual one (Castillo, 2002). Understanding this family interdependence and decision making process (Kodama, McEwen, Liang, & Lee, 2002) may help academic advisors adjust their practice and pedagogy in helping first-year students frame discussions and communications with their families. In the first year, it is important for academic advisors to help Asian Pacific Islander American students and their families understand the total college experience from academic resources such as tutoring, learning, and advising centers; living on or off campus; and balancing work with studying to exploring different major choices and career options. Attention to academic advisors' training and education on the diversity and complexity of the many microcultures within the Asian Pacific Islander community is initially critical for developing teaching and learning environments.

Latino/a Students

To create meaningful learning experiences and ensure academic success, critical attention needs to be focused on Latino/a students' first-year college experiences. Like African Americans and Asian and Pacific Islander Americans, Latinos are not a homogeneous group. There are more than 20 Spanish- and Portuguese-speaking countries in the Western hemisphere and Latinos self-identify based on their country of origin (Brown & Rivas, 1995). It is also helpful to distinguish between those who identify themselves as multigenerational and those who are recent immigrants.

In terms of economic status, few Latino/a students come from families where both parents have attended college and graduate school. They are often first-generation college students. A large number come from working-class, low-income families, where college attendance may not be encouraged or even introduced as an option. If they do attend college, many Latino/a students apply to nearby institutions to be closer to their families (Rendón, 1992). In addition, many Latinos live in predominantly ethnic minority communities (Gonzalez, 2002; Rendón et al., 2004).

Like African American students, Latino/a students also interpret the campus culture of predominantly White students as alienating, unsupportive, isolating, and hostile. It is common for Latino/a students to feel "out of place" and "ignored" (Attinasi & Nora, 1996; Gonzalez, 2002; Hurtado & Carter, 1996).

Attinasi and Nora's (1996) study describes "getting ready" and "getting in" as important concepts to consider in understanding and addressing Latino/a student retention. The getting-ready concept includes college staff communicating with parents about college preparation and expectations of going to college, students' witnessing or not witnessing family members attending college, conversations with high school teachers and counselors about college, and visiting college campuses. The getting-in concept (or cognitive mapping) are the postmatriculation experiences associated with how Latino/a students manage their new environment (Attinasi & Nora). The overall transition in the first year may include experiences such as (a) learning how to manage resources (e.g., time and money), (b) maintaining family support, and (c) finding their "fit" in the college community. Further, Hurtado and Carter (1996) found if Latino/a students made a smooth transition into college in the first year, they are less likely to perceive college as a hostile environment in the second year, which can result in an overall positive sense of belonging in the third year. One Latina student told me:

> More focus should be on commending these students for what they have accomplished thus far. When they enter college, they have a desire to succeed that is not seen or recognized…staying in college is another challenge. A lot of students of color see college as something that has to be done, but they rarely see themselves as who they have become (upon entering college) and who they can become.

For Latino/a students, validating their desire to succeed, encouraging their optimistic outlook (Hernandez, 2000), and recognizing their achievement in the first-year of college is essential to their overall success and retention.

Native American Students

It is important for academic advisors to continually educate themselves and be adaptive to the cultural needs of first-year Native American students who differ from mainstream students. Native Americans, according to Russell (1997), include 557 federally recognized tribes in the US; 220 of them are in Alaska.

There is a notable lack of research and information about Native American student participation, their ability to preserve their cultural integrity, their educational struggles, and how they meet these challenges. Nor do institutions actively engage in specific strategies to encourage Native American students to attend and graduate from college. What we know about Native American participation in higher education is that it has revolved around notions of assimilation. The mission statements of Dartmouth College, the College of William and Mary, and Princeton University described their role as educating and "civilizing" Indian people

(DeJong, 1993; Tierney, 1993; Wright, 1988). Given the effects of colonialism, Native Americans are poverty-stricken, come from inferior education systems, experience more unemployment, have major health concerns, and many live in rural areas where access to postsecondary institutions is difficult (Rendón et al., 2004; Tierney). In this first year, it is critical to understand how Native American students' lives are affected by life on the reservations, their values of harmony with nature, and the degree to which community (i.e., other first-year student of color populations) and tribal goals supersede individual goals.

Multiracial and Biracial Students

Experiences of multiracial and biracial students are very diverse. Specifically in the first year of college, many may encounter and/or establish their multiracial identity within a new environment. It is important to know and understand multiracial and biracial students from their point of reference, i.e., how they view themselves and their experiences. What is critical to consider from a teaching and learning perspective is that there is no endpoint or final resolution to identity development. Various models illustrate that students have their own way of coming to terms with their multiracial heritage.

Renn's (1998) multiracial identity model delineates five patterns describing how students group themselves in terms of their identity. This porous and fluid framework results from the influence of campus culture and peer-to-peer interactions to make sense of their racial identity. One way that first-year students choose to identify themselves racially is to choose one racial category with which to affiliate. A second way involves students moving between their different heritage groups and choosing not to identify with one racial identity all the time. The third approach is identifying themselves as "multiracial" depending on the campus support (i.e., clubs and organizations for multiracial students, mentoring, courses, and/or ongoing programs or events that explore multiracial student identity and experiences). The fourth category includes students who avoid being labeled as belonging to any racial group. The fifth and final category involves students who use one or more of the first four options when different situations suggest different ways of affiliation. One student, identified in this fifth category, told me, "There are times where I need to 'play up' a specific culture of mine during certain settings…it was dependent on what I felt most comfortable with." Pope, Ecklund, Miklitsch, and Suresh (2004) assert that, "how others identify us racially and how we choose to self-identify are essential pieces of the complex issue of racial identity" (p. 162).

Developing a campus community that is welcoming to first-year multiracial and biracial students requires total campus-wide commitment and support to increase interracial contact and provide requisite resources to achieve multicultural competence (Pope et al., 2004). Advisors as educators must strive to make the first year for multiracial and biracial students more meaningful and purposeful. One approach is to first find out where students are in their racial identity formation and how they view themselves and the world around them.

Strategies for Actualizing Learning Communities With Students of Color: Recommended Items for Action

When thinking about advising students of color, it is important to note that there are no set guidelines or clear-cut strategies. Nor should advisors and other university faculty and staff view the experiences and characteristics of all students of color monolithically in order to support their learning. As one student said, "Academic advisors must be able to adjust their technique to the ever-changing needs of students both collectively and individually…a cookie-cutter, one-size-fits-all approach to advising doesn't work." Also, academic advisors must challenge their own stereotypes and biases about students of color, before working with and educating this diverse group. The overarching goal in advising students of color is that it be contextual, ongoing, educational, and developmental for both advisor and advisee. The strategies and recommendations that follow are not just for academic advisors, but for campus-wide consideration to transform education by advocating for the integration of both academic learning and student development. By identifying these areas, academic advisors may reevaluate and/or reaffirm their commitment to being student-focused and learning-centered when working with students of color.

Create a Culture of Caring

Students succeed when they are surrounded by caring professionals who are their advocates. Academic advisors can create a culture of caring and empower students of color by teaching necessary coping and assertiveness skills, problem-solving strategies, and ways of increasing social and academic support (Brown & Robinson Kurpius, 1997). Do not be afraid to specifically ask a student of color, "What do you need in order to learn?" or "How can I serve you?"

Advise the whole student. Academic advising should be more than just offering services. At the onset, students of color enter college with a complex range of family, economic, educational, language, and identity characteristics and issues that warrant our critical attention as educators to work with them holistically. It is our responsibility to learn about their individual, cultural backgrounds and help develop their confidence and competence to navigate campus that they may initially view as unsupportive. Lee (2005) tells us to listen with an open heart and an open mind to the most critical advocates of the communities and that the more challenging these advocates are, the more change may be needed at the institution.

Mentorship. Students of color, particularly in their first year of college, need a person who can help them when they have problems, offer advice, and provide support. Mentors and mentor programs can enhance minority student satisfaction about university life and their academic performance (McMillan & Reed, 1994; Ting, 2000). Intentional mentoring and role modeling is an important aspect to the academic success of students of color. These formal and informal interactions with faculty and staff are essential to academic integration and educational persistence (Tinto, 1993; Wallace, Abel, & Ropers-Huilman, 2000). Therefore, purposeful efforts must be made to connect students of color with members of the campus community as potential mentors who have similar interests and background.

Although there are not enough women and people of color in established positions to serve as mentors (Rodriguez, 1995), academic advisors from any cultural background can successfully provide quality support and service to students of color by showing that they care, personalizing their interactions with students, and genuinely understanding the whole student and their background.

Making Personal Meaning

How students make meaning of their experiences can help us understand what they learn in the classroom (Fries-Britt, Gerald, & Lee, 2005). Asking students to define what being a college student means to them allows educators to align realities to an ideal (Tagg, 2004). In addition, discerning intrinsic versus extrinsic motivations for attending college is meaningful for first-year students of color and can inform their resilience and persistence in college. It is critical, however, to realize that immediate and extended families play a significant role in students' attending and continuing in college (Castillo, 2002). Advisors can help first-year students of color to make meaning of their experiences by discussing options, majors, various career pathways, and involvement opportunities; by helping them make sense of their environment, and how they fit and belong; and by exploring various ways to enhance students' dialogue with their families, professors, and peers.

Intentional Teaching and Learning Efforts

Understand identity development. Tierney (1993) states that minority students need institutions that will create the conditions that help students not only celebrate their cultural and personal histories but also critically examine how their lives are molded and shaped by society's forces. It is important to understand the experiences of students of color through their cultural backgrounds, views, values, and identity development. Advisors play a key role in helping students through this process by educating themselves about the student populations and understanding the lenses through which students look at their experiences and make decisions about their surroundings and relationships. Advisors need to understand different student cultures that exist on their campus. One way to further their understanding would be for academic advisors to be informally assigned to culturally based clubs and organizations. Similar to some advising staff structures whereby academic advisors are assigned liaison responsibilities with colleges or schools across campus, this connection to cultural clubs and organizations would serve as a strong learning link between students' academic advising experience and the relationship with their advisor.

Develop multicultural competencies. Advisors need to possess the appropriate attitudes, knowledge, and skills to support and assist a broad diversity of students. To develop these multicultural competencies, academic advisors must engage in purposeful and ongoing training and education. Communication styles, beliefs, values, worldviews, and perceptions about students of color are just some examples to be explored and embraced. It is also critical to continue to support ethnic studies courses, which help students of color learn about their history, culture, and identity. For continuous education and development, advisors may consider attending or auditing such courses.

Student leadership and growth opportunities. Because of family obligations, financial situation, adjustment to campus life, or academic achievement concerns, first-year students of color may not easily or rapidly get involved in campus activities and leadership opportunities. Academic advisors should actively recruit students of color for leadership opportunities and positions with an advising emphasis, such as peer advisors. Research shows that students who get involved in the overall collegiate experience persist and succeed in college. Students of color need this type of engagement to truly feel connected, which greatly increases their chances for academic success. Advisors can also support first-year students of color by being a resource of information and by actively nominating and including them in various recognition, awards, and scholarship opportunities across campus.

Be in Their World

Interact with students. There are real advantages for advisors to meet with students on more informal levels (e.g., outside their offices). Students see their advisors as "real" people and feel they can connect, while advisors, on the other hand, witness first-hand, and more personally, the world in which their students live. These meetings can occur anywhere including functions, events, programs, or in the local coffee shop. Meeting with students in these types of places encourages a caring environment that is crucial for first-year students of color and their academic success. In addition, academic advisors can connect with student of color communities through on-going, cocurricular experiences as a organization sponsor or participant. For a true teaching and learning relationship to occur, advisors need to be involved in a more holistic approach to student development, encouraging student of color involvement in activities that relate best to their interests.

Meet the families of first-year students of color. Advisors should make a conscious effort to meet the families of students of color during orientation, at prospective student events, move-in days at the residence halls, or at convocation ceremonies. We know that families play a large role for most students of color. Advisors making connections early with students' families in the first year can engage family and student in the learning process and help them understand the values of college life.

Implications for the Profession

Support and provide additional preparation for academic advisors. Institutions and campus leaders must support culturally competent academic advisors with ongoing and purposeful training, speaker series, workshops, and seminars. Professional development is one way to address enhanced preparation. A more drastic approach would be to expand the academic advisor's role to include "helping students of color design a college experience that will lead to the learning outcomes they and the institution seek" (Keeling, 2004, p. 22).

Diversify staff and faculty. First-year students of color in college communities are greatly served by the presence of role models on campus who look just like them. Specifically, for long-term goals of enhancing the performance of student affairs, Sagaria and Johnsrud (1991) posit that it is "essential to increase minority representation at all levels and across all functional areas in student services divisions" (p. 106). We know that students of color can have a mentoring relationship with caring professionals no matter what their racial or cultural background. However, institutional commitment and attention to increasing the recruitment and hiring of staff and faculty of color to serve as necessary role models and mentors is of paramount importance to both minority and majority students.

Involve the student voice in the planning process. All institutions should establish routine ways to hear students voice their concerns, and create opportunities for dialogue. With regard to programs, classes, and events, advisors should allow time for self-reflection and construction of meaning. This may be in the form of forums, portfolios, discussion groups, advising, and mentoring. Faculty and staff should seek students' input in institutional planning, because they experience and benefit from the educational process.

In light of a rapidly changing environment and the growing population of students of color on college and university campuses, staff, faculty, and administrators need to work collectively and collaboratively as educators in creating a nurturing, sustainable learning environment for first-year students of color (Cortese, 2003). Overall institutional commitment from the top down is necessary to transform learning and enhance campus life for first-year students of color.

Conclusion

Academic advisors, as teachers and educators in this learning paradigm, are dealing with issues related to a growing, dynamic, multi-faceted, and complex group of students of color. A successful first year is likely to provide the motivation for students of color to persist until college graduation (Nora, 2003). Academic advisors can be instrumental and successful teachers in improving first-year college retention rates for first-year students of color by actively learning about the cultural contexts and backgrounds of these students and understanding the pre-collegiate and first-year issues they face. Moreover, institutions must consider

> past experience, language and culture as strengths to be respected and woven into the fabric of knowledge production and dissemination…we need to validate students' capacities for intellectual development at the beginning, not at the end, of their academic careers. (Rendón, 1992, p. 62)

We illustrated areas that concern marginalization, community and family obligations, challenging stereotypes, identity, academic achievement barriers, and disadvantages in economics and school systems. These issues require educators and campus leaders to reevaluate student learning and to intentionally transform higher education in the effort to create an enriched and vital community of learners.

To advocate for transformative education means to integrate advising as a form of pedagogy into the students' learning environment. Academic advising is more than just offering a service or providing information; it is a teaching and learning process that helps students construct meaning and purpose from their experiences and choices they make in college and develops their identities. Academic advisors as teachers can make a significant difference in the personal and academic lives of first-year students of color. The success will depend on how well staff, faculty, students, surrounding community, alumni, and families work together. Tinto (1993) argues that college life is a passage from one stage to another and that the entire college experience from admission to graduation depends upon how well the institution can integrate the student into the social and academic fabric of the campus. Student learning is the responsibility of all educators on campus. It is our privilege and responsibility as educators to be sensitive to the role of culture and background that affect student academic achievement. It is our duty to be at the forefront, critically vigilant in creating meaningful learning opportunities for and with our first-year students of color during one of the most challenging and exciting times in their lives.

Author's Note

All student quotes are taken from conversations between the student and Evette Castillo.

References

Almanac. (2004). College enrollment by racial and ethnic group, selected years. *Chronicle of Higher Education*. Retrieved June 28, 2005, from http://chronicle.com/weekly/almanac/2004/nation/0101603.htm

Anderson, J. A. (1995). Toward a framework for matching teaching and learning styles for diverse populations. In R. R. Sims & S. J. Sims (Eds.), *The importance of learning styles: Understanding the implications for learning, course design, and education* (pp. 69-78). Westport, CT: Greenwood Press.

Attinasi, L. C., & Nora A. (1996). Diverse students and complex issues: A case for multiple methods in college student research. In C. Turner, N. Garcia, A. Nora, & L. Rendón (Eds.), *Racial and ethnic diversity in higher education* (ASHE Reader Series, pp. 545-554). Needham Heights, MA: Simon & Schuster Custom Publishing.

Brown, L. L., & Robinson Kurpius, S. E. (1997). Psychosocial factors influencing academic persistence of American Indian college students. *Journal of College Student Development, 38*(1), 3-12.

Brown, T., & Rivas, M. (1995). Pluralistic advising: Facilitating the development and achievement of first-year students of color. In M. L. Upcraft & G. L Kramer (Eds.), *First-year academic advising: Patterns in the present, pathways to the future* (Monograph No. 18, pp. 121-137). Columbia, SC: University of South Carolina, National Resource Center for The Freshman Year Experience & Students in Transition.

Carnevale, A. P. (1999). *Education = success: Empowering Hispanic youth and adults.* Princeton, NJ: Educational Testing Service.

Castillo, E. J. (2002). *Bridges over borders: Critical reflections of Filipino American college students on academic aspirations and resilience.* Unpublished doctoral dissertation, University of San Francisco.

Chew-Ogi, C., & Ogi, Y. (2002). Epilogue. In M. K. McEwen, C. M. Kodama, A. N. Alvarez, S. Lee, & C. T. H. Liang (Eds.), *Working with Asian American college students* (New Directions for Student Services, No. 97). San Francisco: Jossey-Bass.

Cortese, A. D. (2003, March-May). The critical role of higher education in creating a sustainable future. *Planning for Higher Education,* 15-22.

DeJong, D. H. (1993). *Promises of the past: A history of Indian education.* Golden, CO: North American Press.

Fleming, J. (1984). Summarizing the impacts of college on students. In *Blacks in college: A comparative study of students success in Black and White institutions* (pp. 161-194). San Francisco: Jossey-Bass.

Fries-Britt, S., Gerald, D. S., & Lee, Z. S. (2005). Clarion calls for reform and change in postsecondary education. In A. B. Harvey-Smith (Ed.), *The seventh learning college principle: A framework for transformational change* (pp. 1-25). Washington, DC: National Association of Student Personnel Administrators.

Fries-Britt, S. L., & Turner, B. (2001). Facing stereotypes: A case study of Black students on a White campus. *Journal of College Student Development, 42*(5), 420-429.

Gonzalez, K. P. (2002). Campus culture and the experiences of Chicano students in a predominantly White university. *Urban Education, 37*(2), 193-218.

Harvey-Smith, A. B. (2005). *The seventh learning college principle: A framework for transformational change.* Washington, DC: National Association of Student Personnel Administrators.

Helms, J. E. (1990). *Black and White racial identity: Theory, research, and practice.* Westport, CT: Greenwood Press.

Helms, J. E. (1995). An update of Helms' White identity and people of color racial identity models. In J. G. Ponterotto, J. M. Casa, L. A. Suzuki, & C. M. Alexander (Eds.), *Handbook of multicultural counseling* (pp. 181-198). Thousand Oaks, CA: Sage.

Helms, J. E., & Cook, D. A. (1999). *Using race and culture in counseling and psychotherapy: Theory and process.* Boston: Allyn & Bacon.

Hernandez, J. C. (2000). Understanding the retention of Latino college students. *Journal of College Student Development, 41*(6), 575-588.

hooks, b. (2003). *Teaching community: A pedagogy of hope.* New York: Routledge.

Hune, S. (2002). Demographics and diversity in Asian American college students. In M. K. McEwen, C. M. Kodama, A. N. Alvarez, S. Lee, & C. T. H. Liang (Eds.), *Working with Asian American college students* (New Directions for Student Services, No. 97, pp. 11-20). San Francisco: Jossey-Bass.

Hurtado, S., & Carter, D. F. (1996). Latino students' sense of belonging in the college community: Rethinking the concept of integration on campus. In F. K. Stage & G. L. Anaya (Ed.), *College students: The evolving nature of research* (ASHE Reader Series). Needham Heights, MA: Simon & Schuster Custom Publishing.

James, T. (2005). The learning college concept and its compatibility with student affairs. In A.B. Harvey-Smith (Ed.), *The seventh learning college principle: A framework for transformational change* (pp. 27-48). Washington, DC: National Association of Student Personnel Administrators.

Keeling, R. (Ed.). (2004). *Learning reconsidered: A campus-wide focus on the student experience.* Washington, DC: American College Personnel Association, National Association of Student Personnel Administrators.

Kodama, C. M., McEwen, M. K, Liang, C. T. H., & Lee, S. (2002). An Asian American perspective on psychosocial student development theory. In M. K. McEwen, C. M. Kodama, A. N. Alvarez, S. Lee, & C. T. H. Liang (Eds.), *Working with Asian American college students* (New Directions for Student Services, No. 97, pp. 45-59). San Francisco: Jossey-Bass.

Lee, S. (2005, March 15). Reflections on working with Asian American college students. *Net-results, National Association of Student Personnel Administrators' E-zine for Student Affairs Professionals.* Retrieved April 8, 2005, from http://www.naspa.org/NetResults/index.cfm

Lee, W. Y. (2004). Enhancing the first-year experience of African Americans. In L. I. Rendón, M. García, & D. Person (Eds.), *Transforming the first year of college for students of color* (Monograph No. 38, pp. 93-107). Columbia, SC: University of South Carolina, National Resource Center for The First-Year Experience and Students in Transition.

Malveaux, J. (2005, November 3). Dimensions of diversity. *Diverse issues in higher education, 22*(19), 31.

McEwen, M. K. (2003). New perspectives on identity development. In S. R. Komives & D. B. Woodard, Jr. (Eds.), *Student services: A handbook for the profession* (4th ed., pp. 203-233). San Francisco: Jossey Bass.

McEwen, M. K., Kodama, C. M., Alvarez A. N., Lee, S., & Liang, C. T. H. (2002). *Working with Asian American college students* (New Directions for Student Services, No. 97). San Francisco: Jossey-Bass.

McMillan, J. H., & Reed, D. F. (1994). At-risk students and resiliency: Factors contributing to academic success. *The Clearing House, 67*(3), 137-140.

Nora, A. (2003). Access to higher education for Hispanics: Real or illusory? In J. Castellanos & L. Jones (Eds.), *The majority in the minority* (pp. 47-68). Sterling, VA: Stylus Press.

Palmer, P. (1998). *The courage to teach.* San Francisco: Jossey-Bass.

Pascarella, E. T., & Terenzini, P. T. (1998). Studying college students in the 21st century: Meeting new challenges. *The Review of Higher Education, 21*(2), 151-165.

Pope, R. L. (2000). The relationship between psychosocial development and racial identity of college students of color. *Journal of College Student Development, 4*(3), 302-312.

Pope, R. L., Ecklund, T. R., Miklitsch, T. A., & Suresh, R. (2004). Transforming the first-year experience for multiracial/bicultural students. In L. I. Rendón, M. Garcia, & D. Person (Eds.), *Transforming the first year of college for students of color* (Monograph No. 38, pp. 161-174). Columbia, SC: University of South Carolina, National Resource Center for The First-Year Experience and Students in Transition.

Rendón, L. I. (1992). From the barrio to the academy: Revelations of Mexican American "scholarship girl." In L. S. Zwerling & H. B. London (Eds.), *First generation students: Confronting the cultural issues* (New Directions for Community Colleges, No. 80, pp. 55-64). San Francisco: Jossey-Bass.

Rendón, L. I. (2004). Transforming the first-year experience for students of color: Where do we begin? In L. I. Rendón, M. García, & D. Person (Eds.), *Transforming the first year of college for students of color* (Monograph No. 38, pp. 177-184). Columbia, SC: University of South Carolina, National Resource Center for The First-Year Experience and Students in Transition.

Rendón, L. I., García, M., & Person, D. (2004). A call for transformation. In L. I. Rendón, M. García, & D. Person (Eds.), *Transforming the first year of college for students of color* (Monograph No. 38, pp. 3-22). Columbia, SC: University of South Carolina, National Resource Center for The First-Year Experience and Students in Transition.

Rendón, L. I., & Hope, R. O. (1996). *Educating a new majority: Transforming America's educational system for diversity.* San Francisco: Jossey-Bass.

Renn, K. A. (1998). *Check all that apply: The experience of biracial and multiracial college students.* ASHE Annual Meeting Paper, Miami, FL. (ERIC Document Reproduction Services No. ED 427 602)

Rodriguez, Y. E. G. (1995). Mentoring to diversity: A multicultural approach. In M. W. Galbraith & N. H. Cohen (Eds.), *Mentoring: New strategies and challenges* (New Directions for Adult and Continuing Education, No. 66, pp. 69-77). San Francisco: Jossey-Bass.

Russell, G. (1997). *American Indian facts of life: A profile of tribes and reservations.* Phoenix, AZ: Russell Publication.

Sagaria M., & Johnsrud, L. K. (1991). Recruiting, advancing, and retaining minorities in student affairs: Moving from rhetoric to results. *NASPA Journal, 28*(2), 105-120.

Schmader, T., Major, B., & Gramzow, R. H. (2002, Spring). How African American college students protect their self-esteem. *Journal of Blacks in Higher Education, 35,*116-119.

Suzuki, B. (2002). Revisiting the model minority stereotype: Implications for student affairs practice and higher education. In M. K. McEwen, C. M. Kodama, A. N. Alvarez, S. Lee, & C. T. H. Liang (Eds.), *Working with Asian American college students* (New Directions for Student Services, No. 97, pp. 21-32). San Francisco: Jossey-Bass.

Tagg, J. (2004, May-June). Alignment for learning: Reorganizing classrooms and campuses. *About Campus*, 8-18.

Tierney, W. G. (1993). The college experience of Native Americans: A critical analysis. In L. Weis & M. Fine (Eds.), *Beyond silenced voices* (pp. 309-323). Albany, NY: State University of New York Press.

Ting, S. R. (2000). Predicting Asian Americans' academic performance in the first year of college: An approach combining SAT scores and noncognitive variables. *Journal of College Student Development, 41*(4), 442-449.

Tinto, V. (1993). *Leaving college: Rethinking the causes and cures of student attrition* (2nd ed.). Chicago: University of Chicago Press.

Wallace, D., Abel, R., & Ropers-Huilman, B. (2000). Clearing a path for success: Deconstructing borders through undergraduate mentoring. *The Review of Higher Education, 24*(1), 87-102.

Wasson, R. (1990). *Implications from a Black student culture for more effective college teaching: Black voices in the White institution.* Paper presented at the Annual Meeting of the American Anthropological Association, New Orleans, LA.

White, L. S. (1998). "Am I Black enuf fo ya?" Black student diversity: Issues of identity and community. In K. Freeman (Ed.), *African American culture and heritage in higher education research & practice* (pp. 93-119). Westport, CT: Greenwood Publishing Group.

Wright, B. (1988). "For the children of the infidels?": American Indian education in the colonial colleges. *American Indian Culture and Research Journal, 12*(3), 1-14.

Chapter Eleven

Advising First-Year Students With Disabilities

Dick Vallandingham

Students with disabilities arrive at college, like any other student, with misconceptions, fears, and a certain naiveté about the college experience. In addition to these common struggles, students with disabilities face unique challenges regarding to how their disability impacts learning and what accommodations are made in response to the educational impact of their disability.

A disability may impact a student's ability to gain access to, use, store, or retrieve information. Communication skills and receptive or expressive modalities or both may be affected. Deficiencies in social skills may impact the learning environment and learning opportunities. Additionally, the accommodations offered by the college or university in response to the educational needs of the student may be very different from accommodations provided in the K-12 school years. For many first-year students with disabilities, the K-12 school years provided an environment where the complete responsibility for identifying and accommodating students with disabilities was the school system, with the student being almost a "passive" recipient. For these first-year students, the accommodations process at the postsecondary level results in culture shock when it becomes the students' responsibility to self-identify and request accommodations and services related to their disability.

This lack of preparation for such a dramatic change in academic and social environment leaves the student with a disability struggling to find strategies for success. The academic advisor is critical to their ultimate success. Advisors can be an important part of the team that assists the student with addressing issues, and teaches the student how to develop a successful educational plan based on career and life goals. This chapter explores the unique and varied challenges of students with disabilities and the roles the academic advisor must assume to help these students succeed.

Descriptive Research Findings

Several studies have been conducted and reported by the U.S. Department of Education, National Center for Education Statistics (NCES), to provide nationally representative data from two- and four-year institutions about students with disabilities. These reports indicate significant differences in several areas between students with disabilities and the overall student population that may impact the population of first-year students with disabilities.

According to *Profile of Undergraduates in U.S. Postsecondary Institutions: 1999-2000* (Horn, Peter, Rooney, & Malizio, 2002), 9% of undergraduates report having some type of disability. Compared to their counterparts without disabilities, undergraduates who identify themselves as students with disabilities were more likely to have delayed their postsecondary enrollment a year or more after finishing high school, to have lower SAT scores, and to be enrolled in two-year colleges (Horn & Berktold, 1999). In addition, students with disabilities are more likely to be older, men, military veterans, and to have dependents other than a spouse (Horn & Berktold). In this same study, students who reported any disabilities were found to be less likely to have stayed enrolled or earned a postsecondary degree or credential within five years (Horn & Berktold). While students with disabilities were less likely to persist, the study indicated that those who earn a bachelor's degree appeared to have relatively similar labor market outcomes and graduate school enrollment rates as students without disabilities.

An earlier study (Lawrence, Kent, & Henson, 1981) that focused on a longitudinal analysis of first-year college students with disabilities had slightly different findings. The majority of the respondents in their analysis had persisted in college; earned good grades; retained high degree aspirations; were satisfied with college; manifested high self-esteem; and looked forward to being married, having children, and pursuing full-time careers. The study pointed out, however, that differences between disability groups emphasized the need to individualize services especially in terms of accommodations. In this study (Lawrence et al.), age of onset of disability and time of diagnosis were also factors considered. Those students whose disability (or disabilities) had been diagnosed relatively late tended to perform better in college than did those whose disability was diagnosed early. This relationship suggests that those who become disabled early in their lives may "accumulate" educational disadvantages that work against them at the college level.

Most significantly, Lawrence et al. (1981) noted the important role of academic advisors in their study. They concluded that students with disabilities who made use of academic advising were more likely to be satisfied with college and to maintain enrollment. They noted that more than 60% of the total group identified one person whose guidance, support, or confidence in them was central to their success in college. It seems safe to say that academic advising was an important element related to academic success of these students.

Culture Shock of College

Along with the multitude of adjustment issues facing any first-year college student, the first-year student with a disability must often acclimate to a significant shift in expectations, policies, and support services between high school and college environments. The high school environment may have allowed the student to be a somewhat passive participant in the accommodations process, whereas the college environment demands the student to be the active and responsible party in requesting and using accommodations.

IDEA Versus ADA

The federal government regulates K-12 educational environments with significantly different legislation than what applies to colleges. The Individuals with Disabilities Education Improvement Act (IDEA) of 2004 (U. S. Department of Education, 2006) has the mission to provide a free, appropriate, public education in the least restrictive environment for students age 3 - 21 who need special education and related services because of their disability. It is the responsibility of the school district to identify and evaluate students with disabilities at no expense to parents or individuals. Special education services and auxiliary aids must be stipulated in an Individual Education Plan (IEP) with students and their parents as part of the IEP decision-making process.

Colleges and universities, on the other hand, are responsible under the Rehabilitation Act of 1973, Section 504 (U.S. Department of Labor, 2006b) and the Americans With Disabilities Act (ADA, U. S. Department of Justice, 2006) to provide students with disabilities, to the maximum extent possible, the opportunity to be fully integrated into mainstream academic life (Lewis & Farris, 1999). Disability is defined as a physical or mental impairment that substantially limits one or more major life activities. Students must be otherwise qualified and are responsible to identify themselves as having a disability and to provide documentation of the disability. The cost of obtaining appropriate documentation is to be assumed by the student. A comparison of IDEA, Section 504 and ADA is presented in Appendix A of this chapter.

Changing Roles and Responsibilities

First-year students with disabilities find they are expected to move from an intrusive/prescriptive educational approach for accommodations to a self-directed, personally responsible academic environment emphasizing accessibility. Likewise, as students take more responsibility, the parents of these students may feel excluded in this new academic setting. Academic advisors who are faced with teaching students to assume responsibility for their own educational planning and decision making find they may need to help parents understand their changing role in the educational planning and decision-making process (Mellard & Lancaster, 2000).

Academic advisors may need to assist students with disabilities in learning more about their disability. Simply by asking questions about students' strengths and weaknesses, how the students' disability impacts their scholastic work, and what academic strategies the students find to be most beneficial, the advisor can help them learn to become better advocates for themselves and their educational needs. Advisors will find that solid developmental advising approaches provide learning opportunities for the student as an active learner.

Developmental Advising

Advisors should approach the advisement of students with disabilities as an interactive process aimed at the student's development of competencies, autonomy, and purpose (Gordon, 1988). The foundation for success of the advising experience is the development of a relationship between the advisor and the student in which both parties share responsibilities in determining and achieving immediate and long-term goals (Crookston, 1972). Many first-year students with disabilities will look to the advisor to be the source for information regarding academic topics such as academic vocabulary (e.g., "GPA" or a "prerequisite"), academic planning, and programs of study. At the same time, the advisor may look to the student as the information source regarding how their disability impacts their educational experience. As the advising relationship develops, the student will gain knowledge and competency in dealing with academic topics, while the advisor will gain knowledge regarding disability issues and the student's educational strengths and weaknesses.

At the same time the student is gaining knowledge regarding academic planning, the advisor is working with the student to incorporate this academic knowledge into immediate actions and long-term educational and career goals. By helping the student compare academic progress to these goals, the academic advisor can teach the skills necessary to evaluate appropriateness of goals and to modify goals as needed. The student, in turn, gains competencies and moves toward greater autonomy and self-awareness.

Disability Language

In interactions between the advisor and first-year students with disabilities, advisor should use words that are empowering. Word choice is very important in establishing a supportive advising relationship, displaying respect for the individual, and communicating acceptance of the student. Placing the person before the disability (i.e., referring to a student as "a student with a disability" rather than a "disabled student" or a "handicapped student"), avoiding outdated terms like "handicapped" or "crippled," and remembering that disability is a physical or mental impairment and that a handicap is the effect of an impairment or limitation are important guidelines for advisors to keep in mind. With any disability, avoiding negative, condescending words like "victim" or "sufferer" and not referring to an individual by the condition he or she has such as "a quadriplegic" or "an epileptic" are also important. Instead, using terms like "a student with quadriplegia" or "a student with epilepsy" is more appropriate and respectful of the individual.

First-year students with disabilities are not looking for sympathy or pity. Most have accepted their disabilities and their lifestyles; in fact, the alternative means by which they accomplish tasks may be natural for them. For this reason, it is a good idea to ask before offering help and then only if the student appears to need it. Such behavior treats the student as an independent adult.

Advising and Career Exploration

First-year students with disabilities often have limited experience with career options and career planning. Because the prescriptive approach to educational planning is often used prior to college, they may not have had an opportunity to gain experience in educational planning. They may also lack specific strategies to obtain academic success in the college environment. The advisor working with first-year students with disabilities will find that applying the basics of developmental advising will be an extremely important strategy to use in teaching these students how to be successful and independent in these areas (i.e., to develop and assess academic, vocational, social, and personal interest potentials).

Career Exploration

First-year students with disabilities often base their career information on the healthcare professionals they have associated with for treatment or rehabilitation. It is not uncommon, for example, for students with a psychiatric disability to list mental health profession as their career goal or for students with a seizure disorder to want to be paramedics. The advisor for these students will need to introduce career exploration as part of the learning process. In providing a non-restrictive learning experience for career exploration, the advisor will want to emphasize realistic information about employment trends in current and future job markets along with accurate information about educational and certification requirements. As areas of interest emerge, the advisor will want to guide the student in exploring the expected competencies and abilities expected in specific careers, helping the student to examine how their disability might impact the way in which they accomplished such expectations. Advisors should not assume that a disability automatically eliminates a career choice. There are many examples of individuals who have found ways to accommodate for their disability in meeting career expectations—for example, there are chemists who are blind, musicians and pilots who are deaf, guitar players with no arms, and a multitude of other examples of individuals who exceed surface expectations.

The career exploration process for first-year students with disabilities should involve self-exploration and discovery as well as fact-finding about the world of work. Values, interests, and personalities are significant contributors to career satisfaction. Guided discussion, including analysis of academic history, exposure to career options, and the personal experiences of the student, combined with career decision-making tools, such as the Strong Interest Inventory and the Myers-Briggs Type Inventory, provide a basis for facilitating the self-discovery process.

Attainability of career goals for students with disabilities is related to skills and aptitudes, taking into consideration appropriate accommodations. The advisor can help the student learn about essential functions related to specific career options. Advisors should be careful in making assumptions about students' ability, or lack thereof, to accomplish these functions. A good approach is for the advisor, as part of the discussion of competencies and job requirements, to ask the student how they would accomplish the tasks. Often, it is helpful to include the college's disability specialist in the discussion for additional information related to accommodations. For example, information on accommodating chemists who are blind or have other disabilities is available from the American Chemical Society (Kucera, 1993), while the U.S. Department of Labor's Job Accommodations Network of the Office of Disability Employment Policy (U.S. Department of Labor, 2006a) has many resources on job accommodations (see Appendix B of this chapter for additional resources).

First-year students with disabilities may not have had exposure to successful individuals with disabilities in the workforce nor be aware of the areas in which these individuals are working. They may not know that there are pilots and lawyers who are deaf, computer programmers and chemists who are blind, and college professors with schizophrenia. Advisors can encourage students with disabilities to research the topic and, if possible, conduct vocational interviews with successful individuals with disabilities.

Integrative Advising

As with all students, advising first-year students with disabilities moves past exploration into implementation through an interactive educational planning process. It is especially important for the student with disabilities that the advisor teaches them to be active participants in this process. The advisor assists students in interpreting areas of interest and ability, and students identify the accommodation strategies they have used which have led to academic success. As the advisor and students work together in this integrative process, students will have an opportunity to grow in their self-advocacy skills.

Individual student strengths and learning styles, educational impact of specific disabilities, social maturity, and familial factors should be addressed as part of the advising process with these first-year students. Developing an "advising team" of student, advisor, and disability support specialist is often an effective way to create an integrated strategy for students. This team approach will allow the advisor to take advantage of campus professionals focused on accommodating specific disabilities while addressing the informational aspects and specific competencies (e.g., understanding academic vocabulary such as "GPA" and "prerequisite," problem solving, goal setting, time management, progress assessment) aimed at academic success.

Advisors should ensure that the advising environment is positive and supportive. The advisor can make sure that the physical environment of the advising office or setting is accessible for all students. An appropriate advising space will allow for a student using a wheelchair to navigate in and out, will provide tactile signage for a student who is blind, and will ensure privacy of discussions for all students. With individual students, the advisor will want to use accommodations appropriate for the student within advising interactions (e.g., using sign language interpreters or providing written materials in alternative formats).

Disability-Specific Issues

Advisors may find that first-year students with a disability require longer advising appointments. Additional issues regarding accommodation strategies and scheduling considerations will add topics to academic advising discussions. Scheduling of classes and breaks between classes may become important advising issues. First-year students with a physical disability or who are blind might need additional time between classes to move from class to class. First-year students who are deaf often are not accustomed to watching an interpreter for 50 minutes or more and, therefore, need to have the information delivered in shorter segments. First-year students with a psychiatric disability may need time between classes to decompress from intense discussions or check in with college counselors or other contacts regarding emotions and behaviors.

To be a good advisor for the students with disabilities does not mean that the advisor has to be an expert regarding disabilities. Advisors will find that every student with a disability is an individual and should not be stereotyped by the label of their disability. However, some generalizations regarding individuals with certain specific disabilities may help advisors to better understand the students.

Learning Disabilities

Learning disability (LD) is a broad term used to describe the seemingly inexplicable difficulties a person of at least average intelligence has in acquiring basic academic skills. The term is related to several disorders with different causes, symptoms, treatments, and outcomes. Because it is difficult to diagnose or to pinpoint causes, LD is often divided up into three broad categories: (a) developmental speech and language disorders; (b) academic skills disorders; and (c) "other," a catch-all grouping that includes certain coordination and other learning disorders.

According to the National Center for Learning Disability (2006), a learning disorder is a neurological disorder that affects the brain's ability to receive, process, store, or respond to information. This disorder may affect a person's ability to either interpret what they see and hear or to link information from different parts of the brain. These limitations can show up in a variety of ways: (a) as specific difficulties with spoken and written language, (b) as problems with coordination, (c) as self-control issues, or (d) as attention difficulties.

One of the challenges advisors face when working with first-year students with learning disabilities relates to the stigma of the LD label, which they may have gotten in their previous educational experience. These students come to college with a desire to fit in with their peers by not identifying themselves to the college office for disability services, thereby denying themselves appropriate accommodations. This attitude can put the advisor in the position of being the first person on campus to which the student reveals his or her disability. The advisor can be a key person in helping students understand that (a) information regarding their disability is considered confidential, (b) any accommodations provided are to ensure students' access to learning opportunities and to display mastery of the class material, and (c) the competencies expected will be the same as for any other student.

First-year students with learning disabilities may need additional guidance in managing their time and in approaching class assignments effectively. Advisors can help students remember to separate complex assignments into manageable parts. Providing the student with a datebook and teaching them to plot out components of homework assignments within reasonable timelines are valuable strategies to use with these students. Multi-modal teaching techniques such as color-coding important dates and reinforcing advising sessions with written lists or contracts will increase the effectiveness of advising sessions.

Occasionally, academic advisors will be questioned about the fairness of accommodations given students with learning disabilities. For example, extended test time is frequently used for students with learning disabilities. Research studies have demonstrated that normally achieving students performed significantly better than students with learning disabilities under timed conditions. However, when students with learning disabilities are given extra time, there is no statistically significant differences between the two groups. In addition, normally achieving students did not perform significantly better with extra time (Alster, 1997; Runyan, 1991; Weaver, 2000).

Another good strategy for the advisor is to ask students how they process information. It may be easier for some students to function in a quiet environment without distractions. Students with auditory processing disorder may need visual demonstrations of a process or information presented in writing, while students with dyslexia may prefer verbal explanations with extra time allowed for reading.

Mobility/Physical Disabilities

Some students with mobility difficulties will need to consider the travel time between classes as part of the scheduling component of their class registrations. They may need to consider class locations, terrain of the campus, and room accessibility when compiling their class schedules. For these reasons, preferential or early registration may be considered as an accommodation to ensure access to appropriate classes.

Career advising with students with physical disabilities often is a reciprocal learning exercise. Students learn from the advisor the core competencies and basic tasks involved with specific occupations. The advisor, in turn, learns how students approach these tasks and competencies. Both student and advisor may learn from the college disability services professional about new technologies to assist students in accomplishing these tasks.

The advisor working with a student who uses a wheelchair needs to become cognizant of behaviors that could impact the advising relationship. For example, if conversations are to be longer than a few minutes, the advisor should sit at eye level with the student. Students using a wheelchair consider the wheelchair as part of their personal space. Therefore, the advisor should avoid leaning on the wheelchair or moving the wheelchair without first asking if assistance is desired. The advisor also needs to consider wheelchair accessibility of buildings, restrooms, and parking.

Hearing Loss and Deafness

Hearing loss is determined by audiometric testing to determine sensitivity to sound in decibels at different frequency ranges and to evaluate hearing acuity or the ability to discriminate sounds and understand speech. Hearing loss is generally described as slight, mild, moderate, severe, or profound, depending on how well a person can hear the intensities or frequencies mostly associated with speech.

Sensorineural hearing loss results from damage to the nerve endings (hair cells) of the inner ear or the nerves that supply it, ranging from mild to profound and most often affecting the high frequencies more than the low frequencies. Thus, even with amplification to increase the sound level, a person with a sensorineural hearing loss may perceive distorted sounds, sometimes making the successful use of a hearing aid impossible.

Ability to understand speech is an important factor related to loss of hearing sensitivity. Spoken English is made up of low-frequency vowels and high-frequency consonants. Vowels have more intensity (loudness) than consonants, but it is the information from consonants that carry the meaning of speech. The ability to use one's hearing for understanding speech is related to the ability to hear and discriminate high-frequency consonant information.

The educational and social effects of hearing loss are influenced by the degree of hearing loss, speech discrimination abilities, and age of onset of hearing loss. Individuals with moderate-to-severe hearing loss that occurred after language development (after ages 8 to 12) may function well in individual conversational situations but have difficulty in group situations. Since these students often use speech-reading as a receptive language tool, advisors should talk facing the student. When students do not understand a phrase or sentence, advisors may find that re-phrasing is a good strategy, giving students different acoustic, visual, and linguistic information to decipher.

Students with severe-to-profound hearing loss of pre-lingual onset may depend on visual information for their major communication intake path and may present linguistic and cultural challenges for the advisor. These students may use vision as their main receptive communication avenue, either depending on speech reading or using sign language. The sign language used in the United States by most Deaf adults is a conceptually based language called American Sign Language (ASL). (Note: A capital "D" is used in "Deaf" to connote individuals considered "culturally deaf.") ASL is actually a derivative of French sign language, first introduced in the United States in 1817. It is a visual-spatial language with its own grammatical structure, a structure that is closer to the Romance languages than the Germanic roots from which English derived. This basic language structure is further defined by the use of visual and spatial markers within the language to designate such things as time (tense). As with any language, ASL has its own idiomatic expressions. These factors combine to make ASL very different from spoken or written English.

The advisor working with a Deaf student will benefit from the use of a sign language interpreter. The interpreter will ensure that the ideas presented by the advisor in spoken or written English will be translated with conceptual accuracy. When using a sign language interpreter, the advisor will want to look directly at the student, maintaining eye contact, and talking directly to the student rather than through the interpreter.

With both hard-of-hearing and Deaf students, an interactive approach to advising will allow the advisor to determine the level of clarity and understanding occurring in the advising session. Asking the student to repeat or explain information presented in advising sessions and encouraging student questions are helpful strategies.

Vision Loss and Blindness

Vision impairments can result from a variety of causes, including congenital conditions, injury, eye disease, brain trauma, or as the result of other conditions such as diabetes and glaucoma. A person is considered legally blind if his or her corrected vision is no better than 20/200, meaning seeing at 20 feet what others see at 200 feet or having peripheral fields (side-to-side vision) of no more than 20° as compared to normal field of vision of 180°. Of legally blind people, 80 to 90% have some measurable vision or light perception.

Most students who are blind or have vision impairments come to college with strategies and techniques to deal with written materials. The advisor will want to work closely with the college's office of disability services to ensure that advising information is available in alternate formats or in a form that can be accessed via technology such as screenreading programs. Verbal description of visual information will be necessary in the advising session.

In discussing academic plans, the advisor may consider the nature of individual classes. Courses that are extremely visual by nature, unless they are considered essential to a major, can sometimes be handled by recommending another less visually focused one that fits the student's program. However, such substitutions should not be assumed to be necessary for a specific student. By involving the student in the decision process, the advisor may find that there are options available to make the visually focused class accessible for blind students. For example, a blind student wanting to take an art appreciation course to become familiar with the world's great art may be successful with a classroom assistant who is talented at describing visual images and who serves as a visual interpreter or translator. It is possible for a blind student to have an understanding of what a certain painting looks like because the painting can be described. Miniature models of great works of sculpture can be displayed and touched in the classroom. Many museums have tactile galleries and special guided tours for people with visual impairments.

The advisor will want to identify him or herself before making physical contact with a student who is blind. In situations where the student asks for or requires guidance, the advisor will want to offer an arm rather than taking the arm of the student or guiding them by the hand. If the student has a guide dog, the advisor will want to walk on the side opposite to the dog. In either situation, the advisor will want to describe the setting and obstacles, such as steps or cracks in the sidewalk. When directions are given, the directions should be specific and nonvisual.

Psychiatric Disabilities

Mental illness is a term that describes a broad range of mental and emotional conditions that could be considered as one portion of the broader ADA term "mental impairment." The Center for Psychiatric Rehabilitation (1997) uses this definition: "The term 'psychiatric disability' is used when mental illness significantly interferes with the performance of major life activities, such as learning, thinking, communicating, and sleeping, among others" (p. 1).

The number of students with psychiatric disabilities continues to increase. These students have a variety of diagnoses, including depression, bipolar disorder, schizophrenia, and compulsive disorder. In addition to the conditions themselves, medications used in treatment may have side effects that have negative educational impact. The advisor may need to function as a point of contact for the student in providing structure and support.

Advisors may also find that students with a psychiatric disability may need additional information and encouragement regarding good study habits and effective time management. Teaching students how to use a daily planner and how to plan for completing class work is an effective tool. This discussion also allows the advisor to develop a supportive relationship with the student.

As a product of such supportive relationships, the advisor should be a sounding board for students regarding their academic and personal behaviors. Since students with psychiatric disabilities are held to the same code of conduct as other students, honest and caring feedback regarding behavior and classroom expectations can be an important advising tool. Likewise, the advisor should use praise when merited as a method for building self-confidence with students.

The career decision-making component of developmental advising may be especially challenging for first-year students with psychiatric disabilities. It is not uncommon for students to have career goals based on the individuals with whom they have the most contact, namely, mental health professionals. Expanding career choices within the decision-making process, exploring options, and determining skill sets within career areas may need to be major goals of the advising process.

Traumatic or Acquired Brain Injury

First-year students with traumatic brain injury have had damage to the brain usually as the result of trauma, such as an accident or stroke. Some of the learning factors that affect students with learning disabilities also apply to these students. In addition, students with brain injury may have loss of muscle control, difficulty with short-term memory, or poor impulse control.

Creating a supportive relationship with first-year students with traumatic brain injury will be the advisor's best advising tool. This will allow the advisor to assist the student, as needed, with recognizing and understanding social cues and to help the student deal with frustration related to misunderstandings.

Late Onset and Progressive Disabilities

For most first-year students with disabilities, the disability is just one part of who they are as a person and as a part of their self-image. Other students, however, will be newly disabled or have a progressive disability. These students may be involved in varying stages of acceptance, adaptation, and awareness. For these students, the advisor can be a supportive sounding board as they deal with issues related to how they view themselves, and encourage students to explore various roles and various aspects of their personality. The advisor will need to include opportunities for self-exploration in the teaching aspects of advising sessions along with academic planning and career exploration.

Universal Design

A new approach to access called "Universal Design" has emerged that not only addresses the needs of individuals with disabilities but that also attempts to ensure that all products and environments are as usable as possible for as many people as possible regardless of age, ability, or situation. Advisors should be aware of Universal Design as it assumes greater importance as a new paradigm that represents a holistic and integrated approach to design.

The concept of Universal Design arose in the 1990s when a group of architects, product designers, engineers, and environmental design researchers formed the Center for Universal Design at North Carolina State University (Universal Design Education Online, 2006). They developed seven principles that describe characteristics that make designs universally usable:

1. Equitable use
2. Flexible in use
3. Simple and intuitive use
4. Perceptible information
5. Tolerance for error
6. Low physical effort
7. Size and space for approach and use

These concepts have also been applied to teaching and learning. Recent research in neuroscience has shown differences in brain networks involved with information processing and learning (Center for Applied Special Technology, 2006). Based on this research, new approaches to teaching are being proposed using universal design principles for learning (UDL). UDL principles help educators customize their teaching for individual differences in the brain networks. A universally designed curriculum offers:

1. Multiple means of representation to give learners various ways of acquiring information and knowledge

2. Multiple means of expression to provide learners alternatives for demonstrating what they know
3. Multiple means of engagement to tap into learners' interests, challenge them appropriately, and motivate them to learn

Conclusion

Academic advisors working with first-year students with disabilities, while dealing with each student as an individual, may find that they need to include issues impacted by the disability to their advising approach. The students' (and their parents') previous experience with educational accommodations in the K-12 system may influence their expectations of intervention at the college level. The advisor will want to address issues related to adapting to college life with both students and their parents. Career exploration may have been limited or influenced by the experiences of the student, and their knowledge of successful professionals with disabilities may be scant. By providing honest career guidance information, the advisor can help students develop realistic and attainable career goals.

Class scheduling may involve special consideration related to physical needs of the student. Students with a disability may need additional time between classes, opportunities built into the schedule to rest or connect with campus mentor, or consider other specific factors related to students' daily living requirements.

A final word for advisors working with the first-year student with a disability—relax! Asking students what they are comfortable with, what strategies work for them, or what assistance they desire is the best strategy when the advisor is in doubt. Treating each student individually and not making assumptions about abilities based on the disability will help advisors build strong relationships with their advisees. By emphasizing achievements, abilities, and individual qualities while providing honest feedback about academic performance and individual behavior, the advisor will be able to develop a healthy advisor-student relationship focused on student success and learning.

References

Alster, E. H. (1997). The effects of extended time on algebra test scores for college students with or without learning disabilities. *Journal of Learning Disabilities, 30*(2), 222-227.

Center for Applied Special Technology. (2006). *What is universal design for learning?* Retrieved May 8, 2006, from http://www.cast.org

Center for Psychiatric Rehabilitation. (1997). *What is psychiatric disability and mental illness?* Retrieved August 8, 2005, from http://www.bu.edu/cpr/reasaccom/whatis-psych.html

Crookston, W. H. (1972). A developmental view of academic advising as teaching. *Journal of College Student Personnel, 13*(1), 12-17.

Gordon, V. N. (1988). Developmental advising. In W. R. Habley (Ed.), *The status and future of academic advising: Problems and promise* (pp. 104-115). Iowa City, IA: American College Testing Program.

Horn, L., & Berktold, J. (1999). *Students with disabilities in postsecondary education: A profile of preparation, participation, and outcomes* (NCES 1999-187). Washington, DC: National Center for Education Statistics, U.S. Department of Education, U.S. Government Printing Office.

Horn, L., Peter, K., Rooney, K., & Malizio, A. (2002). *Profile of undergraduates in U.S. postsecondary institutions: 1999-2000* (NCES 2002-168). Washington, DC: National Center for Education Statistics, U.S. Department of Education, U.S. Government Printing Office.

Kucera, T. J. (Ed.). (1993). *Teaching chemistry to students with disabilities* (3rd ed.). Washington, DC: American Chemical Society.

Lawrence, J., Kent, L., & Henson, J. (1981). *The handicapped student in America's colleges: A longitudinal analysis.* Washington, DC: U.S. Department of Education. (ERIC Document Reproduction Services No. ED 226 694)

Lewis, L., & Farris, E. (1999). *An institutional perspective on students with disabilities in postsecondary education* (NCES 199-046). Washington, DC: National Center for Education Statistics, U.S. Department of Education, U.S. Government Printing Office.

Mellard, D., & Lancaster, S. (2000). *A parent's guide to college. Individual accommodations model.* Lawrence, KS: University of Kansas, Center for Research on Learning.

National Center for Learning Disability. (n.d.). *LD InfoZone.* Retrieved April 7, 2006, from http://www.ncld.org

Runyan, M. K. (1991). The effect of extra time on reading comprehension scores for university students with and without learning disabilities. *Journal of Learning Disabilities, 24*(2), 104–108.

Universal Design Education Online. (2006). *About Universal Design.* Retrieved May 8, 2006, from http://www.udeducation.org

U. S. Department of Education. (2006). *IDEA 2004 resources.* Retrieved June 26, 2006, from http://www.ed.gov/policy/speced/guid/idea/idea2004.html

U.S. Department of Justice. (2006). *Information and technical assistance on the Americans With Disabilities Act.* Retrieved June 26, 2006, from http://www.usdoj.gov/crt/ada/adahom1.htm

U.S. Department of Labor. (2006a). *Job accommodations network.* Retrieved June 26, 2006, from http://www.jan.wvu.edu/

U.S. Department of Labor. (2006b). *Section 504, Rehabilitation Act of 1973.* Retrieved June 26, 2006, from http://www.dol.gov/oasam/regs/statutes/sec504.htm

Weaver, S. M. (2000). The efficacy of extended time on tests for postsecondary students with learning disabilities. *Learning Disabilities, 10*(2), 47-56.

Appendix A

Comparison of the IDEA, Section 504, and the ADA

	IDEA	**Section 504**	**ADA**
Mission	To provide a free, appropriate, public education in the least restrictive environment.	To provide people with disabilities, to the maximum extent possible, the opportunity to be fully integrated into mainstream American life.	To provide all people with disabilities broader coverage than Section 504 in all aspects of discrimination law.
Scope	Applies to public schools.	Applies to any program or activity that receives federal financial assistance.	Applies to public or private employment, transportation, accommodations, and telecommunications regardless of whether federal funding is received.
Coverage	Only those students age 3-21 who need special education and related services because of their disability.	All qualified people with disabilities regardless of whether special education services are required in public elementary, secondary, or postsecondary settings.	All qualified people with disabilities, and qualified non-disabled related to or associated with a person with a disability.
Disability Defined	A listing of disabilities is provided in the act, including specific learning disabilities.	No listing of disabilities is provided, but criteria including having any physical or mental impairment that substantially limits one or more major life activities, having a record of such impairment, or being regarded as having such an impairment.	Same as Section 504.
Identification Process	Responsibility of school District to identify through "Child Find" and evaluate at no expense to parent or individual.	Responsibility of individual with disability to self-identify and provide documentation. Cost of evaluation must be assumed by the individual, not the institution.	Same as Section 504.
Service Delivery	Special education services and auxiliary aids must be stipulated in the Individual Education Plan.	Services, auxiliary aids, and academic adjustments may be provided in the regular education setting, arranged for by special education coordinator or disabled student services provider.	Services, auxiliary aids, and accommodations arranged for by the designated ADA coordinator. Accommodations must not pose an undue hardship to employers.

Table continued p. 170

Table 1 continued

	IDEA	Section 504	ADA
Funding	Federal funds are conditional on compliance with IDEA regulations.	No authorization for funding is attached to this civil rights statute.	Same as Section 504.
Enforcement Agency	Office of Special Education and Rehabilitative Services in the U.S. Department of Education.	Office of Civil Rights in the U.S. Department of Education.	Primarily in the U.S. Department of Justice, in conjunction with the Equal Employment Opportunity Commission and Federal Communications Commission. May overlap.

Appendix B

Web Resources

Abilities
    http://www.ncds.org
ABLEDATA database of assistive devices
    http://www.abledata.com/
Attention Deficit Disorder organization
    http://www.addresources.org/
Alliance for Technology Access
    http://www.ataccess.org/
American Council of the Blind
    http://www.acb.org/
American Printing House for the Blind
    http://www.aph.org/
Apple Accessibility
    http://www.apple.com/accessibility/
Association on Higher Education and Disability (AHEAD)
    http://www.ahead.org/
Brain Injury Association of America
    http://www.biausa.org/
Cornucopia of Disability Information
    http://codi.buffalo.edu/
Diversity World
    http://www.diversityworld.com/Disability/index.htm
Epilepsy Foundation of America
    http://www.epilepsyfoundation.org/
Heath Resource Center/Clearinghouse on Postsecondary Education
    http://www.heath.gwu.edu

IBM Accessibility Center
>   http://www-03.ibm.com/able/product_accessibility/ibmfocus.html

Individual Accommodations Model
>   http://das.kucrl.org/iam.html

International Dyslexia Association
>   http://www.interdys.org

Job Accommodation Network
>   http://janweb.icdi.wvu.edu/

LD Online – web site on Learning Disabilities
>   http://www.ldonline.org/ld_indepth/postsecondary/

Learning Disabilities Association of America
>   http://www.ldaamerica.org/

Medline Plus
>   http://www.nlm.nih.gov/medlineplus/mentalhealth.html

Mental Health America
>   http://www.nmha.org

Microsoft Accessibility
>   http://www.microsoft.com/enable

Multiple Sclerosis Foundation
>   http://www.msfacts.org

Muscular Dystrophy Association
>   http://www.mdausa.org

National Alliance on Mental Illness
>   http://www.nami.org

National Center for Learning Disabilities
>   http://www.ncld.org/

National Federation of the Blind
>   http://www.nfb.org/nfb/Default.asp

National Institute of Neurological Disorders and Stroke
>   http://www.ninds.nih.gov/

Net Connections for Communication Disorders and Sciences
>   http://www.communicationdisorders.com

On-line Books
>   http://digital.library.upenn.edu/books/

Reasonable Accommodations for People with Psychiatric Disabilities
>   An online resource for employers and educators
>   http://www.bu.edu/cpr/reasaccom/employ-read-macdon.html

Recording for the Blind and Dyslexic
>   http://www.rfbd.org

Roadmaps and Rampways: Profiles of students with disabilities in Science, Mathematics, Engineering, and Technology
>   http://ehrweb.aaas.org/entrypoint/rr/index.html

Tourette's Syndrome Association
>   http://www.tsa-usa.org/

United Cerebral Palsy
>   http://www.ucp.org

WebXACT's free service tests web pages for quality, accessibility, and privacy
>   http://webxact.watchfire.com/

Chapter Twelve

Advising First-Year Honors Students

Marion Schwartz

Honors students are the most talented and committed students on a campus. However, their academic strengths do not mean that they have no issues or concerns. In fact, they have unique needs and challenges that makes the role of the academic advisor critical in helping the students acculturate to honors work. Advisors not only help them to choose courses, but they also encourage the attitudes and skills appropriate for honors learning, as they nurture the students through their transition to college and lay the foundations for the future. This chapter discusses various considerations for helping incoming honors students, focusing first on orientation and scheduling, then on planning ahead, and finally on adjusting to college. The chapter appendix provides a checklist to help advisors apply these considerations to their own advising.

Who Are Honors Students?

The literature suggests that it is difficult to generalize about honors students (Achterberg, 2004), in part because they exhibit a wide range of talents and personality traits. This is particularly true because there are so many different kinds of honors programs offered at so many different institutions. Some researchers have attempted to generalize about the students in terms of personal traits (i.e., dominance, risk-taking, emotional stability) or personality type among honors students (Clark, 2002), but the issues honor students face may be the result of pressures from their environment rather than personal characteristics. It is not even possible to say that honors students are all excellent learners, because some of them have coasted through high school without being tested and come to college with limited study skills. All the advisor can assume is that honors students are willing to engage in a higher level of work than their peers.

At the same time, students are influenced by the kind of honors program they join. Each program attracts students consistent with its own strengths and mission—whether they are specially committed scholars at a prestigious liberal arts college or ambitious adults at a community college. Thus, advisors should be aware of whom their institutions recruit for their honors programs. Depending on its goals, an institution may recruit honors students who meet any combination of the following criteria:

◇ Excellent performance in high school or previous college work (i.e., good grades and advanced classes)
◇ Leadership in high school activities

◇ High scores on standardized tests
◇ Excellent application essays
◇ Strong responses in individual and group interviews
◇ Strong letters of recommendation from high school or college teachers
◇ Self-selection for more challenging work
◇ Research potential in special programs
◇ Special talent in the arts
◇ Awards or other recognition for community service
◇ High achievement under difficult circumstances such as low socioeconomic status or disability

Knowing which of these criteria define the honors class is one way to understand one's advisees.

But the students are not simply defined by their honors program; therefore, it is important that advisors are sensitive about stereotyping their advisees (Kem & Navan, 2006). Before meeting their students, advisors can learn about each one individually by obtaining admissions information, especially qualitative data like essays or interviews. Finally, when a student arrives at the office, advisors can dig deeper, asking about their hobbies, their social life, their shaping experiences, their fears, all the things that make them complex individuals.

What is an Honors Education?

Honors education is the place where the institution embodies its own educational ideals for its most talented and committed students. The structure of the program establishes certain expectations for the students, such as taking honors courses, living in an honors learning community, serving the public, or completing an original project (National Collegiate Honors Council, 2005). The honors courses usually encourage active learning, critical thinking, and integration of knowledge from different spheres (Gabelnick, 1986). They may take the form of small-class discussions or interdisciplinary or team-taught seminars. They may use problem-based learning pedagogies or require students to conduct research or develop other creative works. Outside the classroom, honors programs may offer honors-specific living arrangements, dedicated meeting space, social occasions, celebrations, cultural events, leadership training, and forums for the discussion of public issues. By choosing elements such as these for its honors program, the institution tells the students what they think an intellectual person should be.

To help their new students get started, honors advisors need to know what their own program offers, the rationale for each feature, and how the parts work together.

Getting Oriented

When students arrive on campus, they need a strong introduction both to the institution and to the honors program. If honors advisors contribute to the orientation, they should include information for students about:

◇ Program requirements, such as completing certain course work or projects, especially as these obligations relate to scholarships
◇ Special academic and professional opportunities, such as early class scheduling, special advising, extended library privileges, and grants for research or study abroad
◇ Available resources, such as listservs or newsletters that connect students

Another important factor in orientation is setting the appropriate tone for incoming students. Planners should choose language and activities consistent with the goals of the program. For example, if the college recruits high-achieving returning adults who intend to enter new technical fields, the meeting can provide an overview of these new fields and a networking system so that students can contact each other. On the other hand, if the college recruits potential Rhodes Scholars, the orientation might have a major award winner speak to the students about her experience.

The best consultants on orientation may be advanced standing honors students. Once they have been thoroughly trained to understand the goals of the program, peer assistants can help design the activities, explain the messages, and facilitate discussions. Ideally, they continue to be a resource for students throughout the year.

For the honors advisor who does not help with orientation, it is still important to know what goes on so that students hear consistent messages. The advisor may have to fill in specific details about honors work that were not part of the general introduction. At the same time, no one can cover everything. Advisors must judge what information can wait until later in the semester.

Scheduling for the First Semester

An honors semester schedule is a work of art—a balance of honors and non-honors study, of work and play, of present and future goals, of major and minor interests. Honors advisors should help their new students keep all these concerns in perspective.

Honors Work

Advisors should help students from overreaching—reproducing their high school year of eight advanced placement classes—and underachieving—avoiding honors work altogether for fear that it will hurt their grades. Honors contract courses (i.e., doing an extra project in a non-honors course to get honors credit) are not recommended in the first year, because honors students should first adjust to college-level work and get to know their peers in honors classes. They can take contract courses later in their majors.

Advanced Placement

Students who bring in advanced credit from the College Board Advanced Placement examinations, college-in-high school, academic summer camp, or the International Baccalaureate may be tempted to skip ahead. Advisors need to know exactly what credit has been granted by the institution and help students decide thoughtfully how they wish to use this credit. While there are appropriate reasons for acceleration, students should not assume that because they studied something in high school, they have mastered the topic.

General Education

Some honors students have little patience for anything outside of a narrow area of interest. If their program requires general education, advisors can help them broaden their focus by explaining in some depth the purposes of general education. Some students will need concrete examples of how these requirements relate to their goals. Some will need imaginative course choices or projects in core classes, for example, an engineer might choose a philosophy of science class for the humanities requirement, a paper on Galileo in western civilization, or a project on daVinci in art history (Schwartz, 2005).

Integration

Honors students have the intellectual agility to apply material from one course to the understanding of another. For example, an honors course might require that all incoming students study the Middle East from the perspective of cultural history, natural resources, internal politics, and international relations. If the honors program does not offer an interdisciplinary seminar, advisors can help students create their own integration by taking concurrent courses in related areas. In this case, it will be the honors advisor rather than the teachers who will coach the students to see connections across the disciplines.

Substitutions

Many honors programs allow students to modify the letter of the law to meet the spirit more creatively. Thus students might substitute an upper-level course in the humanities for a lower-level western civilization course or find a community service placement to meet a diversity requirement. Advisors can help students grasp the purpose of the requirements so that they can initiate their own appropriate substitutions as they grow into the curriculum.

Future Plans

If students eventually want to graduate early, study abroad, or apply for graduate school, some preparations may be necessary in the first year. For instance, students may need a higher level of math for graduate study than their undergraduate major requires. Or they may want to start a course sequence early to allow for early graduation or for a semester away from campus. In some cases, institutions start grooming scholarship candidates as early as the first year, with recommendations for leadership or cultural experiences. Advisors should be aware of the students' plans and their curricular implications.

Exploration

While the first course schedule assumes a certain academic direction, honors advisors should expect all their incoming students to spend some time exploring, whether or not they have a stated major goal. Gordon notes that multi-talented students, many of whom are honors students, may find it difficult to choose among their various strengths (cited by Saunders & Ervin, 1984). On the other hand, because of their accelerated academic work and the intense involvement of their families, some honors students zero in on a direction too early, without a chance to develop their own ideas. The process of exploration can help them confirm their goals even if they don't change them. Advisors can introduce their students to the common tools for exploration (e.g., inventories and reflections to elicit self-knowledge, information sources to find out about programs, and sorting strategies to help process the information). Then advisor and advisee can analyze the information together to set priorities. The advisor's job is to help the student make decisions based on solid information and clear thinking. For an example of a curriculum for exploration, see Penn State's Navigator (The Pennsylvania State University, 2005b), also described in chapter 5.

Some honors students may resolve their many interests by combining majors or minors, a strategy that is most practical when the fields are related or the students bring in substantial advanced placement credit. Thus, journalism students could complete concurrent majors in political science or Latin American studies without too much trouble, especially if they arrive with advanced credit. Other combinations may be more challenging, such as film production and business, or geography and art. Honors advisors need extensive knowledge of their institution and a vision for the possibilities when they guide students beyond well-trodden pathways.

Some students will try to avoid setting any priorities by combining three or four majors. Advisors can help them understand that their education will not end when they receive a diploma. Their collateral interests will be expressed in the cocurriculum, in undergraduate minors, or in their career or avocations after graduation.

If the student has a clear educational focus that does not fit into a major offered by the home institution, honors advisors can suggest an open-ended program for which the students supply the structure. At first, this may look attractive, especially to the independent-minded student, but it takes work to think through a good proposal and research to find the appropriate course work. During the first year, the honors advisor has to decide whether the student's interests could actually be worked into a discipline-based major, and, if not, whether the institution has the resources to handle the project through an open-structured program. For example, if the student loves engineering and theater and wants to relate them, is it worthwhile to major in both? If not, can they be combined in a general studies program? Will the student be allowed to take the relevant courses from both departments? Who will supervise the work? After consulting with departmental representatives, the advisor must decide whether to (a) encourage the student to draft a proposal for the self-designed major including a list of relevant courses with a rationale for each one, (b) insist that the student let go of the goal and pursue a more conventional degree, or (c) suggest transferring to a different institution where the student's plan could be implemented.

In many institutions, the time allotted for exploration is limited. Advisors should monitor the process to make sure that students do not explore too long and miss declaring their major altogether. This issue may be further complicated by advanced work: Either the institution or the student may insist that 40 credits of AP work automatically implies early acceptance into a major and early graduation. But honors advisors can observe their students' developmental progress as well as their major exploration to see whether accelerated degree plans are appropriate. If so, they can help students plan a first-year curriculum to make it work. If not, they can convince the student (or the major department) that even with sophomore or junior standing, the student is not ready to commit to the major.

Research

Research may seem unlikely in the first year, but some honors programs, such as the Stars Program at Yale University (2006), require students to begin a research program even before they begin their first semester. First-year advisors should know whether their institution provides research opportunities to first-year students, particularly in the natural and social sciences. If so, how do students find out about them? What do students need to do before they take advantage of these opportunities?

Research may not be appropriate for everyone. Students need a foundation in their discipline and in related general areas to understand the relationship between their work and the larger scheme of things. As guardians of the students' education, honors advisors should help them plan courses that will provide a context for research—a way to know the difference between the trivial and the significant and to grasp implications outside the discipline.

If students do choose to pursue a research project this early in their college career, the honors advisor can help them sift through the opportunities available and find an appropriate mentor, someone ready to include undergraduates as serious members of the research group. However, other tasks, such as getting to know the academic community, cannot be neglected for the sake of a narrow project in their discipline (Schwartz, Black, Castillo, & White, 2003), so advisors can help students determine the appropriate degree of commitment to research programs in their first year.

Engaging With the Community

Honors students should know that learning and giving go together. Indeed, the privileges offered by an honors program often assume that graduates will give back to the rest of the world (Davis, 1989). The honors advisor can encourage them to participate in the various communities around them.

First of all, honors students in a fully developed program belong to an honors community, designed to provide them a challenging but safe place in which to grow. When their students are sharing honors housing, advisors can recommend study sessions, book reading groups, in-house policy debates, or speakers. When the students live off-campus, advisors can make sure they know about the honors lounge or study room where they can meet other students for discussion. When honors students develop friendships with their peers, they have a support group to help celebrate their triumphs and cope with any setbacks.

Building community is particularly important for minority students. Perry (2003) notes that for African Americans, who frequently feel that their intellectual ability is under scrutiny, the educational model of competitive individualism is particularly harmful. African American students need to hear from one another and from their families and communities of origin that pursuing ambitious academic goals is part of their heritage. Some honors programs may be dedicated to minority achievement and, thus, particularly able to provide exemplars and celebrations of various scholarly traditions. However, such content enriches the cultural experience of all honors students, regardless of race. By their encouragement and presence at honors celebrations, advisors can show that they take these intellectual traditions seriously.

The honors community is not the only group on campus and may not be the most important one for all honors students. Some will want to stay close to the students they know from high school or non-honors classes. Some will want to continue with the community service organization in which they were involved in high school—i.e., charities, public issue groups, or religious organizations (Kem & Navan, 2006). Therefore, honors advisors should ensure that their first-year students know about campus activities and leadership training opportunities outside the honors program.

Finally, there is the world beyond national borders. If honors students are the ones most likely to assume leadership roles in their professions, they will be particularly obliged to deal with the implications of global culture. In the first year, they may not study abroad, but they can learn about international issues on campus, perhaps at honors events with an international focus. They may also help work with students from abroad, offer practice in speaking English, attend cultural heritage festivals, watch foreign movies, join a language club, and listen to international speakers. Whether or not they travel, their honors advisors can mentor them to be citizens of the world.

Tools for Learning

Part way through the semester, some first-year honors students will be shocked to realize that they know very little about how to study. Advisors can encourage students to accept help from the writing center or math tutor, or teach them to say "no" to yet another club meeting. They may also have to coach them about how to take notes in a lecture. In small group discussions, some students will need to learn how to participate and write at the same time, not to mention mastering the civility appropriate to serious intellectual discussion. Listening carefully to others, staying on point, taking turns, respecting the different speaking styles of men and women are skills worth cultivating.

Finally, honors students should be ready to learn collaboratively, as one purpose of an honors program is to provide mutual support and stimulation for committed students (Clark, 2002). According to Light (2001), the students who succeed in science are those who work together on their class assignments. They are more likely to persist at solving frustrating problems, and they cover the material more efficiently. These students may also experiment with different strategies to get the most out of group learning, with the understanding that cultural styles for sharing will differ (Perry, 2003). If honors students are dubious because of previous experiences with collaborative learning, they might read Bruffee's (1993) persuasive epistemology in which he argues that knowledge is a communal activity, best developed in critical conversation.

Adjustment

Honors students are not immune to adjustment issues; many will suffer the usual adjustment problems of other students their age. At the same time, they may also be more vulnerable to academic-related stress, especially with regard to issues of control and failure (Callard-Szulgit, 2003). For the student who feels overwhelmed by too much work, the honors advisor can

- ◇ Listen carefully to the student's current obligations
- ◇ Discuss with the student the relative importance of each obligation and help him or her prioritize
- ◇ Discuss what obligations can be reduced or eliminated
- ◇ If possible, help the student negotiate extra time to complete assignments
- ◇ Help the student develop a realistic schedule that accommodates the rest of the work and includes breaks for eating, sleeping, and down time
- ◇ Follow up to see how the schedule is working

For the student who feels devastated by a low grade or some other academic setback, the advisor can

- ◇ Listen carefully for any evidence of exaggeration in the student's account of the failure and ensure that students clarify the situation with the instructor
- ◇ Discuss the possible consequences of the poor result, now and in the future; what is the worst potential outcome?
- ◇ Help the student find ways to cope with the outcomes, whether to improve their performance or to shift direction

The point of such intervention is to get students beyond emotional paralysis (The Pennsylvania State University, 2005a). If there is any doubt about the student's state of mind, advisors should refer them to counseling.

Outside influences on honors students can also contribute to adjustment problems. Because they have been so successful at socially valued endeavors, honors students may depend more than other traditional-aged students on their parents' good opinions. They feel obliged both to keep up the image of high achievement and to maintain the scholarship that goes with it. Honors advisors should be aware of the pressures their first-year students work under and be ready to support them as they struggle towards personal independence. A full-blown identity crisis calls for counseling.

Minority students in predominantly White institutions face all these issues and more. If the students have been recruited because their academic potential exceeds their social resources, Perry (2003) suggests that the institution help cultivate the missing social capital—the behaviors and assumptions that are expected of people in the academic community. Academic advisors should be aware of opportunities their program provides for students to gain cultural ease.

Race brings up another adjustment issue—the burden many students feel as representatives of their gender or ethnic group. Honors students tend to identify with their academic work more than others. High-achieving students are vulnerable to negative effects from stereotyping as are many students in particular micropopulations. In a series of experiments, Steele, Perry, and Hillard (2003) demonstrated that when committed students feel their work on any given task may be taken to confirm a stereotype, they perform dramatically worse. For instance, given an academic task that was designed to be too hard (i.e., college first-year students doing a difficult section of the Graduate Record Examination), Black and White students performed about equally well when they thought it was a study of problem-solving strategies in general, but Black students dropped to about two thirds of White results when they thought it was a test of their innate intellectual ability. Steele says that giving students confidence builders, such as an introductory activity in which they were guaranteed success, does not help. However, when the students are held to high standards of achievement and are told explicitly that these standards are rigorous, they are more likely to believe in their own success. Further, Steele et al. cites a study by Aronson, Fried, and Good showing that students who learned that intelligence is improvable with study received significantly higher grades than those who were not given that information.

Conclusion

Advising honors students can be enormously gratifying. Those with wide-ranging interests pull advisors out of the routine and into new possibilities. Those who achieve high goals give everyone cause for celebration. Those who aim to improve the world sustain our faith in the human enterprise.

But honors students require a great deal of their advisors. Many will be naïve about the new academic world they are entering. It takes work on the advisor's part to network with faculty, to read up on the profession, to imagine creative academic opportunities, and to advocate for appropriate privileges, such as upper-level course work and research. Once the advisor has learned all this extra information, there's more time required to talk about the advantages and disadvantages of each option. Everything is complicated. But it is just this commitment to finding the most fulfilling, effective, or ambitious plan that makes working with honors students so rewarding. The payoff comes as the students discover the extent of their intellectual capacities.

References

Achterberg, C. (2004). Characteristics of honors students. In J. Buck (Ed.), *Student characteristics matter*. University Park, PA: The Pennsylvania State University, Division of Undergraduate Studies.

Bruffee, K. A. (1993). *Collaborative learning: Higher education, interdependence, and the authority of knowledge*. Baltimore: Johns Hopkins University Press.

Callard-Szulgit, R. (2003). *Perfectionism and gifted children: Parenting and teaching the gifted*. Lanham, MD: Scarecrow Press.

Clark, L. (2002). A review of the research on personality characteristics of academically talented college students. In C. L. Fuiks & L. C. (Eds.), *Teaching and learning in honors* (pp. 7-20). Lincoln, NE: University of Nebraska, National Collegiate Honors Council.

Davis, H. E. (1989, Fall). Elitism and honors: A catechism and some propositions. *Forum for Honors, 14*(4), 1-23.

Gabelnick, F. (1986). Curriculum design: The medium is the message. In P. G. Friedman & R. C. Jenkins-Friedman (Eds.), *Fostering academic excellence through honors programs* (pp. 75-86). San Francisco: Jossey-Bass.

Kem, L. & Navan, J. L. (2006). Gifted students in college: Suggestions for advisors and faculty members. *NACADA Journal, 26*(2), 21-28.

Light, R. (2001). *Making the most of college: Students speak their minds.* Cambridge, MA: Harvard University Press.

National Collegiate Honors Council. (2005). *Basic characteristics of a fully developed honors program.* Retrieved on July 9, 2006, from http://www.nchchonors.org/basic.htm

The Pennsylvania State University. (2005a). *Counseling and psychological services.* Retrieved December 22, 2005, from http://www.sa.psu.edu/caps/assisting_students.shtml

The Pennsylvania State University. (2005b). *The DUS Navigator: A guide for educational planning.* Retrieved December 21, 2005, from www.psu.edu/dus/navigate

Perry, T. (2003). Freedom for literacy and literacy for freedom: The African-American philosophy of education. In T. Perry, C. Steele, & G. Hilliard, III, *Young, gifted, and black: Promoting high achievement among African-American students* (pp. 1-87). Boston: Beacon Press.

Saunders, S., & Ervin, L. (1984). Meeting the special advising needs of students. In R. B. Winston, T. K. Miller, S. C. Ender, T. J. Grites, & Associates (Eds.), *Developmental academic advising: Addressing students' educational, career, and personal needs* (pp. 250-286). San Francisco: Jossey-Bass.

Schwartz, M. (2005). *Advising for general education.* University Park, PA: The Pennsylvania State University, Division of Undergraduate Studies.

Schwartz, M., Black, I., Castillo, E., & White, L. (2003, September). The role of advising in undergraduate research, *The Mentor: An On-Line Journal of Academic Advising.* Retrieved December 9, 2005, from http://www.psu.edu/dus/mentor/

Steele, C., Perry, T., & Hillard, A. (2003). Competing theories of group achievement. In T. Perry, C. Steele, & G. Hilliard, III, *Young, gifted, and black: Promoting high achievement among African-American students* (pp. 52-86). Boston: Beacon Press.

Yale University. (2006). *STARS: Science, technology, and research scholars.* Retrieved July 5, 2006 from http://www.yale.edu/stars/

Appendix

Questions for the Honors Advisor

The body of this chapter deals with honors advising in general terms. In order to help advisors take practical steps towards preparing for their own students, a list of questions based on each section of the text is offered. The organization is roughly chronological. It moves from getting background information about the program and the students to orientation and planning the first semester course schedule, to exploring and finding a niche as the first semester begins, to dealing with problems that may arise, both academic and emotional.

Questions about the honors program and students:

- ◇ What is the mission of our honors program? How is it related to the whole institution?
- ◇ What are the criteria for admission to our honors program? What goals do we set? Who is our typical honors student?
- ◇ What is an honors course at my institution? What attitudes and skills do my students need to thrive in honors?
- ◇ What are the privileges and obligations of our honors students? How do they contribute to meeting student goals?
- ◇ Who are my honors students? What information can I gather about them? What do they want from their education?

Questions about orientation:

- ◇ What is absolutely essential for our incoming honors students to know before they begin the school year?
- ◇ What is our honors orientation program? How can I reinforce the messages of orientation in sessions with individual students?

Questions about the first-semester schedule:

- ◇ What is an appropriate honors work load? How will honors obligations be met?
- ◇ What role will general education play in my students' first semester?
- ◇ What advanced work have my students completed? How does my institution accept it? How will each student use it in the building of a coherent educational plan?
- ◇ What opportunities do my students have for integrating material from two or more courses?
- ◇ Should my students make use of substitutions in their first year? If so, what is appropriate?
- ◇ Once the schedule is put together, does it make sense as a whole?

Questions about exploration:

- ◇ What is this student's major preference? Has the student declared choices too early? Does the student need more information to make a sound choice?
- ◇ What other interests does the student bring to the table? Can this student's education be enriched by adding other academic directions without compromising the primary one? How can the requirements be managed most effectively? Who approves of combinations, substitutions, and waivers?
- ◇ If this student does not have clearly focused goals, what tools are available to help with the decision process?
- ◇ When does the student have to make a final decision? What are the implications of waiting too long?
- ◇ Given the students' backgrounds and goals, does it make sense to accelerate the choice of a major?

Questions about research:

- ◇ Is research likely to play a role in this student's undergraduate education? Why or why not?
- ◇ What resources inform our students about research opportunities? Does this student know how to use them?

⬦ What kind of research is appropriate for a student entering the institution? How can I find a good match between students and research mentors?

⬦ If research is not appropriate at this time, how will we plan the student's first-year classes to lay the foundations for future research? Does the student need any specific training in lab procedures, materials handling, or survey skills? Who would provide it?

Questions about engaging the community:

⬦ What means does our program offer to nurture an honors community? What opportunities are most relevant to first-year students?

⬦ How does our program address the needs of minority students? How does it make use of minority resources to educate non-minority students?

⬦ How does our program recognize the needs of honors commuter students and non-traditional students?

⬦ What activities outside the honors program are most relevant for my students? How can they learn leadership skills to contribute to these groups? How can they start a new group to continue a previous interest?

⬦ How do my students learn more about study or service abroad?

⬦ What international activities do we offer on this campus? How can this student participate in such activities?

Questions about learning skills:

⬦ What are the particular challenges that honors students face in managing their time?

⬦ What study skills are appropriate for honors work?

⬦ What resources are available when my students need academic help?

⬦ What techniques will help my students get the most out of collaborative learning?

Questions about adjustment:

⬦ What are the critical moments for honors students in our academic calendar?

⬦ If we have an honors residence hall, what resources does it offer for supporting students? How do students contact key people?

⬦ What accommodations does the honors program offer to students in trouble? If my students struggle with failure, what positive outcomes can I imagine with them?

⬦ How do I refer students for counseling if necessary?

⬦ How do we nurture achievement and high standards among our diverse honors population?

Questions about the advisor's development:

⬦ What satisfactions do I gain from working with honors students?

⬦ What faculty, staff, and other resources can I call on to extend my knowledge?

Chapter Thirteen

Adapting Learning Theory to Advising First-Year Undecided Students

Melinda McDonald and George E. Steele

More than any other group of first-year students, undecided students may gain the most from a learning approach to academic advising. First-year students enter institutions with concerns that range from how to make a smooth transition from high school to college academics to how to deal with roommate problems and homesickness. Some students are able to efficiently balance academics with cocurricular pursuits and social interests, while others struggle with managing multiple activities and keeping academics a priority. First-year undecided students are not only coping with typical developmental issues that all first-year students face, but they are also concerned with being "unwilling, unable, or unready" to make educational and/or occupational decisions (Gordon, 1995b, p. x).

Establishing an effective advising relationship with students early in the first year can facilitate academic adjustment and create a connection to the institution. Nutt (2000) states, "The successful one-to-one advising relationship can be a major factor in a student's decision to remain in college and be academically successful" (p. 226). In addition, an effective advising relationship is key to engaging first-year, undecided students in the process of learning about themselves and how to explore academic majors and career fields.

An initial step in the advising process with undecided students may involve assuring them that it is acceptable and normal to be undecided. Oftentimes, undecided students believe that they are the only ones having difficulty deciding on a major. Providing factual information about numbers of undecided students entering the institution and data regarding the percentage of students who change their majors can be helpful to students who believe all their peers have selected a major. Emphasizing to students that there are advantages to remaining open to new academic possibilities is a useful way to reframe students' concerns. Being undecided gives students the opportunity to explore academic options and the world of work and to learn about who they are before deciding on a major. Undecided students are often relieved to know that there are exploration and decision-making processes to help them choose a major and learn about careers. Students need to know that they will be supported throughout the exploration process and that their advisor is approachable, knowledgeable, and helpful. Advisors who create an advising relationship that is open and conducive to learning will be rewarded by undecided students' interest in engaging in the advising process.

The focus of this chapter is to help advisors who work with this special population of students to achieve success using a teaching approach (see chapter 1). We will begin with a literature review that focuses on what advisors need to know about first-year undecided students to be effective within a teaching-learning paradigm. This literature also provides useful conceptual and practical considerations for working with these students. Next we will apply Krumboltz's (1996) social-learning theory to the advising process for first-year undecided students. Bloom, Mesia, and Krathwohl's (1964) cognitive and affective taxonomy of learning and the Association of College and Research Libraries (ACRL, 2000) *Information Literacy Competency Standards for Higher Education* will be presented as frameworks for developing learning objectives and assessing outcomes. Finally, we will include a series of suggestions for advising practitioners who work with first-year undecided students.

Relevant Research Related to Undecided Students

The research literature available for undecided students is perhaps one of the richest areas of research on students in higher education. This literature contains many studies that describe characteristics of undecided students that help advisors' gain valuable insights about issues that can impede or influence these students' learning. Kimes & Troth (1974), for example, studied the relationship between career decisiveness and trait anxiety. They concluded that high anxiety-prone individuals, compared to those who are less anxious, may have more difficulty in making occupational choices. When Gianakos & Subich (1986) reviewed sex-role orientation, they found that androgynous individuals were more undecided than those with traditional sex-role orientations. Other studies (Appel, Haak, & Witzke, 1970; Fuqua, Seaworth, & Newman, 1987; Mau, 1995) share similar findings. Self-efficacy is used to describe the confidence one has to successfully master specific tasks associated with career decision making. Taylor and Betz (1983) studied self-efficacy in relationship to comfort with decision making and generally found that students undecided about academic and vocational choice have lower self-efficacy compared to decided students. These studies represent a small sample of psychological, sociological, and cultural factors that can influence first-year undecided students.

However, these studies must be placed in context. After reviewing the research literature through the early 1990s that concentrated on comparing "undecided" students with "decided" students, Lewallen (1993) declared that much of it was "conflicting and confusing" (p. 11). In this regard, he agreed with studies that found undecided students to be a heterogeneous group with few similarities (Baird, 1967; Gordon, 1995b; Hagstrom, Skovholt, & Rivers, 1997; Holland & Holland, 1977). Steele (2003) encourages advisors to become familiar with this extensive literature because it provides rich sources of theoretical frameworks and concepts. This research information is not only intellectually rewarding, but it also outlines the assets and barriers that can benefit or impede a student's progress during the exploration process.

One body of work that is especially relevant when advising undecided students is related to the difference between the concepts of "undecidedness" and "indecisiveness" (Appel et al., 1970; Goodstein, 1965). In any advising session, it is important for an advisor to assess whether the student is having difficulty with making academic and occupational decisions or has difficulty with decision making in general. Teaching and advising approaches can be readily and effectively used with first-year undecided students who are indecisive; however, they may include referral to counseling services for more in-depth assistance (Larson & Heppner, 1995). Indecisive students often show high levels of anxiety along with other social or psychological problems (Gaffner & Hazler, 2002; Salamone, 1982; Van Matre & Cooper, 1984). Even though relevant information is present and realistic options understood, indecisive students still find it difficult to make a commitment to a particular course of action. Few students manifest these extreme characteristics; therefore, advisors who work with undecided students must be careful not to be judgmental about students who take longer to explore options than other students.

Definitions of Decided and Undecided Students

Some researchers have concentrated on defining sub-types of undecided and decided students (Newman & Fuqua, 1990; Savickas & Jorgourna, 1991). Typically, these studies use multiple variable approaches to help identify clusters of students who share similar character-istics. These studies can help advisors group undecided students, based upon their personality characteristics and decision-making abilities. Gordon (1998) proposed seven groups of decided and undecided students, after reviewing 15 studies examining this issue (Table 1). Gordon identifies the similarities and differences among each of these groups. Central to understand-ing her groupings is the view that decidedness and undecidedness lie on a continuum rather than as separate states. Certainly no student fits perfectly into one group. However, the seven groups can help advisors begin to focus on and help students "mindfully" identify and address potential perceived barriers. To illustrate this point, let us compare the advisor focus for two different types: (a) students who are identified as "developmentally undecided" and (b) those identified as "tentatively undecided." The developmentally undecided students are dealing with the normal developmental tasks involved in the major/career decision-making process. They need to gather pertinent information about themselves and the world of work and develop decision-making skills. They may be multipotential, that is, they are interested and competent in many areas. Advising strategies for these first-year students would include a general introduction to the exploration process that includes self-assessment, academic information, occupational information, and decision making. Such strategies would also be tempered by the realization that these students need time to explore and help with processing what they have discovered. When working with tentatively undecided students (see Table 1), an advisor's focus might shift to meet these students' greater need to address issues of valuing and value clarification as it relates to work and non-work activities, rather than emphasize the entire career decision-making process. When compared to "developmental undecided" students, "tentatively unde-cided" students tend to be more mature, have better self-esteem, and indicate greater comfort with themselves. Perhaps because of this, they perceive fewer barriers to achieving their goals but need assistance in weighing which goals to pursue.

Social Learning Theory Applied to Advising

Krumboltz's (1996) social learning theory of career decision making (SLTCDM) has impor-tant implications for advising undecided first-year students. The main premise of his theory can be explained by understanding the role that unique learning experiences play in an individual's career choice(s). These learning experiences are labeled as either instrumental or associative.

Instrumental learning results from a behavior that has been positively or negatively reinforced. Following a speech to a class, a student is told that her oral communication skills are excellent and is given an "A" on both the content and the delivery of her speech. This feedback leads to greater self-efficacy about oral communication skills, which provides incentive for spending more time on speech class and improving communication skills. The result is increased satisfaction with oral communication and a decreased need for reinforcement. Conversely, a student who does not perform well in speech class and receives negative feedback may learn to dislike giving speeches and end up avoiding any class or activity that involves giving a speech.

Table 1
Summary of Degree of Decided and Undecided Students

Degree of Decidedness	Characteristics	Advice/Strategy
Very decided	These students feel good about themselves, believe that they have personal control over their lives, and see themselves as making good decisions regarding their future.	While they are capable of implementing choices or making plans, advisors still may need to review the exploration process with them.
Somewhat decided	These students have some doubts about their decisions and have higher levels of state and trait anxiety and lower levels of self-clarity, decisiveness, and self-esteem than their very decided peers. They may have made premature choices because of external pressures.	By taking time to encourage these students to explore their concerns, advisors can help these students confirm their original choice or identify a well-grounded alternative.
Unstable decided	These students exhibit high goal instability, a high level of anxiety, and a lack of confidence in their ability to perform adequately. They may also experience ambivalence about their choices and believe that because a decision has been made they have no reason to seek help to confirm or to change their direction.	Advising strategies would include discussing student's career-development history allied with the goal of improving their decision-making skills.
Tentatively undecided	These students feel comfortable with themselves, have a strong sense of personal esteem, and are more vocationally mature. They may exhibit a vocational direction and are often intuitive decision makers. They do not perceive barriers to achieving their goals and are confident that a decision will be made when it feels right to do so.	Advisors can help these students establish a plan to explore and discuss the relationship of values to work and non-work tasks and concerns about commitment.
Developmentally undecided	These students are dealing with the normal developmental tasks involved in the major/career decision-making process. They need to gather pertinent information about themselves and the world of work and develop decision-making skills. They may be multi-potential; that is, they may need to be interested and competent to succeed in many areas.	Advising strategies would include traditional psycho-educational and career planning interventions.

Table 1 continued

Degree of Decidedness	Characteristics	Advice/Strategy
Seriously undecided	These students have low levels of vocational identity, self-clarity, and self-esteem. They have limited knowledge of educational and occupational alternatives and may be looking for the "perfect" choice. They may be seeking occupational information to support the choice.	In addition to traditional psycho-educational and career planning interventions, advisors may need to refer these students to personal counseling due to the scope of their problems.
Chronically indecisive	These students have excessive anxiety that permeates many facets of their lives. They are often distressed, unclear about their career options, and depend on other's assistance and approval when making decisions.	Advisors may need to refer these students to long-term counseling rather than begin academic and career advising with them.

Source. Gordon, 1998. Reprinted with permission.

Associative learning involves learning through either direct or vicarious experience in which there is an emotional aspect associated with the experience. A student may be very interested in the field of physical therapy as a result of his or her own direct experience working with a physical therapist after an accident. The student has a positive association with his or her experience as a patient being treated by a physical therapist and, therefore, is interested in pursuing the occupation. An individual may learn more about physical therapy by reading about the occupation, watching a movie about the role that a physical therapist has in rehabilitating athletes after an injury, or interviewing a physical therapist who works with the elderly. An interest or disinterest in physical therapy may result from any of these vicarious activities.

The type and variety of learning experiences that an individual is exposed to is dependent on social, cultural, and economic circumstances and geography. Therefore, learning experiences vary from one individual to the next. "People form their self-observation generalizations and task-approach skills from a limited set of possible experiences" (Krumboltz, 1996, p. 60). In addition, there is a wide range of feedback for learning experiences that impacts whether a student continues or abandons an activity. Learning experiences (positive or negative) or the lack of learning experiences may lead to indecision about occupational choice. While learning experiences are a primary focus of the SLTCDM, Mitchell and Krumboltz (1996) acknowledge that innate and developmental processes also play a role in the career choice process.

Facilitating Learning in the Advising Process

According to Krumboltz (1996), "The goal of career counseling is to facilitate the learning of skills, interests, beliefs, values, work habits, and personal qualities that enable each client to create a satisfying life within a constantly changing work environment" (p. 61). Similarly, the goal of academic advising is to facilitate learning. Undecided students must learn about themselves—their interests, abilities, beliefs, and values—and to understand that how they define themselves today will not necessarily be how they define themselves tomorrow. They also need to know about the variety of academic disciplines that are available to them, what the different curricula consists of, and how to prepare for these fields. Occupational information is also needed in order to understand the nature of work in a particular career field as well as what qualifications are needed to enter and succeed in a particular job. Decision-making skills must be learned in order to take the steps necessary to declare a major and to realize goals.

The SLTCDM provides a basis for examining how we advise undecided students and asking ourselves what could we be doing differently to help our students learn about themselves and the vast array of academic and career resources. Krumboltz (1996) contends that interest inventories should be used primarily as an opportunity to discuss developing new interests. Many first-year undecided students have been exposed to a limited number of academic and occupational experiences from which they could develop interests (Gordon, 1995b). These students need to be encouraged to take courses in a variety of subject areas to test academic fields to which they have never been exposed. Many times, undecided students are reluctant to select a major because they cannot see the connection between the academic choice and an occupation. Learning more about occupations and testing those occupations need to be an important component of the exploration process. Computers offer increasingly innovative ways to experience and understand the world of work. The Virtual Job Experience (VJE) is an interactive job simulation that gives users an opportunity to realistically test occupations (Krumboltz, Vidalakis, & Tyson, 2000). Career-related web sites offer vast resources for students seeking information about occupations (see chapter appendix). Internships and part-time jobs that are career-related may be the best type of experience for students to get a first-hand look at a particular occupation or career field.

Similar to interests, aptitudes are viewed as "skills that have been learned to date" (Mitchell & Krumboltz, 1996, p. 254). Current aptitudes can be used as a starting point for discussing how to develop new skills and abilities. A first-semester student, who has a low ACT/SAT quantitative score and an interest in business, should not (necessarily) be discouraged from pursuing a business major. Curricular requirements need to be outlined with a particular emphasis on quantitative courses and what steps need to be taken to achieve success in those subjects. Academic resources in terms of tutoring, study groups, and study skills courses should be discussed; and goals should be set to include these resources. Since many business programs are selective, academic progress should be monitored closely.

Challenging and Grounding Beliefs and Addressing Values

One of the biggest barriers that advisors face in working with undecided students is the set of beliefs about majors and careers that students hold. Beliefs such as "there is a single 'right' occupational choice for everyone" and "the choice of a major or career is irreversible" can prevent students from exploring and taking the necessary steps to declare a major. These types of absolutes lead students to the conclusion that even if there was a major in which they were interested, they would not know that it was the right major for them. This belief becomes more difficult to counter if the student also believes that they will be doing this particular occupation for the rest of their lives. Advisors need to help undecided students examine their belief systems and counter erroneous beliefs with factual information. (See the information literacy discussion in the next section of this chapter, which focuses on the acquisition and evaluation of information.)

Faulty beliefs that are more ingrained may call for strategies that include consistent repetition, positive statements, and ongoing support (Krumboltz, 1992).

Values are an important component in the career decision-making process for any student. For some first-year undecided students examining what is most important to them is the key to declaring a major. This is particularly true with students who have multiple interests and abilities and cannot decide in which academic field or occupation they are most interested. However, the process of values clarification can be frustrating for some first-year undecided students who are coping with developmental issues as well as academic uncertainty. Simply helping students to define values, to understand the differences between personal and work values, and to explain the role that values play in the choice of major and career can be a good first step. Some traditional-age, first-year students will find this discussion difficult due to limited exposure to life and work experiences. Acknowledging this fact as well as the fact that values continue to change over a lifespan may help students accept that they may not know which values are most important to them right now.

Assessing Learning Outcomes

Krumboltz (1996) proposes that career counselors use learning outcomes as criteria of success instead of solely focusing on career choice. "Criterion measures will include assessment of attempts to learn new behaviors, revised thoughts, and more comfortable emotional reactions" (Krumboltz, 1996, p. 75). Similarly, undecided students see advisors with one goal in mind—to get help with choosing a major. While choice of major is one objective of the advising process, there are additional learning objectives that need to be delineated and incorporated into the process. Spight (2005) contends that advising undecided students is a process involving learning and development. "It includes learning outcomes and competencies involving information acquisition, critical thinking, decision making, and integration and application of the knowledge gained" (Spight, p. 14). These types of competencies are essential for students in preparing for a changing work world as well as an uncertain economy. Within a teaching-learning paradigm of advising undecided students, the primary focus is not on the single event of choosing a major, but rather on teaching life skills and developing student learning (Spight).

Bloom et al. (1964) identified and defined domains of learning in three general categories. The *cognitive* domain addresses the development of mental skills. The *affective* domain addresses growth in the area of emotions, feelings, and values, and the *psychomotor* domain addresses activities or physical skills. All three of these domains share the characteristic of having categories that are not absolutes, but points of reference, starting from the simplest behavior and moving to the most complex. These domains have been commonly used by educators to help them analyze and evaluate the questions and activities they ask their students to engage in to help guide and assess critical thinking.

When working with undecided students, an advisor will address all of these domains in the advising process. However, the greatest focus is with the cognitive and affective domains. To highlight these interactions, Tables 2 and 3 describe the stages identified by Bloom et al. (1964) for the cognitive and affective domains and provides examples of the type of question or activity an advisor might ask a student. Also identified on these charts are examples of key words, which help us associate words we use to define or frame a question or an activity for a stage in a domain. For example, when we use terms such as "defines," "describes," or "identifies," we are asking students to operate at the *knowledge* stage in the cognitive domain. Good teaching and advising should challenge and support a student to engage in the exploration process at

Table 2

Bloom's Cognitive Domain* Applied to Academic Advising

Definition	Examples	Key Words
Knowledge: Recall data	◇ Describe how the course catalog can be used through its two different media: print and hypertext. ◇ List three resources at the institution where occupational information can be found.	defines, describes, identifies, knows, labels, lists, matches, names, outlines, recalls, recognizes, reproduces, selects, states
Comprehension: Understand the meaning, translation, interpolation, and interpretation of instructions and problems; state a problem in one's own words	◇ Summarize the similarity and differences for the course requirements of three majors that interest you. ◇ Describe in your own words the academic and career exploration model discussed in class.	comprehends, converts, defends, distinguishes, estimates, explains, extends, generalizes, gives examples, infers, interprets, paraphrases, predicts, rewrites, summarizes, translates
Application: Use a concept in a new situation or use an abstraction unprompted; apply what was learned in the classroom to novel situations in the workplace	◇ Review the courses you have taken to date, and apply them to three different major requirements you are considering. ◇ Use the *Occupation Outlook Handbook* to list skills necessary for any occupation you wish to select, state how you have used these skills in the classroom or through extracurricular activities, internships, or your employment during the past year.	applies, changes, computes, constructs, demonstrates, discovers, manipulates, modifies, operates, predicts, prepares, produces, relates, shows, solves, uses
Analysis: Separate material or concepts into component parts so that its organizational structure may be understood; distinguish between facts and inferences	◇ Review the courses you have taken to date and those you plan to take for the next three terms. How would you categorize them based on the structure of the general education requirements? ◇ Use a concept map to diagram your analysis. ◇ After your two informational interviews with our institution's alumni in the occupational field you selected, how does their description of their occupation compare with what you have read about it in the *Occupation Outlook Handbook*?	analyzes, breaks down, compares, contrasts, diagrams, deconstructs, differentiates, discriminates, distinguishes, identifies, illustrates, infers, outlines, relates, selects, separates

Table 2 continued

Definition	Examples	Key Words
Synthesis: Build a structure or pattern from diverse elements with emphasis on creating a new meaning or structure	◇ After reviewing courses in the Course Bulletin and circling those that interest you, compile a list of departments from which these courses are offered. ◇ After interviewing three seniors, in a major of your choice, summarize those characteristics they identified that contribute to one being a "successful student" in the major. ◇ After reviewing the results of your *Self-Directed Search*, how would you interpret the list of occupations that appear based on the value, interest, and ability surveys you took?	categorizes, combines, compiles, composes, creates, devises, designs, explains, generates, modifies, organizes, plans, rearranges, reconstructs, relates, reorganizes, revises, rewrites, summarizes, tells, writes
Evaluation: Make judgments about the value of ideas or materials	◇ After reviewing a list of extracurricular activities, justify which ones would provide you with the best means of acquiring work-related skills that you need. ◇ After reviewing all of the information you have collected about academic majors; which major would challenge you the most? Which one would you enjoy the most? Explain how your responses to these two questions are similar or different.	appraises, compares, concludes, contrasts, criticizes, critiques, defends, describes, discriminates, evaluates, explains, interprets, justifies, relates, summarizes, supports

*The cognitive domain involves knowledge and the development of intellectual skills.
Source. Clark, 2005. Reprinted with permission.

Table 3

Bloom's Affective Domain* Applied to Academic Advising

Definition	Examples	Keywords
Receiving phenomena: Awareness, willingness to hear, selected attention	◇ Describe three academic majors you never heard of before you attended the academic information session. ◇ Name three occupations that you became familiar with while you were in elementary school.	asks, chooses, describes, follows, gives, holds, identifies, locates, names, points to, selects, sits, erects, replies, uses
Responding to phenomena: Active participation on the part of the learners; attends and reacts to a particular phenomenon; learning outcomes may emphasize compliance in responding, willingness to respond, or satisfaction in responding (motivation).	◇ Listen to a presentation of academic majors and read curricular information on three for further investigation. ◇ Present to peer support group three occupations that are under consideration, and discuss the action steps taken for exploration this week.	answers, assists, aids, complies, conforms, discusses, greets, helps, labels, performs, practices, presents, reads, recites, reports, selects, tells, writes
Valuing: The worth or value a person attaches to a particular object, phenomenon, or behavior. This ranges from simple acceptance to the more complex state of commitment. Valuing is based on the internalization of a set of specified values, while clues to these values are expressed in the learner's overt behavior and are often identifiable.	◇ Take an occupational values inventory, and select and explain your choice of the top three selections. ◇ Engage in the academic and career exploration process, and actively seek and study information pertaining to selected major and occupational selections.	completes, demonstrates, differentiates, explains, follows, forms, initiates, invites, joins, justifies, proposes, reads, reports, selects, shares, studies, works
Organization: Organizes values into priorities by contrasting different values, resolving conflicts between them, and creating an unique value system. The emphasis is on comparing, relating, and synthesizing values.	◇ Create an academic plan in harmony with abilities, interests, and beliefs. ◇ Prioritize time effectively to balance academic, social, and work demands.	adheres, alters, arranges, combines, compares, completes, defends, explains, formulates, generalizes, identifies, integrates, modifies, orders, organizes, prepares, relates, synthesizes

Table 3 continued

Definition	Examples	Keywords
Internalizing values (characterization): Has a value system that controls their behavior. The behavior is pervasive, consistent, predictable, and most importantly, characteristic of the learner. Instructional objectives are concerned with the student's general patterns of adjustment (personal, social, emotional).	◇ Complete and hand in academic work for credit that displays the highest standards of academic integrity. ◇ Practice the professional ethical standards established by the occupation of choice.	acts, discriminates, displays, influences, listens, modifies, performs, practices, proposes, qualifies, questions, revises, serves, solves, verifies

*Affective: This domain includes the manner in which we deal with things emotionally, such as feelings, values, appreciation, enthusiasms, motivations, and attitudes.
Source. Clark, 2005. Reprinted with permission.

the more complex stages. When advisors do this, they are helping students learn at the highest levels and assisting their institution to achieve the mission of educating students.

Today, there is another way advisors who work with undecided students can see their efforts correspond to the larger educational mission of the institution. Clearly, one of the greatest changes in advising in the past decade has been the use of the Internet to provide information, resources, and tools for self-assessment and academic and career exploration. Evaluating the information is important for grounding academic and career beliefs. Much work has been done by the Association of College and Research Libraries (ACRL) in the area of developing students' information literacy. The ACRL web site states that information literacy

> encompasses more than good information-seeking behavior. It incorporates the abilities to recognize when information is needed and then to phrase questions designed to gather the needed information. It includes evaluating and then using information appropriately and ethically once it is retrieved from any media, including electronic, human, or print sources. The responsibility for helping people become information literate is best shared across an institution, as is clearly indicated in the Competency Standards. (ACRL, 2000)

Reviewing the general standards for information literacy created by ACRL (Table 4) shows that there is a relationship between these standards and Bloom et al.'s (1964) cognitive and affective domains. By looking at the performance indicators listed under each of the competency standards, learners interact with the Internet using the more complex behavior identified by Bloom et al. The first performance indicator listed under Competency Standard One is: "The information literate student defines and articulates the need for information." This performance indicator is similar to the *knowledge* stage in the cognitive domain and the "Responding to Phenomena" in the affective domain by Bloom et al.

Table 4

ACRL's Information Literacy Competency Standards for Higher Education

Standards	Performance Indicators
	The information-literate student
Competency Standard One: The information literate student determines the extent of the information needed.	◇ defines and articulates the need for information ◇ identifies a variety of types and formats of potential sources for information ◇ considers the costs and benefits of acquiring the needed information ◇ reevaluates the nature and extent of the information needed
Competency Standard Two: The information literate student accesses needed information effectively and efficiently.	◇ selects the most appropriate investigative methods or information retrieval systems for accessing the needed information ◇ constructs and implements effectively designed search strategies ◇ retrieves information online or in person using a variety of methods ◇ refines the search strategy if necessary ◇ extracts, records, and manages the information and its sources
Competency Standard Three: The information literate student evaluates information and its sources critically and incorporates selected information into his or her knowledge base and value system.	◇ articulates and applies initial criteria for evaluating both the information and its sources ◇ compares new knowledge with prior knowledge to determine the value added, contradictions, or other unique characteristics of the information ◇ determines whether the initial query should be revised
Competency Standard Four: The information literate student, individually or as a member of a group, uses information effectively to accomplish a specific purpose.	◇ understands many of the ethical, legal, and socioeconomic issues surrounding information and information technology ◇ acknowledges the use of information sources in communicating the product or performance

Source. Association of College and Research Libraries, 2000. Reprinted with permission.

How we work with students' beliefs provides a good example to illustrate the relationship between Krumboltz's (1996) learning theory and the use of the ARCL (2000) *Information Literacy Competency Standards for Higher Education*. As addressed previously, some ungrounded beliefs can paralyze the exploration process. Most advisors who have worked with undecided first-year students have encountered some variation of the unrealistic starting salary expectation or the unwillingness to consider a particular academic major because there is not a clear relationship between the major and an associated occupation. Clearly, when working with undecided first-year students, we should be encouraging them to ground these beliefs with evidence while reinforcing the process itself. An example to encourage this activity would be using web sites that offer examples of starting salaries or ones that show what occupations graduates of particular majors pursue. The ARCL standards provide numerous teachable moments for advisors. For example, the standards suggest that advisors need to be concerned with assisting students ground unfounded beliefs and consciously realize the cognitive and affective decisions they are making as a result of using information from the Internet. For the interested reader, Rockman (2004) provides additional strategies for integrating information literacy with instruction.

Teaching computer skills throughout students' postsecondary career is critical. Levy and Murnane (2004) identified five categories of work: (a) expert thinking, (b) complex communication, (c) routine manual, (d) routine cognition, and (e) non-routine manual. Of these five, the first two, expert thinking and complex communication occupations will see growth in the future economy. Both of these categories share two major characteristics: (a) most of the occupations within each requires a postsecondary education, and (b) the occupations in these categories will use computers to complement tasks they will perform. Some of the general tasks that define these categories include:

◇ Problem-solving in which there is no rule-based solutions (expert thinking)
◇ Interacting with humans to acquire information, to explain it, or to persuade others of its implications for action (complex communication)

By using the Internet as a tool in the exploration process, advisors can help students access a rich resource of academic and occupation information. By approaching its use in a critical inquiry-based method, advisors can help students integrate this technology into their decision making processes thus advancing with the educational mission of the institution for life-long learning and assisting their students with demonstrable career-related skills.

The critical thinking that occurs between an undecided student and an advisor can be more thoughtfully planned using Bloom's taxonomy (Clark, 2005) and the ACRL's information literacy guidelines (2000). In the end, an advisor who is familiar with these constructs can interact and create a more purposeful academic and career exploration for undecided students.

The Art of Teaching First-Year Undecided Students

Gordon (1984) describes educational planning as "a process in which each college student is involved in self-assessment, exploring and integrating academic and career alternatives, and making decisions that are personally relevant for the present and for the future" (p. 123). Helping students to achieve this goal calls for multiple approaches, resources, and tools. A series of suggestions are listed below.

◇ Use a variety of media instead of relying solely on dialogue and conversation. This is also a helpful way to address differences in students' learning styles.
◇ Remember that not all students are the same.
◇ Do not expect all students to complete the exploration process at the end of their first year at a level and depth that shows the most complex behaviors associated with Bloom's cognitive and affective domains.
◇ Students should be encouraged to explain their thinking and how they arrive at conclusions. Expect students to be able to explain their decisions using Bloom's taxonomy (Clark, 2005) and the ACRL's (2000) information literacy guidelines as reference. This process can help them learn good decision making.

◇ Expect some students to change their minds. The process is not linear. There are false starts and hypotheses that are not confirmed by action. These are key moments for support and challenge.

◇ Expect some decided first-year students to become undecided. As the literature suggests, declaration of a major does not necessarily mean that a thorough decision was made or that some first-year decided students actually explored their initial choice.

◇ Remember advisors always play an important role.

◇ Assist students with developmental issues when undecided students declare a major and begin working with an advisor in a "declared area" after the first year. The heart of these issues will involve decision making and the models presented here.

◇ Engage the larger institutional community for assistance by recruiting alumni and seniors to volunteer as resources for information interviewing. One-on-one informational interviews help students move beyond text- or Internet-based sources by having students conduct interviews that can help highlight personal perspectives.

◇ Invite librarians to assist by helping students learn more about the relationship between information literacy and their academic assignments. Work with other faculty to design appropriate in-class assignments that facilitate the major and career exploration process with an academic discipline.

◇ Be aware of the influence parents and other family members may have on the undecided student. More than past generations, the current generation of students (the Millennial generation) tends to make decisions jointly with their parents (Howe & Strauss, 2003). Develop advising strategies for working with undecided students and their parents.

◇ View creating resources that assist undecided students as part of curriculum development. An example would be pulling together resources such as lists of seniors or alumni in specific majors for informational interviewing.

◇ Create a student mentoring program by using sophomore- and junior-level students who have engaged in the exploration process to facilitate peer learning and support.

◇ Provide and encourage other forms of support.

◇ Use living-learning programs for undecided students in the residence halls to build a support system and facilitate adjustment. Use a student-produced blog that focuses on sharing experiences related to the exploration process to provide additional means of support. Hold office hours in person or through technology and conduct programming designed to help students explore in the residence halls.

◇ Consider organizing the links and resources based on a decision-making model when designing a resource web site (McDonald & Steele, 1998).

◇ Use the Internet as an active tool. Develop activities and lessons that help guide a student to use higher levels of cognitive and affective reasoning skills. Use the Internet as a resource for self-assessment, academic, and occupational information. While many Millennials feel comfortable using technology, they may not be familiar with using it in a scholarly environment. Use information literacy guidelines as a context for enriched and critical learning.

◇ Remind students of the mental processes they are using to reach decisions. Help them be aware and model good critical-thinking skills.

◇ Consider using Instant Messenger as an additional mode of communicating with students for quick questions and "just-in-time" responses.

◇ Develop a podcast for delivering information and promoting advising services.

Summary

Undecided first-year students may benefit the most from a learning approach to academic advising. Some undecided students are overwhelmed by the number of academic options that exist and become paralyzed during the exploration process, while other undecided students may be reluctant to choose a major for fear it may be the wrong major. Some undecided students may have ideas about certain majors, but need time to explore and gather information before they commit to a particular major. Uncertainty can be anxiety provoking for these students; nevertheless, it can also be viewed as a prime opportunity for students to learn about themselves and the decision-making process.

Institutions need to know how undecided students are labeled and viewed. Those institutions that encourage (or require) students to declare a major at matriculation may be sending a message that it is wrong to be uncertain. Tinto (2004) suggests that such a view is shortsighted. Institutions that do not address the advising needs of special populations of students, including undecided students, may be impacted adversely in terms of retention (Tinto). In reality, most traditional-aged, postsecondary students have been exposed to a limited number of academic subjects and occupations. As a logical consequence, many students who enter higher education as declared will change their minds during their postsecondary career. Gordon (1995a) states that "The first year in college should be the time when students begin to lay the foundation for a lifetime of career choices and maintenance" (p. 99). Teaching undecided first-year students a process for making academic and career decisions should be a priority at all institutions.

References

Appel, V., Haak, R., & Witzke, D. (1970). Factors associated with indecision about collegiate major and career choice. *Proceedings, American Psychological Association*, 667-668.

Association of College and Research Libraries (ACRL). (2000). *Objectives for information literacy instruction: A model statement for academic librarians*. Retrieved May 17, 2006, from http://www.ala.org/ala/acrl/acrlstandards/informationliteracycompetency.htm

Baird, L. (1967). *The undecided student—How different is he?* (ACT Research Report, No. 2). Iowa City, IA: American College Testing Program.

Bloom, B. S., Mesia, B. B., & Krathwohl, D. R. (1964). *Taxonomy of educational objectives* (vols. 1-2). New York: David McKay.

Clark, D. (2005). *Learning domains or Bloom's taxonomy*. Retrieved May 23, 2005, from http://www.nwlink.com/~donclark/hrd/bloom.html

Fuqua, D. R., Seaworth, T. B., & Newman, J. L. (1987). The relationship of career indecision and anxiety: A multivariate examination. *Journal of Vocational Behavior, 30*(2), 175-186.

Gaffner, D. C., & Hazler, R. J. (2002). Factors related to indecisiveness and career indecision in undecided college students. *Journal of College Student Development, 4*(3), 317-326.

Gianakos, I., & Subich, L. M. (1986). The relationship of gender and sex-role orientation to vocational undecidedness. *Journal of Vocational Behavior, 29*(1), 42-50.

Goodstein L. (1965). Behavior theoretical views of counseling. In B. Steffre (Ed.), *Theories of counseling* (pp. 140-192). New York: McGraw-Hill.

Gordon, V. (1984). Educational planning: Helping students make decisions. In R. B. Winston, Jr., T. K. Miller, S. C. Ender, T. J. Grites, & Associates (Eds.), *Developmental academic advising: Addressing students' educational career, and personal needs.* (pp. 123-146). San Francisco: Jossey-Bass.

Gordon, V. (1995a) Advising first-year undecided students. In M. L. Upcraft & G. L. Kramer, (Eds.), *First-year academic advising: Patterns in the present, pathways to the future* (Monograph No. 18, pp. 93-100). Columbia, SC: University of South Carolina, National Resource Center for The Freshman Year Experience and Students in Transition.

Gordon, V. (1995b). *The undecided college student: An academic and career advising challenge.* Springfield, IL: Charles C. Thomas.

Gordon, V. N. (1998). Career decidedness types. *The Career Development Quarterly, 46*(4), 386–403.

Hagstrom, S. J., Skovholt, T. M., & Rivers, D. A. (1997). The advanced undecided college student: A qualitative study. *NACADA Journal, 17*(2), 23–30.

Holland, J. L., & Holland, J. E. (1977). Vocational indecision: More evidence and speculation. *Journal of Counseling Psychology, 24*(4), 404-414.

Howe, N., & Strauss, W. (2003). *Millennials go to college—Strategies for a new generation on campus: Recruiting and admissions, campus life, and the classroom.* Washington, DC: Life Course Associates and American Association of Collegiate Registrars and Admissions Officers (AACRAO).

Kimes, H. G., & Troth, W. A. (1974). Relationship of trait anxiety to career decisiveness. *Journal of Counseling Psychology, 21*(4), 277-280.

Krumboltz, J. D. (1992). *Challenging troublesome career beliefs.* Ann Arbor, MI: Clearinghouse on Counseling and Personnel Services. (ERIC Document Reproduction Services No. ED 347 481)

Krumboltz, J. D. (1996). A learning theory of career counseling. In M. L. Savickas & W. B. Walsh, (Eds.), *Handbook of career counseling theory and practice* (pp. 55-79). Palo Alto, CA: Davies-Black.

Krumboltz, J. D., Vidalakis, N., & Tyson, J. (2000). *Virtual Job Experience: Try before you choose.* Paper presented at the meeting of the American Educational Research Association, New Orleans, LA. (ERIC Document Reproduction Services No. ED 442 961)

Larson, L. M., & Heppner, P. P. (1995). The relationship of problem-solving appraisal to career decision and indecision. *Journal of Vocational Behavior, 26*(1), 55-65.

Levy, F., & Murnane, R. J. (2004). *The new division of labor.* Princeton, NJ: Princeton University Press.

Lewallen, W. C. (1993). The impact of being "undecided" on college-student persistence. *Journal of College Student Development, 34*(2), 103-112.

Mau, W. (1995). Decision making style as a predictor of career decision making status and treatment gains. *Journal of Career Assessment, 3*(1), 89-99.

McDonald, M. L., & Steele, G. E. (1998, Winter). The growing role of web-based advising, *The Keystone, Newsletter of the Wadsworth College Success Series, 5*.

Mitchell, L. K., & Krumboltz, J. D. (1996). Krumboltz's learning theory of career choice and counseling. In D. Brown, L. Brooks, & Associates (Eds.), *Career choice and development* (pp. 233-280). San Francisco: Jossey-Bass.

Nutt, C. (2000). One-on-one advising. In V. N. Gordon & W. R. Habley (Eds.), *Academic advising: A comprehensive handbook* (pp. 220-227). San Francisco: Jossey-Bass.

Newman, J. L., & Fuqua, D. L. (1990). Further evidence for the use of career subtypes in defining career status. *Career Development Quarterly, 39*(2), 176-188.

Rockman, I. F., & Associates. (2004). *Integrating information literacy into higher education curriculum: Practical models for transformation.* San Francisco: Jossey-Bass.

Salamone, P. R. (1982). Difficult cases in career counseling: II – The indecisive client. *Personnel and Guidance Journal, 60*(8), 496-499.

Savickas, M. L., & Jorgourna, D. (1991). The Career Decision Scale as a type of indicator. *Journal of Counseling Psychology, 38*(1), 85-90.

Spight, D. B. (2005). Letter to the editor: The pros and cons of solution-focused advising with the undecided student: A reply to Mayhall and Burg. *NACADA Journal, 25*(1), 14-15.

Steele, G. E. (2003). A research-based approach to working with undecided students: A case studies illustration, *NACADA Journal, 23*(1 & 2), 10-20.

Taylor, K. M., & Betz, N. E. (1983). Application of self-efficacy theory to the understanding and treatment of career indecision. *Journal of Vocational Behavior, 22*(1), 63-81.

Tinto, V. (2004). *Student retention and graduation: Facing the truth, living with the consequences.* Retrieved May 23, 2005, from http://www.pellinstitute.org/publications.html

Van Matre, G., & Cooper, S. (1984). Concurrent evaluation of career indecision and indecisiveness. *Personnel and Guidance Journal, 62*(10), 637-639.

Appendix

Examples of Career Web Sites

America's Career InfoNet – Contains current market and occupational trends, employment opportunities, demographic and economic data; searchable
http://www.acinet.org/acinet/

Career Choices – Canadian site for exploring occupations; alphabetical detailed description of occupational choices
http://www.umanitoba.ca/counselling/careers.html

Future Jobs – Canadian site that contains national occupational trends and outlooks, listings of field of study with accompanying career outlook including salary expectations
http://www.hrdc-drhc.gc.ca/redirect_hr.html

Occupational Outlook Handbook – A comprehensive searchable career database; each description includes required training and education, current salary trends, work environment, employment trends and related occupations
http://stats.bls.gov/oco/

O*Net – The Occupational Information Network (O*NET) and O*NET OnLine were developed for the US Department of Labor by the National O*NET Consortium. Features include: accessing occupational information, conducting a skills match to find occupations, and conducting a cross-walk career search
http://www.doleta.gov/programs/onet/

US Census Bureau – Includes income statistics and demographic and economic information related to career opportunities and job trends
http://www.census.gov/hhes/www/income/income.html

Chapter Fourteen

First-Generation College Students: First-Year Challenges

Ruth A. Darling and Melissa Scandlyn Smith

As educators we do these students no great favor should they become—out of our own awareness—confused, frightened, and alienated, only to drift away and drop out. If we…mean for them to stay and not become attrition statistics, we need a keener understanding of the sensibilities and concerns they bring with them and of the difficulties they encounter along the way (London, 1989, p. 118).

First-generation students are a growing and diverse campus population. In the fall of 2003, 14.9 million undergraduate students enrolled in postsecondary institutions nationwide (National Center for Education Statistics, 2005). The exact percentage of these students who fit the first-generation student profile is unclear, but existing research places the figure at anywhere between 31% (Somers, Woodhouse, & Cofer, 2004) and 45% (McConnell, 2000) of the higher education population. Regardless, this percentage translates into a formidable segment of the student population, a population that has more difficulty being successful in the postsecondary environment. These students bring with them unique characteristics, needs, and expectations that impact their daily campus life and their successful progress toward degree attainment. This chapter will examine the student characteristics and issues first-generation students face as they attempt to navigate our institutional cultures and offer appropriate academic advising strategies and learning outcomes for them. In addition, we will review resources available for those who advise first-generation students.

Characteristics of First-Generation College Students

The term "first-generation college student" has taken on more than one meaning in current research, depending on the parameters of researchers' projects. In simplest terms, a first-generation college student is an undergraduate whose parents have no college experience (McConnell, 2000). There have always been first-generation students, but, in the last few decades, this student population has become a topic drawing the serious attention of faculty, administrators, and staff within postsecondary education. First-generation college students tend to share certain characteristics, falling into two categories: (a) those attributable to the group as they finish high school and (b) those that develop during their enrollment in institutions of higher education. Research on first-generation students as they graduate and enroll in higher education institutions (Ishitani, 2003; Lohfink & Paulsen, 2005; Ting, 1998; Warburton, Bugarin, & Nuñez, 2001) indicates the following similarities:

◇ They tend to be from low-income families.
◇ They tend to be members of racial or ethnic minority groups, particularly Hispanic or African American.
◇ They are more likely to be female than male.
◇ They tend to have lower college entrance examination scores.
◇ They tend to be less well prepared academically for college.
◇ They perceive that they are lacking support from those at home, including family and friends.

These factors, alone or in combination with each other, put first-generation students at a disadvantage before they ever step onto campus.

Once their education is underway, these students take on an additional set of characteristics. Research (Chen, 2005; London, 1989, 1992; Pascarella, Pierson, Wolniak, & Terenzini, 2004; Richardson & Skinner, 1992; Somers et al., 2004) suggests these students develop the following traits:

◇ They have lower first-semester and first-year grade point averages (GPA) than their classmates.
◇ They are more likely to drop out during the first year.
◇ They are more likely to attend classes part-time and work full-time.
◇ They tend to experience cultural difficulties in the transition; they often feel marginalized by both the culture they are leaving behind and the one that they are joining.
◇ They encounter lower faculty expectations and have lower self-esteem.
◇ They are more likely to enroll in a two-year institution or community college.
◇ They are more likely to leave without a degree.

Coupling these characteristics with those the students might bring with them from high school and home puts these students at a distinct disadvantage as they attempt to navigate our campuses and engage in postsecondary learning.

First-Year Challenges

Family values, race and ethnicity, socioeconomic status, learning skills, the ability to navigate the culture, and finding connections within that culture are issues that bring daily challenges to first-generation students. Each of these issues influence how these students approach life in the institution and in their academic programs and have a direct relationship to their persistence and graduation rates.

First-generation students come from families with parents who have no experience with higher education. This is a disadvantage in three ways. First, family members of first-generation students have no knowledge of the higher education system; therefore, they cannot guide their students in the same way as parents with college experience can (Horn & Nuñez, 2000; Pascarella et al., 2004). Second, the students have issues with challenging the role assignments that have been a part of their family values, which leads to guilt, shame, and confusion when they begin to change because of their college experiences (Lara, 1992; Lohfink & Paulsen, 2005; London,

1989, 1992; Orbe, 2004; Somers et al., 2004). Third, because of their background they tend to view college as something they have to do to get a better job or prepare for a specific career; they do not view a college education in relation to any kind of personal development (Hahs-Vaughan, 2004; Lee, Sax, & Kim, 2005; Longwell-Grice, 2003; McConnell, 2000; Nuñez, 1998; Richardson & Skinner, 1992). Most students do seek out higher education to further their careers, but first-generation students are more likely to report this as the sole reason they enroll. They do not identify higher education as providing anything other than the path to a better lifestyle than what their parents have.

Race and ethnicity, in combination with first-generation status, are related to how well students succeed in the institutional structure. We have already established that students from racial and ethnic minority groups are more likely to be first-generation college students; they are also more likely to attend community college, attend in nontraditional ways (i.e., part-time attendance or breaks in attendance), encounter low faculty expectations, have lower self-concepts and feelings of support (Dennis, Phinney, & Chuateco, 2005; Lohfink & Paulsen, 2005; Richardson & Skinner, 1992).

Socioeconomic status also plays a role in the attendance and success of this population. Being from lower-income families affects their behaviors: They work more hours, often off campus, to fund their education and their family expenses. They are more likely to receive financial aid than other students but are wary of incurring debt, so they often work off-campus instead of borrowing money. The type of financial aid they receive, therefore, affects how connected they become to the campus. They are much more likely to be involved in campus life when their financial aid package consists primarily of grants, work-study funds, and any other funds besides student loans. They also seek specific academic programs that are located close to their homes and are low in cost so that they can maintain their financial responsibilities and their family connections (Lohfink & Paulsen, 2005; Longwell-Grice, 2003; Nuñez, 1998; Orbe, 2004).

Individual learning skills affect all college students, but first-generation students are less likely to have mastery in these areas. Self-regulation skills, such as good time management and study skills, empower students and engage them in the process of learning. Williams and Hellman (1998) show that the link between these skills and academic success is strong and that there is a need to teach these skills to the first-generation students who feel they are lacking in these areas. Naumann, Debora, and Gutkin (2003) raise the importance by suggesting that self-regulated learning is the most significant factor that relates to GPA for first-generation students, i.e., the greater the skills, the higher the GPA.

First-generation students are often less prepared academically for college. Some first-generation students lack learning skills or foundational knowledge because of their course selection, both in secondary school and in college. Horn and Nuñez (2000) report that the path to academic success begins in middle school. They show that students who take high school level algebra in the eighth grade and take advanced math classes in high school are significantly more likely to enroll in college, particularly in a four-year institution. First-generation students are far less likely to do either. Horn and Nuñez attribute this, in part, to the difference in parent involvement in secondary school curriculum programs. Parents who attended college are more involved in their students' class choices than parents who did not attend college.

Research shows that parents' educational level also relates to the college coursework and their students' choice of major. First-generation students complete fewer courses during their first year, including fewer courses in humanities, fine arts, math, science, computer science, history, and foreign languages (Chen, 2005; Pascarella et al., 2004;). Warburton et al. (2001) and Chen also show that first-generation students are more likely to major in either a vocational or technical field, a social science, or in business or management than to choose a major in a "high-skill" field (Chen, p. v) or in a field that might be perceived to be low-earning. These factors, coupled with lack of academic preparedness and self-regulation skills, are strongly related to long-term educational outcomes and persistence to a bachelor's degree.

The ability to navigate the college culture is another skill that is necessary for success, but first-generation students are often poorly prepared to do this. Before entering college, these students have little information about application procedures and financial aid opportunities, and their parents are not in a position to be of assistance (Horn & Nuñez, 2000; Pascarella et al., 2004). Richardson and Skinner (1992) demonstrate that first-generation students need someone to explain the bureaucracy of the college administration, as they find it both intimidating and confusing. Once they arrive at college, they often perceive faculty and administrators as relatively indifferent to them and sometimes even hostile (Longwell-Grice, 2003).

The final challenge for first-generation students is connection to the college culture. Not only are many first-generation students unable to navigate the college structure and culture, they are also not attempting to become a part of it. As these students tend to be older, have family responsibilities, and work and live off-campus, they are more likely to come to campus only to attend classes. Richardson and Skinner (1992) indicate that immersion in the student role is critical for student success. Several other researchers (e.g., Lee et al., 2004; Lohfink & Paulsen, 2005; Longwell-Grice, 2003; Olenchak & Hebert, 2002) report that students who are intentionally drawn into the college environment, both inside and outside of the classroom, get more out of their college experience, face fewer challenges, and are more likely to succeed than those who are not integrated. Pascarella et. al (2004) found that although first-generation students are less likely to be involved in campus activities, they reap much greater rewards from this kind of involvement than other students do. At the same time, it is necessary to remember the "dual socialization" process referred to by Lohfink and Paulsen (2005) "that is both the connection to their native cultures, family life, and family support as well as to those aspects of college life that serve to benefit them" (p. 420).

Academic Advising Models, Strategies, and Approaches

First-generation college students have challenges in their first college year because of past experiences and perspectives. It is critical for academic advisors to consider the broader issues when working with these students (e.g., family values, low socioeconomic status, limited preparation). Academic advisors and administrators can be instrumental at all levels in addressing the needs of first-generation students and developing academic advising strategies and approaches that serve as frameworks for discussion, program implementation, and assessment. The literature on first-generation college students clearly presents issues that reach across four-year and two-year institutions, academic affairs and student affairs, to institutional research and community/high school relations. The following campus advising strategies and approaches take the form of a plan or an approach to implement at the individual, departmental, or institutional level and involve campus-wide collaborations and partnerships.

Establish a group on campus that has a shared interest in the academic success of first-generation college students. This group could range from only advising colleagues to a campus-wide enrollment management committee. Broader participation (e.g., faculty, academic advisors, first-year seminar instructors, student affairs staff, institutional research staff, and first-generation students) might result in a more informed and strategic use of campus programs and resources as well as a shared knowledge base that focuses on first-generation students and their needs. The purpose of such a group might be to assess the campus culture relative to the first-generation student population and to recommend advising and programmatic implications and initiatives.

Use institutional data concerning first-generation students. Most institutions have offices of institutional research that might already collect data on who the first-generation students are, or the admissions office might collect similar data on the admission application. It is important to identify the population and basic demographics, perhaps unique to your institution, before designing and initiating new efforts. Because the first-generation population is so diverse, efforts need to focus on the unique characteristics of the students and of the institution itself. It is important to consider if the national demographics and the literature on first-generation students provide information that might be useful in local, institutional initiatives and methods of gathering data.

Explore opportunities for pre-college enrollment academic advising. The literature reviewed at the beginning of this chapter clearly indicates that high academic aspirations begin with middle and high school curriculum selection and early major/career information. Partnering with admissions counselors and recruiters might provide opportunities for advisors to meet with prospective first-generation students and parents as well as high school guidance counselors who work with the families and students. Information concerning majors and careers, high school pre-requisite requirements for successful college learning, and academic advising and support services available on the campus will help better prepare both parents and students for the transition to college. Such efforts also begin the "relationship" building with academic advisors that is viewed as critical by first-generation students.

As noted by Richardson and Skinner (1992), collaborative efforts among an area's secondary schools, community colleges, and universities to develop summer bridge programs, academic support services, and networking groups for first-generation students entering postsecondary institutions is found to contribute to academic success and persistence. Academic advisors and administrators could partner with surrounding secondary and postsecondary institutions to design and implement bridge programs that emphasize academic success strategies for both pre-college coursework as well as for future academic work in college.

Provide comprehensive academic advising during summer orientation programs. Academic advisors need to create learning outcomes for orientation advising that are realistic and address the immediate needs of students—especially first-generation students who might possess little knowledge of college learning, curricula, and academic daily life. What the students should learn and accomplish during that first orientation advising session varies by campus and within departments but should be thoughtfully addressed by advisors and administrators.

Of main concern should be an assessment of the students' academic preparedness and appropriate placement in first-year courses based on that assessment. As previously discussed, first-generation students are academically at risk due to a lack of academic preparedness and lack of the academic skills (i.e., time management, study skills, reading college texts) needed to be successful at the college level. As a result, these students typically have a lower first-term GPA than other students. A thoughtfully crafted first-year schedule based on an accurate assessment of strengths and weaknesses is critical to the success of this particular group of students. Students also need to know and understand the basic "survival" skills of the first several weeks on campus—how to contact academic advisors, where to get textbooks, and where classrooms are located.

The transition model and the novice-to-expert model discussed in the first chapter are helpful frameworks to review when designing this first orientation advising experience. These models emphasize the importance of developing an academic plan with the students as they enter and move through their first year. In addition, the models focus on the relationship between the student and advisor as one that continues over time. Again, this approach emphasizes the first-generation students' need to establish a strong academic contact that provides validation, "that they can do college-level work, that their ideas and opinions have value, that they are worthy of the attention and respect of faculty, staff and peers alike" (Terenzini et al., 1994, p. 70).

Adopt appropriate advising models. Within the institutional structure, academic advisors have a special role in the academic and social lives of their first-generation students. First-generation students sometimes rely on their academic advisors for non-academic guidance when they feel that they are missing this kind of support from their families. They want to build a trusting relationship with their advisor based on the advisor's understanding of their past experiences and background. They rely on their advisor to have a comprehensive knowledge of campus programs and to help them access those resources (Sickles, 2004).

Somers et al. (2004) propose that academic advisors work in combination with personal and career counselors to address first-generation issues in a comprehensive manner. The complicated issues brought to campus by the students require a network of support from various units across campuses. Academic advisors can offer students strategies to help them adjust to the educational environment. Such strategies include helping students find a focus for their studies within diverse curriculum options, recommending that students find peer support groups, and suggesting that students minimize the size of the campus by finding certain physical areas on campus to which they can retreat (Richardson & Skinner, 1992). Reducing the size of the larger community could involve referring the students to an academic club within a certain major, seeking membership in a living/learning community, joining an organization that matches the student's interests, or simply utilizing a study lounge designated for commuter students.

Again, in the first chapter of this monograph, the author introduces two models that provide practical ways the academic advisor can teach first-year students about the transition into college life. These models clearly address the issues encountered by first-generation college students by focusing on the experiences the students bring to college, how the students interpret their first year based on those experiences, and the need for academic advisors to teach students how to make new meanings of their experiences that connect with the collegiate culture. At various points during the first year, it is important that the students begin to understand the following:

◇ The nature of college learning
◇ The meaning and purpose underlying the curriculum (i.e., general education requirements, potential majors, and electives)
◇ The resources available to explore majors and careers
◇ The academic support programs available (i.e., "early alert" academic warning program, study skills, and time-management seminars)
◇ The various ways to connect to the academic community through discipline-oriented clubs and organizations
◇ The academic criteria that might be attached to financial aid packages
◇ The social opportunities that connect the curricular to the cocurricular such as activities that focus on diversity, cultural programs, lecture series, and recreational clubs

Connect through first-year seminars. The transition from orientation to advising during the first year is often when first-generation students experience a disconnect from our campus communities. First-year seminars that emphasize advisors' early and continued contact with first-generation students help bridge the gaps in experience and knowledge that many of these students experience. Continued emphasis on connecting with instructors and academic skill-building opportunities is critical during the first year, as is a continued assessment of the student's academic progress or lack thereof.

The first-year seminar instructor can serve as a guide in the process of helping the student find programs, additional campus resources, and peer groups that provide the connections necessary for academic success and a sense of belonging to the campus community. As noted earlier, there is a rich representation of racial and ethnic diversity among first-generation students. Helping these students integrate into the larger community and create meaningful connections and relationships with peers, faculty, and staff is critical to how well these students adjust to campus life and achieve academic success.

First-year seminars can serve as a vehicle for connecting first-generation students to the campus and college learning by:

◇ Providing opportunities for students to engage in campus-based activities with their peers
◇ Connecting the academic and cocurricular with the home and family experiences of the students
◇ Using peer mentors who serve as role models and provide a consistent source of support throughout the first year
◇ Incorporating a strong emphasis on academic success skills (i.e., time management, study skills, college reading, test taking skills, wellness) into the seminars
◇ Familiarizing students with the mission and purpose of the institution and using academic advisors to teach students how the curriculum connects to the larger context as well as to the individual students' academic goals and experiences

Serve as the first-generation students' advocate and as a campus educator. Academic advisors and administrators are in a unique position to provide information about first-generation students to various campus constituencies. First-generation students first come to the attention of academic advisors and administrators because of their lower rate of academic progress and the various academic challenges they face. Often, low retention rates appear on our reports, representing students already lost from our institutions.

As cited in the literature review, professors, instructors, and other academic contacts are critical to first-generation students and how they connect with our campus cultures. Academic advisors and administrators could develop and teach seminars that bring faculty, graduate teaching assistants, academic advisors, and first-year seminar instructors together to focus on the demographics, the diversity, and the academic concerns of this student group. The understanding and knowledge gained by the participants would enrich the campus learning environment for the first-generation student population and provide a clearer picture of a particular campus' first-generation population and their specific needs. The same information would benefit student affairs and student services colleagues as they consider services and programming initiatives that are more non-traditional in nature.

Serving as an advocate and educator can reach beyond the campus boundaries to the homes and families of first-generation students. Many institutions are supporting parent's associations with staff who keep in touch with parents and provide a network for communication. Reaching out to parents and family members through such organizations helps families better understand the nature of home-to-college transitions. Academic advisors and administrators can write articles for family/parent newsletters or for web sites that focus on first-generation transition issues, and they can serve as speakers for parent groups.

Conclusion

The final phrase of London's (1989) quote on page one of this chapter summarizes how we, as academic advisors and administrators, must move to critically address the needs of the first-generation college students on our campuses. This chapter presents national data and research that describe first-generation students and the characteristics they bring to our campuses, characteristics that often result in concerns that make it difficult for these students to be academically successful. Models, strategies, and approaches are proposed that assist the academic advisor and advising administrator in the design and implementation of programs focusing on first-generation students. Campus-wide collaborations with colleagues in student affairs, student services, and institutional research are also suggested. In the research study conducted by Lohfink and Paulsen (2005), they indicate that first-generation students are more likely to persist if they are engaged in academic activities. As academic advisors and administrators, we are uniquely positioned within our institutions to connect first-generation students with our educational communities in ways that provide opportunities for them to be academically successful and to earn their degrees.

References

Chen, X. (2005). *First generation students in postsecondary education: A look at their college transcripts* (NCES 2005-171). Washington, DC: National Center for Education Statistics, U.S. Department of Education, U.S. Government Printing Office.

Dennis, J. M., Phinney, J. S., & Chuateco, L. I. (2005). The role of motivation, parental support, and peer support in the academic success of ethnic minority first-generation college students. *Journal of College Student Development, 46*(3), 223-236.

Hahs-Vaughan, D. (2004). The impact of parents' education level on college students: An analysis using the beginning postsecondary students longitudinal study 1990-92/94. *Journal of College Student Development, 45*(5), 483-500.

Horn, L., & Nuñez, A. (2000). Mapping the road to college: First-generation students' math track, planning strategies, and context of support. *Education Statistics Quarterly, 2*(1). Retrieved August 30, 2005, from http://nces.ed.gov/programs/quarterly/vol_2/2_1/q5-1.asp

Ishitani, T. T. (2003). A longitudinal approach to assessing attrition behavior among first-generation students: Time-varying effects of pre-college characteristics. *Research in Higher Education, 44*(4), 433-449.

Lara, J. (1992). Reflections: Bridging cultures. In L. S. Zwerling & H. B. London (Eds.), *First-generation students: Confronting the cultural issues* (pp. 65-70). San Francisco: Jossey-Bass.

Lee, J. J., Sax, L. J., & Kim, K. A. (2005). Understanding students' parental education beyond first-generation status. *Community College Review, 32*(1), 1-20.

Lohfink, M. M., & Paulsen, M. B. (2005). Comparing the determinants of persistence for first-generation and continuing-generation students. *Journal of College Student Development, 46*(4), 409-428.

London, H. B. (1989). Breaking away: A study of first-generation college students and their families. *American Journal of Education, 97*(1), 144-170.

London, H. B. (1992). Transformations: Cultural challenges faced by first-generation students. In L. S. Zwerling & H. B. London (Eds.), *First-generation students: Confronting the cultural issues* (pp. 5-12). San Francisco: Jossey-Bass.

Longwell-Grice, R. (2003). Get a job: Working class students discuss the purpose of college. *The College Student Affairs Journal, 23*(1), 40-53.

McConnell, P. J. (2000). What community colleges should do to assist first-generation students. *Community College Review, 28*(3), 75-87.

National Center for Education Statistics. (2005). *Enrollment in postsecondary institutions, fall 2003; Graduation rates 1997 & 200 cohorts; and financial statistics, fiscal year 2003.* Washington, DC: U.S. Department of Education. Retrieved September 1, 2005, from http://nces.ed.gov/pubs2005/2005177.pdf

Naumann, W. C., Debora, B., & Gutkin, T. B. (2003). Identifying variables that predict college success for first-generation college students. *Journal of College Admission, 181*, 4-9.

Nuñez, A. (1998, November). *First-generation students: A longitudinal analysis of educational and early labor market outcomes.* Paper presented at the Annual Meeting of Association for the Study of Higher Education. Miami, FL.

Olenchak, F. R., & Hebert, T. P. (2002). Endangered academic talent: Lessons from gifted first-generation college males. *Journal of College Student Development, 43*(2), 195-212.

Orbe, M. P. (2004). Negotiating multiple identities within multiple frames: An analysis of first-generation college students. *Communication Education, 53*(2), 131-149.

Pascarella, E. T., Pierson, C. T., Wolniak, G. C., & Terenzini, P. T. (2004). First-generation college students: Additional evidence on college experiences and outcomes. *Journal of Higher Education, 75*(3), 249-284.

Richardson, R. C., Jr., & Skinner, E. F. (1992). Helping first-generation minority students achieve degrees. In L. S. Zwerling & H. B. London (Eds.), *First-generation students: Confronting the cultural issues* (pp. 29-44). San Francisco: Jossey-Bass.

Sickles, A. R. (2004). *Advising first-generation students.* Retrieved June 29, 2005, from http://www.nacada.ksu.edu/Clearinghouse/AdvisingIssues/1st_Generation.htm

Somers, P., Woodhouse, S., & Cofer, J. (2004). Pushing the boulder uphill: The persistence of first-generation college students. *NASPA Journal, 41*(3), 418-435.

Terenzini, P. T., Rendón, L. I., Updraft, M. L., Millar, S. B., Allison, K. W., Gregg, P. L., et al. (1994). The transition to college: Diverse students, diverse stories. *Research in Higher Education, 35*(1), 57-73.

Ting, S. (1998). Predicting first-year grades and academic progress of college students of first-generation and low-income families. *Journal of College Admission, 158*, 14-23.

Warburton, E. C., Bugarin, R., & Nuñez, A. (2001). *Bridging the gap: Academic preparation and postsecondary success of first-generation students* (NCES 2001-153). Washington, DC: National Center for Education Statistics, U.S. Department of Education, U.S. Government Printing Office.

Williams, J., & Hellman, C. (1998). Investigating self-regulated learning among first-generation community college students. *Journal of Applied Research in the Community College, 5*(2), 83-87.

Appendix

Additional Resources for Advisors and Administrators

There are several federal agencies and programs that provide data and research on first-generation students as well as federally-funded programs housed on campuses of higher learning. These include:

⋄ The National Center for Education Statistics (NCES) at http://nces.ed.gov
⋄ Office of Postsecondary Education at http://www.ED.gov/index.jhtml
⋄ TRIO Programs
  ⋄ Ronald E. McNair Post-Baccalaureate Achievement Program
  ⋄ Student Support Services
  ⋄ Talent Search
  ⋄ Upward Bound
  ⋄ Upward Bound Math-Science.

Local and area resources to consider include summer bridge programs at both four-year and two-year institutions, admissions offices, and institutional research units.

Chapter Fifteen

Advising Lesbian, Gay, Bisexual, and Transgender First-Year Students

Casey Self

Every academic year, academic advisors have a wealth of information to teach all new students, while being sensitive to the diverse populations of students they serve. In the case of advising lesbian, gay, bisexual, and transgender (LGBT) students, many academic advisors may not be exposed to the needs and issues of these students as they are to other diverse identities such as race/ethnicity, ability level, religion, and socioeconomic class.

In most cases, institutions of higher education explicitly promote the value of attracting diverse student populations to our campuses. This value is evident in specific recruiting strategies that target underrepresented populations and marketing brochures that highlight academic and student services designed to assist these populations. Most recruiting efforts and marketing strategies, however, do not target LGBT students. Therefore, it is even more critical that LGBT students, once they arrive on campus, learn about resources that may assist them in their academic and social success.

For the purposes of this chapter, the terms lesbian (L) and gay (G) will be used to include those students, faculty, and staff who are attracted (romantically and/or sexually) to someone of the same sex or gender, the former with women and the latter with men. Bisexual (B) is used to include individuals who are attracted to individuals with similar and differing sex or gender. Transgender (T) will be used to describe those individuals with varying gender identity and/or expression different from what was assigned at birth. Students, faculty, and staff within the transgender community may identify themselves as lesbian, gay, bisexual, or heterosexual. When discussing and working with the LGBT community, it is imperative to recognize the diversity of gender and sexual orientation or identity for each individual.

Depending on a variety of issues such as rural/urban location, campus size, and values, universities and colleges vary in the level of support they offer their LGBT populations. Academic advisors should educate themselves on the campus climate regarding support for LGBT students and staff. An initial indication of support is evident in the campus non-discrimination policy and the inclusion (or exclusion) of sexual orientation and gender identity and expression in that policy. Other indicators of inclusiveness are the availability of domestic partner benefits for LGBT employees, a visible LGBT resource center and/or staff member designated to assist LGBT students, faculty, and staff, and an active SafeZone educational program.

Academic advisors have a tremendous opportunity to teach LGBT students about general resources. Advisors also have an opportunity to teach other professionals across campus the importance of welcoming our LGBT students immediately upon their arrival on campus through one-on-one appointments, providing information in office publications, or simply displaying LGBT-friendly materials such as a campus SafeZone placard.

First-Year Advising and the LGBT Student

First-year LGBT students arriving on campus may also be traditional-aged students, returning adults, transfer students, students with disabilities, athletes, and students with identifiable racial, ethnic, and religious affiliations. Society generally recognizes differences in people based on physical appearance. However, identifying LGBT students is not always possible through visual cues. LGB students who are comfortable with their sexual identity may provide visual indications such as clothing, jewelry, or buttons that demonstrate LGBT pride or community affiliation. Transgender students may wear clothing and style their hair as either masculine or feminine style dictates or mix the two. There are many symbols LGBT community members may use to identify themselves including rainbow-colored items, pink/black/purple triangles, and male/female gender symbols. Some LGBT students may be uncomfortable showing signs of public affection with their significant others while on campus. Other students will be "out and proud" and will leave no room for assumptions about their sexual orientation. Advisors may even observe, over time, the process of a students' coming out (i.e., acknowledging to others and/or themselves their LGBT identity) and their changing levels of comfort expressing their sexual and/or gender identity. Academic advisors may also observe multiple progressions of identity as a student develops.

First-year students may indicate they are struggling with issues regarding their sexual orientation/gender identity to academic advisors. Good academic advising interactions promote the development of a relationship between the advisor and student. In time, students may be comfortable enough with their advisor to begin sharing their feelings and possibly seek assistance.

New Student Orientation Programs

Many students experience their new campus and meet their academic advisors through orientation programs. Orientation is often viewed as "sealing the deal" in the student recruitment process by some, while others consider orientation as the official beginning of the college experience at that institution. In either case, first-year LGBT students need to see their LGBT community at orientation programs in the summer and immediately upon arrival in the fall. Advisors should teach students not only about academic programs, policies, and procedures, but also include other general information about the campus resources and support networks for all students, including LGBT students. Providing LGBT information, along with other resources in general, communicates inclusion without having the task of attempting to identify students who might be interested in these specific resources.

Major/Department/College Affiliation

Academic advisors who work with specific academic programs should be aware of any resources or programs for LGBT students in that academic arena. Advisors should also be aware of regional or national organizations specifically recruiting LGBT students into specific academic or career programs. One example of this is the law school admissions council publication, which invites LGBT student applications to law school. If there is a lack of information, academic advisors should encourage the development of resources that are focused on getting LGBT students into all fields.

Advisor Role in the Coming-Out Process

First-Year LGB Students

A common issue for LGB students is their comfort level with their sexual identity and their willingness to share this information with others. Academic advisors should be generally aware of LGB issues yet understand that the ultimate goal is not to have students feel pressured in any way to disclose their sexual identity in the advising setting. Conversations regarding sexual orientation should be initiated by the student and not by an academic advisor. If the student initiates conversations regarding sexual orientation, advisors should listen and offer appropriate referrals to students when necessary. Academic advisors also need to be careful not to allow stereotypical behaviors (e.g., attire, body mannerisms, and tone of voice) of a student to lead them to make assumptions about the student's sexual identity.

Academic advisors should enhance their understanding of the coming-out process. Exposure to sexual identity development models may provide insight for advisors who are seeking additional information. Evans, Forney, and Guido-DiBrito (1998) provide an overview of a variety of LGB identity-development models and address cultural issues for Hispanic, African American, Asian, and Native American LGB identity development. The Fassinger Model (Fassinger & Miller, 1997; McCarn & Fassinger, 1996) (see Table 1) describes two parallel developmental branches, Individual Sexual Identity and Group Membership Identity. This model attempts to demonstrate LGB development that is more inclusive of demographic and cultural influences such as cultural norms pertaining to gender expression and family roles, and less reliant in identity disclosure as a marker of developmental maturity. An individual's sexual identity, as any identity, is developed and personalized through non-linear experiences of contact, exposure, experimentation, representation, support, and community. Fassinger's model traces an individual's experiences with external forces and community contacts as well as internally through insight, perspective, effect, and comprehension. A person can be at any "location" on either branch of the model at any point in time as exposure and growth occur.

First-Year Transgender Students

Transgender students are often the most misunderstood college students by both LGB and heterosexual communities. Lees (1998) states "transgender persons are those not comfortable living within the confines of the social stereotypes of gender as applied to themselves…genitals do not determine identity" (p. 37). College may be the first opportunity for students to express gender or sexual identity issues openly. Academic advisors should be prepared to work with first-year students who may be at any stage of gender and sexuality identity development. Advisors need to demonstrate sensitivity and respect for students as they progress through their individual identity development. For example, it is appropriate to ask any student directly if they have a preferred name/pronoun other than what is on the student record.

Transgender identity development is difficult to communicate and understand completely by many individuals, including individuals who are experiencing the process. There is currently very little research completed regarding transgender identity development; however, some work is in progress. It may take a great deal of time for individuals to become comfortable expressing their identity in public and communicating their specific needs. Beemyn, Domingue, Pettitt, and Smith (2005) assist institutions in making their campus transgender-inclusive with specific

Table 1

Fassinger Model

Phases	Individual Sexual Identity	Group Membership Identity
Awareness	This phase describes an awareness of feeling different from the heterosexual norm; affective states are likely to include confusion, fear, and/or bewilderment.	This phase involves a new awareness of the existence of different sexual orientations in people. This realization often forces the individual to acknowledge that heterosexism exists and is likely to produce confusion and bewilderment.
Exploration	This phase involves exploration of strong (often erotic) feelings about other same-sex people or a particular same-sex person; affective states are likely to include longing, excitement, and wonder, as hitherto unknown aspects of one's sexuality are discovered.	In this phase, the individual is exploring his or her own attitudes toward gay/lesbian people as a group, as well as the possibility of membership in that group. This exploration is likely to produce anger, anxiety, and guilt due to an increasing awareness of heterosexism, but many individuals exploring the existence of other gays/lesbians also will experience a new found excitement, curiosity, and joy.
Deepening or Commitment	This phase involves a deepening of sexual and emotional self-knowledge, crystallization of choices about sexuality (e.g., deciding to relate exclusively to same-sex partners) and the recognition that preferred forms of intimacy imply certain things about identity. Since the context in which this deepening knowledge occurs is largely heterosexist and homophobic, moving through this phase may require addressing some of the group membership tasks in the other branch of the model. It is likely that anger and sadness as well as acceptance and self-assurance will occur.	This phase involves a deepening commitment to involvement in the lesbian/gay community, with increased awareness of the possible consequences that entails. These experiences are likely to be affectively reflected in a combination of excitement, pride, and rage, and for many, intense identification with the gay/lesbian community and rejection of heterosexual society.
Internalization or Synthesis	In this phase, the individual fully internalizes same-sex desire/love as a part of overall identity, a sense of internal consistency is likely to be manifested, characterized by unwillingness to change preferences and contentment and pride about those preferences.	The gay/lesbian individual has fully internalized his or her identity as a member of an oppressed group into his or her overall self-concept. This synthesis will be reflected in feelings of comfort, fulfillment, security, and an ability to maintain one's sense of self as gay or lesbian across contexts, and it is likely that some identity disclosure will have occurred, depending on individual circumstances.

Source. McCarn & Fassinger, 1996; Fassinger & Miller, 1996.

suggestions ranging from beginning efforts such as providing a list of gender-neutral bathrooms available on campus, to advanced efforts like creating a transgender clinic or healthcare team to provide comprehensive care to transgender students.

Entering first-year LGBT students are first and foremost new students. Academic advisors understand that one's sexual or gender identity does not prohibit the student from experiencing more common issues facing first-year students such as living away from home for the first time and making new friends. LGBT students need to feel welcome, included, and have a sense of belonging on their new campus just like heterosexual students.

Student Advocacy

LGBT students may experience discrimination or harassment from other students or faculty/staff and may need assistance identifying campus resources to assist in these unfortunate situations. Advisor awareness of campus ombudspersons, student advocates, bias response procedures, student clubs and organizations, and SafeZone offices (campus LGBT allies) could be essential in these cases. Advisors may also be a resource regarding specific policies and procedures that may directly affect LGBT student.

Medical/Compassionate Withdrawals

Many institutions have policies that allow students who are dealing with serious medical, psychological, and personal issues that are not within the students' control to withdraw from classes at the approval of specific institution designees. Academic advisors are usually the primary source of information regarding these types of procedures for students in need. Institutional personnel who are authorized to make decisions regarding these types of decisions should be sensitive to LGBT issues that might warrant granting withdrawals such as being cut off from parental support, homelessness, domestic violence, poor health, depression, and/or being suicidal.

Student Records

Institutions of higher education generally have policies and procedures regarding changing academic records. Transgender students may require academic advising assistance for many reasons, including changing their names and changing gender labels in official university records. As more institutions adopt gender identity/expression in non-discrimination policies, procedures for changing official academic records need to be in place.

Career Exploration for First-Year LGBT Students

As many first-year students begin their higher education experience, they are also beginning to explore career options and opportunities. Many academic advisors have some form of career development or career exploration as part of their advising responsibilities, while others rely on campus career services offices as referrals. Providing career exploration assistance for LGBT students may result in questions advisors are not able to readily answer such as: Can I get fired just for being perceived as LGBT in my state? Should I "out" myself on my résumé? Do some companies actively recruit LGBT candidates?

Workplace discrimination based on sexual orientation or gender identity and expression occurs with little to no legal recourse. The Human Rights Campaign reports in 34 states, it is legal to fire someone based on their sexual orientation. In 44 states, it is legal to do so based on gender identity (Human Rights Campaign, 2005). However, many companies, colleges, and some cities and states, include sexual orientation and/or gender identity in non-discrimination policies and offer domestic partner benefits. Advisors and institutions exploring legal issues regarding transgender students may find additional resources provided by the Transgender Law and Policy Institute (2005). Students may also perceive specific academic programs or careers to be more gay friendly. Regardless, it is always in the best interest of the student to choose academic programs and careers based on overall interest and ability.

Advisor Training and Professional Development

Preparing academic advisors to perform their numerous responsibilities is a complex process. Early in this process, academic advisors should be exposed to diversity issues related to their specific campus. Academic advisors are committed to helping students with a multitude of identities achieve their academic goals. Information and details regarding campus resources and support networks for LGBT students should be in all academic advising training outlines. The following is a suggested list of topics to include.

- ◇ Counseling and support groups available on campus
- ◇ Student and faculty/staff clubs and organizations on campus
- ◇ NACADA Lesbian, Gay, Bisexual, Transgender, and Allies (LGBTA) Concerns Commission
- ◇ Institution policies and procedures that specifically affect LGBT students and staff (e.g., non-discrimination policies, bias response procedures, emergency funds)
- ◇ Ally offices on campus that provide specific support to LGBT students and staff (e.g., Multicultural Student Center, Affirmative Action Office, and LGBT Student Center Coordinator)
- ◇ LGBT curriculum opportunities on campus (e.g., certificates, minor/major programs)
- ◇ Off-campus resources for LGBT students (e.g., alumni groups, counseling services, mentor programs)

Each academic advising office should also identify at least one person on staff to establish liaison relationships with the LGBT community on campus. This liaison will provide updates on issues and campus events for the LGBT community. Maintaining open communication and establishing positive relationships with LGBT campus community members will communicate commitment to diversity, specifically to LGBT students. Advisors on some campuses will need to rely more on local community resources if the institution does not provide these resources. Communities that do not have adequate local resources may need to rely more on web resources. Advisors may also be able to call upon family members, friends, and co-workers to assist in the process of becoming more informed about LGBT issues.

LGBT Academic Programs

New students looking for inclusion of LGBT students and staff on a campus need look no further than the curriculum at the institution. LGBT studies programs and specific classes addressing LGBT issues on campuses is a positive indication the campus administration is supportive of the LGBT community. Academic advisors in all departments should familiarize themselves with LGBT curriculum opportunities available to students such as a general listing of LGBT-related courses each semester (e.g., NYU Fall 2006 Sex & Gender Course Guide, 2006). Advisors should also be careful not to assume that all LGBT students will be interested in these opportunities nor that only LGBT students may express interest in these classes or programs. Many heterosexual students are arriving on our campuses having significant exposure to LGBT individuals and culture through friends, family members, and other personal experiences. Academic advisors will play a key role in helping students understand how they can enhance their academic credentials by taking classes or enrolling in programs that focus on the LGBT community.

Academic advisors may also receive questions from students about knowledge of specific faculty or departments. Students may hear rumors of homophobic faculty members or departments or about a particular department being run by the "lesbian or gay mafia." While many questions of this nature may be based on rumors, advisors should be sensitive to what students say and be willing to help direct students to appropriate resources or individuals to get truthful information about faculty, staff, and departments. Improving campus climate for LGBT students, faculty, and staff, starts by addressing these concerns, dispelling rumors, and promoting inclusion and acceptance. Advisors also play the important role of challenging students to look past their own stereotypes to make course, major, and instructor selections based on more meaningful criteria than rumors or popularity.

Recommendations and Conclusion

Academic advisors and/or advising centers may take a number of steps to enhance their knowledge and resources for LGBT students and fellow staff members.

◇ Be inclusive when creating and updating office brochures, publications, web pages, and workshop presentations, and while planning office functions using inclusive terminology such as "spouse/ partner" or "significant other" rather than terms assuming heterosexual relationships.
◇ Identify advising office staff members who are willing to become office liaison with LGBT community on your campus. This office liaison can assist in keeping your staff up-to-date on events, issues, and important dates for the LGBT community.
◇ Include LGBT student/community issues in academic advisor training and professional development programs for new and continuing advisors on your campus. Each campus and community may be different when addressing LGBT students, and advisors need to be aware of these differences.
◇ Use NACADA listservs, conference workshop presentations, and the LGBTA Concerns Commission web page that provide an abundance of resources for academic advisors who work with LGBT students.
◇ Conduct a search on campus web pages for "gay and lesbian" or "LGBT." Is it easy or difficult for students to find positive LGBT-related information about the campus and what it has to offer? Educate campus agencies about how our institutions communicate messages of inclusion or exclusion of LGBT students simply by how readily accessible we make information available about their community.
◇ Create a paper or electronic file of LGBT resources on campus or in community that will be quickly accessible during academic advising appointments. This document may be maintained by a campus coordinator for LGBT students, student leaders, or campus counseling center. It may be necessary to create this list with the assistance of members from the LGBT community.

First-year students experience a wide range of emotions and issues. In an ideal world, dealing with one's sexual and/or gender identity would be no more stressful than dealing with general roommate issues, homesickness, or choosing a major. Unfortunately, our society has yet to allow the exploration of one's sexual and/or gender identity to be "normal" in most circumstances, especially when dealing with non-heterosexual and/or gender variant identities. Until this time arrives, academic advisors need to play a critical role in making sure first-year LGBT students feel included and welcome.

Author's Note

Special thanks to Jessica Pettitt (JessicaPettitt.com) for her assistance in making this chapter possible.

References

Beemyn, B., Dominque, D., Pettitt, J., & Smith, T. (2005). Suggested steps to make campuses more trans-inclusive. *Journal of Gay and Lesbian Issues in Education, 3*(1), 89-94.

Evans, N. J., Forney, D., & Guido-DiBrito, F. (1998). *Student development in college: Theory, research, and practice.* San Francisco: Jossey-Bass.

Fassinger, R. E. (1998). Lesbian, gay, bisexual identity and student development theory. In R. L. Sanlo (Ed.), *Working with lesbian, gay, bisexual, and transgender college students: A handbook for faculty and administrators* (pp. 13-22). Westport, CT: Greenwood Press.

Fassinger, R .E., & Miller, B. A. (1997). Validation of an inclusive model of homosexual identity formation in a sample of gay men. *Journal of Homosexuality, 32*(2), 53-78.

Human Rights Campaign. (2005). *Employment non-discrimination act.* Retrieved April 24, 2006, from http://www.hrc.org/Template.cfm?Section=Employment_Non-Discrimination_Act

Lees, L. J. (1998). Transgender on our campuses. In R. L. Sanlo (Ed.), *Working with lesbian, gay, bisexual, and transgender college students: A handbook for faculty and administrators* (pp. 37-43). Westport, CT: Greenwood Press.

McCarn, S. R., & Fassinger, R. E. (1996). Revisioning sexual minority identity formation: A new model of lesbian identity and its implications for counseling and research. *The Counseling Psychologist, 24*(3), 508-534.

New York University. (2006) *Fall 2006 sex & gender course guide.* Retrieved April 24, 2006, from http://www.nyu.edu/lgbt/sgguidef06.html

Poynter, K. (Producer) & Wang. C. (Director). (2003). *SAFE on campus DVD: A training and development resource for lesbian, gay, bisexual and transgender safe space ally programs* [Motion Picture Case Studies]. Durham, NC: Duke University.

Transgender Law and Policy Institute. (2005) *Welcome to the Transgender Law and Policy Institute.* Retrieved April 24, 2006 from http://www.transgenderlaw.org/

Appendix

LGBT Web Resources

American College Personnel Association's Standing Committee for Lesbian, Gay, Bisexual, and Transgender Awareness
    http://www.myacpa.org/sc/sclgbta/
Human Rights Campaign: Working for lesbian, gay, bisexual, and transgender equal rights
    http://www.hrc.org
LGBT Financial Aid Opportunities
    http://www.lgbtcampus.org/resources/financial_aid.html

LGBT Studies Programs
    http://www.lgbtcampus.org/resources/lgbt_studies.html
LGBT symbols
    http://www.lambda.org/symbols.htm
National Academic Advising Association (NACADA) LGBTA Concerns Commission
    http://www.nacada.ksu.edu/Commissions/C18/index.htm
National Association of Student Personnel Administrators (NASPA) GLBT Issues Knowl-
    edge Community
    http://naspa.org/communities/kc/community.cfm?kcid=7
National Consortium of Directors of LGBT Resources in Higher Education
    http://www.lgbtcampus.org/
Resource Guide to Coming Out: For Gay, Lesbian, Bisexual, and Transgender Americans
    http://www.hrc.org/Content/ContentGroups/Publications1/Resource_Guide_To_
    Coming_Out1/Resource_Guide_to_Coming_Out_09072004.pdf
SafeZone Programs
    http://www.lgbtcampus.org/resources/safe_zone_resources.htm
Transgender Law & Policy Institute
    www.transgenderlaw.org
Transgender 101: An introduction to issues surrounding gender identity and expression
    http://www.hrc.org/Content/NavigationMenu/HRC/Get_Informed/Issues/
    Transgender_Issues1/Transgender_101/Transgender_101.htm

Section Four

Summary, Recommendations, and the Future

Chapter Sixteen

Challenges and Recommendations for Today's Advisors

Eric R. White, Betsy McCalla-Wriggins, and Mary Stuart Hunter

In these early years of the 21st century, higher education finds itself facing many challenges. The issues confronting higher education are, in many cases, the same as those facing academic advising. Consequently, academic advising professionals continually strive to understand the context within which they function and examine advising theories and practices so they can respond positively.

Several themes are prevalent in academic advising circles today. Without rejecting its history outright, leaders in the field are working to move advising from what it has been, to what it potentially can be. The following challenges can provide guidance as advising professionals attempt to improve advising for the benefit of students and for the benefit of their institutions.

What benefits do students gain from engaging in a relationship with an academic advisor?

Academic advising has shifted to learning-centered approaches to education as has the academy. To suggest that academic advisors should function as college and university instructors, that is, as teachers, moves the profession of academic advising beyond the traditional counseling and human services paradigms that have long dominated the field. In reality, academic advising is one of the most learner-centered activities on a college or university campus, for the outcomes of advising are ultimately about what the student has learned in the higher education environment.

Many learning outcomes are realized when a fully functioning academic advising program is in place. While colleges and universities have the latitude to determine their own learning outcomes, a well-developed academic advising program will include a set of articulated goals, which may include intellectual growth, effective communication, realistic self-appraisal, clarified values, career choices, leadership development, independence, social responsibility, appreciation of diversity, and educational and personal goals. Thus, intentionally articulating and disseminating student-learning objectives to the campus community can challenge advising professionals, and, at the same time, move the status of advising to a more central station in the campus culture.

How can a campus achieve effective academic advising?

It is not enough for an institution to define a set of outcomes. The assessment movement, closely aligned with accountability, calls upon academic advising to find ways to measure whether these outcomes have been achieved. Ways to measure observable behaviors and ways to query students via surveys or in focus groups need to be developed. Both qualitative and quantitative approaches to assessment need to be explored to better understand the entire learning process for today's students.

How is technology being used at institutions to support the learning goals of academic advising, including those for the distance learner?

While many fields were leery of the new technologies for the classroom, academic advising quickly grasped the power of technology to free advisors from the more tedious aspects of their work. The electronic degree audit, for one, has become a staple for academic advisors. Any institution without an electronic degree audit continues to saddle the academic advisor with tasks that technology can accomplish in a fraction of the time. The challenge, now, is to turn technology into a "teaching and learning machine" rather than simply a purveyor of information.

Advanced technologies have detached advising from the process of registration. This separation allows advising to reconceptualize itself. Once freed of the routine, advising now can take up the challenge of examining itself from a student-centered, learning outcomes perspective. While academic advising continues to embrace the use of technology, the struggle to guarantee that the advisor, not the technology, determines the parameters of professional behavior will no doubt continue.

Advising students at a distance provides special challenges. Historically, advising has been a face-to-face interaction. But, the arrival of the distance learner, a phenomenon encouraged by the technological advances in instructional methods, has forced advising to rethink the face-to-face session, provide analogs for this approach within available technological resources, and develop new protocols for advising students without seeing advisees in person. This challenge, in combination with the instructional challenge of teaching students at a distance, will continue to grow.

Do advisors at institutions know who their students are, what unique needs they may have, and how to best work with various groups to support their success?

Exploring alternative methods of instruction to meet the demands of a changing college-going population is another challenge facing higher education. Specifically, it means that advisors must assist a much more diverse group of students. Consequently, academic advising must examine the characteristics of these students and determine what approaches to advising achieve which outcomes.

Many chapters in this monograph specifically address the wide demographic range of students entering our colleges and universities. Each one of these micropopulations has advising needs that must be addressed. The significance of meeting such needs is heightened given the higher attrition rates for many of these groups in the first year. Academic advising must continue to explore student characteristics, recognizing not only that students often represent more than one group, but that they are also unique individuals who may possess few or none of the characteristics typically associated with a micropopulation. They may even resent the assumption that they are associated with a specific micropopulation based on a few shared characteristics.

At the same time, academic advisors must keep abreast of the research in the advising field and issues facing these groups during their first-year college experience. As more research is conducted, academic advisors may have to consider altering approaches to advising or instituting additional assessment measures to determine whether the designated outcomes are being achieved.

The amount of attention paid to the characteristics of unique micropopulations of students on our campuses should be one of the hallmarks of a student-centered institution. Understanding the needs of students and establishing an environment that acknowledges students as paramount in the learning process are critical if an institution aspires to be student- and learning-centered. Academic advising, as a core activity in higher education, contributes to the student centeredness of a college or university, because, when done well, academic advising approaches each student as an individual, and assures that the goals and aspirations of that student are addressed and, hopefully, achieved. In this way, academic advising can prepare students for their lives as citizens. The relationship between a well-crafted education and students' accomplishments as citizens contributing to society is significant. Academic advisors, then, become central in the students' lives, urging students to consider opportunities perhaps never thought of before and challenging their students' preconceived notions of the purpose of higher education. When an institution claims to be student- and learning-centered, then it needs to have professionals who have the time, the education, the experience, and desire to respond to students.

What research is being conducted on campuses to support the supposition that the academic advising program is truly student-centered and enhances student retention and progress towards graduation?

Retention, as an issue, continues to be a challenge at American colleges and universities. Where once survival-of-the-fittest mentality sufficed (and, indeed, still is prevalent on some campuses), the vast majority of colleges and universities have come to realize that it makes good sense to enable success for those students who have been admitted. In addition, it is more cost effective to retain students than to recruit new students. As tuition at institutions of all types continues to rise and as public institutions discuss adopting various aspects of privatization, the need to retain as many students as possible becomes more critical. Institutions look to many of its processes to increase retention, and academic advising is often considered as very significant.

Academic programs that do not take into account students' interests and abilities, their need to work to pay for their education, and their learning patterns surely put unnecessary burdens on students and no doubt assist, rather than prevent, students in leaving higher education. But the exact relationship between quality academic advising and retention is not yet empirically clear and additional research on this subject must be undertaken.

How does the campus environment reinforce the connections between academic and career advising?

While academic advising continues to carve out a specific niche in higher education, it shares goals with career advising. Understanding the similarities and differences between these two activities will continue to dominate the academic advising community. Further refinements will be made as the scholarship of academic advising addresses where the boundaries may exist.

The call for student centeredness has entered the language of higher education. Academic advising, with its focus on one-to-one sessions with students and addressing the unique academic needs of each student, is well equipped to respond to this call. Student centeredness also implies that the institution is responsive to student learning. Academic advising thus finds itself at the core of this student-centered imperative. Understanding the impact of academic advising on students with regard to choice of major, use of university resources, participation in internships and education abroad, and life after college are some of the areas that present themselves for research.

What educational background is expected of advisors, and what ongoing
professional development opportunities are supported for those who advise?

Another significant challenge relates to the preparation of academic advisors. Although the field of academic advising traces it origins to the early 19th century in American history, it is only recently that advising has gained recognition not only as a functional area of responsibility but also as a field with its own theories, practices, statement of core values, and standards of professional behavior. With these important basics in place, the next logical step would be an academic curriculum.

Graduate schools have now developed courses in academic advising, where some hold permanent standing and some are taught as special topics. Currently, Kansas State University's College of Education offers a 15-credit academic advising graduate certificate program. The completion of this certificate requires a foundation course in academic advising along with courses in multicultural advising, career counseling, the college student and the college environment, and learning principles.

The logical progressions beyond certifications are graduate degree programs. As more monographs, empirical research articles, and books on academic advising are published, the faster the move toward full professional status. The significant nexus of academic advising and the first-year experience thus becomes one of the major foci for the advising profession. This monograph serves as a foundation and text for current practitioners and scholars, and perhaps, most importantly, for future academic advisors who now deliberately choose to become academic advisors rather than serendipitously falling into the field, as did many a generation ago.

What pressures exist from agencies and situations beyond the campus?

Challenges for academic advisors are not limited to those on the campus. Other challenges come from beyond the campus, as well. Regional accrediting agencies' emphasis on the assessment of learning outcomes and the need to better understand the nature of advising has taken on even greater urgency. With financial resources to support public education now more scarce than ever before, having to justify staffing and programmatic offerings is to be expected. The ways in which academic advising articulates its mission, especially within the context of learning outcomes, will help place academic advising as central to the mission of higher education.

Recommendations

The significant challenges facing higher education and academic advisors for first-year students can be overwhelming. However, here are some very specific recommendations that an individual advisor can implement. Each one can have a very positive impact on first-year students.

1. Articulate what first-year students will learn from the advising process. Be very intentional about the goal for each advising interaction and publish these through multiple channels so that both advisors and students know what is expected and what learning outcomes are to be achieved.
2. Identify what first-year activities support the curriculum, pedagogy, and outcome components of the advising experiences and connect specific advising activities to each

component. This effort reinforces with advisors and students that academic advising is a multidimensional process and not just "course selection."

3. Determine if there is a college-wide or institutional plan for first-year advising initiatives and who is responsible. A key to success is having a plan and a person with specific responsibility for its implementation. If this exists, meet with that person. If this does not exist, then initiate negotiations to implement such a position.

4. Identify possible departmental, college, and/or institutional barriers to effective first-year advising initiatives. Being able to address both the real and perceived barriers will increase the probability that advising initiatives will be supported.

5. Collaborate with others across the institution. Reach out to those who are committed to quality advising experiences for first-year students. Share your ideas and ask about what they are doing. Identify how to support each other and brainstorm new ways to work together.

6. Develop assessment plans/activities for all phases of the advising process. Unless there is an assessment plan for all the learning outcomes identified for the advising sessions, it will never be clear if the stated goals have been met. Information is power. In this day of very limited resources, those who have data to show that their initiatives make a positive difference for first-year students are much more likely to continue to get those limited resources.

7. Engage in research on academic advising experiences for first-year students. In assessment planning, consider some research objectives. Academic advising on all campuses will be greatly enhanced and become more credible as quality research is presented and published.

8. Recognize all those who provide quality academic advising for first-year students.

9. Identify passions and strengthen skills. Whether it is working one-on-one with students, developing new advising programs, creating new technologies, or supervising and developing a staff, identify where skills need to be enhanced. If advisors are going to talk with students about life-long learning, they need to be role models.

10. Access external resources such as the National Resource Center for The First-Year Experience and Students in Transition, NACADA, and other professional groups. With the power of technology, multiple professional development opportunities are available online. Set aside at least an hour a week checking those resources.

11. Acknowledge the power of one. Look at what can be done differently within an advisor's sphere of influence. Even if the department, college, or system cannot change, the advisor can behave differently and, thus, improve academic advising with first-year students.

As it has over the past decades, academic advising will continue to evolve and develop as long as there are students at colleges and universities. The editors of this monograph encourage and challenge readers to not be satisfied with the status quo of advising on campus and in individual departments. Critically examine the current status of advising and tirelessly work toward improvement at each opportunity. The future holds great promise for the credibility of the profession and the influence that academic advisors can have on the education of all students.

Introduction
to the Appendices

The National Academic Advising Association Board of Directors endorses three documents that champion the educational role of academic advising in a diverse world. The three documents are

◇ Concept of Academic Advising
◇ Statement of Core Values
◇ Council for the Advancement of Standards (CAS) in Higher Education Standards and Guidelines for Academic Advising

These sets of guiding principles affirm the role of academic advising in higher education, thereby supporting institutional mission, while at the same time, anticipating the needs of 21st century students, academic advisors, and institutions.

They can be used for a variety of purposes including professional development of academic advisors and program assessment. They also can be used when implementing a new advising program or revising a current one.

Academic advising is carried out by a vast array of individuals, including faculty and staff members. These guiding principles are intended for use by all who advise.

These documents support all categories of institutions with every type of advising delivery system. Intentionally, they do not address every detail and nuance of academic advising. Rather they should be used as starting points and references for a discussion of academic advising, providing the framework for a coherent approach to implementing a well-functioning academic advising program that would meet any specified institutional goals.

Appendix A

Concept of Academic Advising

National Academic Advising Association (NACADA)

Academic advising is integral to fulfilling the teaching and learning mission of higher education. Through academic advising, students learn to become members of their higher education community, to think critically about their roles and responsibilities as students, and to prepare to be educated citizens of a democratic society and a global community. Academic advising engages students beyond their own world views, while acknowledging their individual characteristics, values, and motivations as they enter, move through, and exit the institution. Regardless of the diversity of our institutions, our students, our advisors, and our organizational structures, academic advising has three components: curriculum (*what* advising deals with), pedagogy (*how* advising does what it does), and student learning outcomes (the *result* of academic advising).

The Curriculum of Academic Advising

Academic advising draws primarily from theories in the social sciences, humanities, and education. The curriculum of academic advising ranges from the ideals of higher education to the pragmatics of enrollment. This curriculum includes, but is not limited to, the institution's mission, culture and expectations; the meaning, value, and interrelationship of the institution's curriculum and co-curriculum; modes of thinking , learning, and decision making; the selection of academic programs and courses; the development of life and career goals; campus/community resources, policies, and procedures; and the transferability of skills and knowledge.

The Pedagogy of Academic Advising

Academic advising, as a teaching and learning process, requires a pedagogy that incorporates the preparation, facilitation, documentation, and assessment of advising interactions. Although the specific methods, strategies, and techniques may vary, the relationship between advisors and students is fundamental and is characterized by mutual respect, trust, and ethical behavior.

Student Learning Outcomes of Academic Advising

The student learning outcomes of academic advising are guided by an institution's mission, goals, curriculum, and co-curriculum. These outcomes, defined in an advising curriculum, articulate what students will demonstrate, know, value, and do as a result of participating in academic advising. Each institution must develop its own set of student learning outcomes and the methods to assess them. The following is a representative sample. Students will:

◇ Craft a coherent educational plan based on assessment of abilities, aspirations, interests, and values
◇ Use complex information from various sources to set goals, reach decisions, and achieve those goals
◇ Assume responsibility for meeting academic program requirements
◇ Articulate the meaning of higher education and the intent of the institution's curriculum
◇ Cultivate the intellectual habits that lead to a lifetime of learning
◇ Behave as citizens who engage in the wider world around them

Summary

Academic advising, based in the teaching and learning mission of higher education, is a series of intentional interactions with a curriculum, a pedagogy, and a set of student learning outcomes. Academic advising synthesizes and contextualizes students' educational experiences within the frameworks of their aspirations, abilities and lives to extend learning beyond campus boundaries and timeframes.

Revised 2006.

Appendix B

The Statement of Core Values of Academic Advising

National Academic Advising Association (NACADA)

The National Academic Advising Association (NACADA) is comprised of professional and faculty advisors, administrators, students, and others with a primary interest in the practice of academic advising. With diverse backgrounds, perspectives, and experiences, NACADA members advise in a variety of settings and work to promote quality academic advising within their institutions.

NACADA recognizes and celebrates the contributions of professional, faculty, paraprofessional, and peer advisors to the advising profession. NACADA acknowledges the complex nature of higher education institutions and the role academic advising plays within them, the wide variety of settings and responsibilities of academic advisors, and advisors' diverse backgrounds and experiences. NACADA provides a Statement of Core Values to affirm the importance of advising within the academy and acknowledge the impact that advising interactions can have on individuals, institutions, and society.

The Statement of Core Values consists of three parts: (1) Introduction, (2) Declaration, and (3) Exposition, a descriptive section expanding on each of the Core Values. While each part stands alone, the document's richness and fullness of meaning lies in its totality.

The Statement of Core Values provides a framework to guide professional practice and reminds advisors of their responsibilities to students, colleagues, institutions, society, and themselves. Those charged with advising responsibilities are expected to reflect the values of the advising profession in their daily interactions at their institutions.

The Statement of Core Values does not attempt to dictate the manner in or process through which academic advising takes place, nor does it advocate one particular advising philosophy or model over another. Instead, these Core Values are the reference points advisors use to consider their individual philosophies, strengths, and opportunities for professional growth. Furthermore, the Core Values do not carry equal weight. Advisors will find some Core Values more applicable or valuable to their situations than others. Advisors should consider each Core Value with regard to their own values and those of their institutions.

Advising constituents, and especially students, deserve dependable, accurate, timely, respectful, and honest responses. Through this Statement of Core Values, NACADA communicates the expectations that others should hold for advisors in their advising roles. Advisors' responsibilities to their many constituents form the foundation upon which the Core Values rest.

Declaration

1. Advisors are responsible to the individuals they advise.

Academic advisors work to strengthen the importance, dignity, potential, and unique nature of each individual within the academic setting. Advisors' work is guided by their beliefs that students:

⬦ Have diverse backgrounds that can include different ethnic, racial, domestic, and international communities; sexual orientations; ages; gender and gender identities; physical, emotional, and psychological abilities; political, religious, and educational beliefs
⬦ Hold their own beliefs and opinions
⬦ Are responsible for their own behaviors and the outcomes of those behaviors
⬦ Can be successful based upon their individual goals and efforts
⬦ Have a desire to learn
⬦ Have learning needs that vary based upon individual skills, goals, responsibilities, and experiences
⬦ Use a variety of techniques and technologies to navigate their world.

In support of these beliefs, the cooperative efforts of all who advise include, but are not limited to, providing accurate and timely information, communicating in useful and efficient ways, maintaining regular office hours, and offering varied contact modes.

Advising, as part of the educational process, involves helping students develop a realistic self-perception and successfully transition to the postsecondary institution. Advisors encourage, respect, and assist students in establishing their goals and objectives.

Advisors seek to gain the trust of their students and strive to honor students' expectations of academic advising and its importance in their lives.

2. Advisors are responsible for involving others, when appropriate, in the advising process.

Effective advising requires a holistic approach. At many institutions, a network of people and resources is available to students. Advisors serve as mediators and facilitators who effectively use their specialized knowledge and experience for student benefit. Advisors recognize their limitations and make referrals to qualified persons when appropriate. To connect academic advising to students' lives, advisors actively seek resources and inform students of specialists who can further assess student needs and provide access to appropriate programs and services. Advisors help students integrate information so they can make well-informed academic decisions.

3. Advisors are responsible to their institutions.

Advisors nurture collegial relationships. They uphold the specific policies, procedures, and values of their departments and institutions. Advisors maintain clear lines of communication with those not directly involved in the advising process but who have responsibility and authority for decisions regarding academic advising at the institution. Advisors recognize their individual roles in the success of their institutions.

4. Advisors are responsible to higher education.

Academic advisors honor academic freedom. They realize that academic advising is not limited to any one theoretical perspective and that practice is informed by a variety of theories from the fields of social sciences, the humanities, and education. They are free to base their work with students on the most relevant theories and on optimal models for the delivery of academic advising programs. Advisors advocate for student educational achievement to the highest attainable standard, support student goals, and uphold the educational mission of the institution.

5. Advisors are responsible to their educational community.

Academic advisors interpret their institution's mission as well as its goals and values. They convey institutional information and characteristics of student success to the local, state, regional, national, and global communities that support the student body. Advisors are sensitive to the values and mores of the surrounding community. They are familiar with community programs and services that may provide students with additional educational opportunities and resources. Advisors may become models for students by participating in community activities.

6. Advisors are responsible for their professional practices and for themselves personally.

Advisors participate in professional development opportunities, establish appropriate relationships and boundaries with advisees, and create environments that promote physical, emotional, and spiritual health. Advisors maintain a healthy balance in their lives and articulate personal and professional needs when appropriate. They consider continued professional growth and development to be the responsibility of both themselves and their institutions.

Exposition

Core Value 1: Advisors are responsible to the individuals they advise.

- ◇ Academic advising is an integral part of the educational process and affects students in numerous ways. As advisors enhance student learning and development, advisees have the opportunity to become participants in and contributors to their own education. In one of the most important potential outcomes of this process, academic advising fosters individual potential.
- ◇ Regular student contact through in-person appointments, mail, telephone, e-mail, or other computer-mediated systems helps advisors gain meaningful insights into students' diverse academic, social, and personal experiences and needs. Advisors use these insights to assist students as they transition to new academic and social communities, develop sound academic and career goals, and ultimately, become successful learners.
- ◇ Advisors recognize and respect that students' diverse backgrounds are comprised of their ethnic and racial heritage, age, gender, sexual orientation, and religion, as well as their physical, learning, and psychological abilities. Advisors help students develop and reinforce realistic self-perceptions and help them use this information in mapping out their futures.
- ◇ Advisors introduce and assist students with their transitions to the academic world by helping them see value in the learning process, gain perspective on the college experience, become more responsible and accountable, set priorities and evaluate their progress, and uphold honesty with themselves and others about their successes and limitations.

◇ Advisors encourage self-reliance and support students as they strive to make informed and responsible decisions, set realistic goals, and develop lifelong learning and self-management skills.

◇ Advisors respect students' rights to their individual beliefs and opinions.

◇ Advisors guide and teach students to understand and apply classroom concepts to everyday life.

◇ Advisors help students establish realistic goals and objectives and encourage them to be responsible for their own progress and success.

◇ Advisors seek to understand and modify barriers to student progress, identify ineffective and inefficient policies and procedures, and work to affect change. When the needs of students and the institution are in conflict, advisors seek a resolution that is in the best interest of both parties. In cases where the student finds the resolution unsatisfactory, they inform students regarding appropriate grievance procedures.

◇ Advisors recognize the changing nature of the college and university environment and diversity within the student body. They acknowledge the changing communication technologies used by students and the resulting new learning environments. They are sensitive to the responsibilities and pressures placed on students to balance course loads, financial and family issues, and interpersonal demands.

◇ Advisors are knowledgeable and sensitive regarding national, regional, local, and institutional policies and procedures, particularly those governing matters that address harassment, use of technology, personal relationships with students, privacy of student information, and equal opportunity.

◇ Advisors are encouraged to investigate all available avenues to help students explore academic opportunities.

◇ Advisors respect student confidentiality rights regarding personal information. Advisors practice with an understanding of the institution's interpretation of applicable laws such as the Federal Educational Rights and Privacy Act (FERPA).

◇ Advisors seek access to and use student information only when the information is relevant to the advising process. Advisors enter or change information on students' records only with appropriate institutional authorization to do so.

◇ Advisors document advising contacts adequately to meet institutional disclosure guidelines and aid in subsequent advising interactions.

Core Value 2: Advisors are responsible for involving others, when appropriate, in the advising process.

◇ Academic advisors must develop relationships with personnel critical to student success including those in such diverse areas as admissions, orientation, instruction, financial aid, housing, health services, athletics, academic departments, and the registrar's office. They also must establish relationships with those who can attend to specific physical and educational needs of students, such as personnel in disability services, tutoring, psychological counseling, international study, and career development. Advisors must also direct students, as needed, to experts who specialize in credit transfers, cocurricular programs, and graduation clearance.

◇ Because of the nature of academic advising, advisors often develop a broad understanding of an institution and a detailed understanding of student needs and the resources available to help students meet those needs. Based upon this understanding:

◇ advisors can have an interpretative role with students regarding their interactions with faculty, staff, administrators, and fellow students, and

◇ advisors can help the institution's administrators gain a greater understanding of students' needs.

◇ Students involved in the advising process (such as peer advisors or graduate assistants) must be adequately trained and supervised for adherence to the same policies and practices required of the professional and faculty advisors and other specially trained staff advising in the unit/institution.

Core Value 3: Advisors are responsible to their institutions.

◇ Advisors work in many types of higher education institutions and abide by the specific policies, procedures, and values of the department and institution in which they work. When circumstances interfere with students' learning and development, advisors advocate for change on the advisees' behalf with the institution's administration, faculty, and staff.

◇ Advisors keep those not directly involved in the advising process informed and aware of the importance of academic advising in students' lives. They articulate the need for administrative support of advising and related activities.

◇ Advisors increase their collective professional strength by constructively and respectfully sharing their advising philosophies and techniques with colleagues.

◇ Advisors respect the opinions of their colleagues; remain neutral when students make comments or express opinions about other faculty or staff; are nonjudgmental about academic programs; and do not impose their personal agendas on students.

◇ Advisors encourage the use of models for the optimal delivery of academic advising programs within their institutions.

◇ Advisors recognize their individual roles in the success of their institutions and accept and participate in institutional commitments that can include, but are not limited to, administrative and committee service, teaching, research, and writing.

Core Value 4: Advisors are responsible to higher education in general.

◇ Advisors accept that one goal of education is to introduce students to the world of ideas in an environment of academic freedom. Advisors demonstrate appreciation for academic freedom.

◇ Advisors base their work with students on the most relevant theoretical perspectives and practices drawn from the fields of social sciences, the humanities, and education.

◇ One goal of advising is to establish, between students and advisors, a partnership that will guide students through their academic programs. Advisors help students understand that learning can be used in day-to-day application through exploration, trial and error, challenge, and decision making.

◇ Advisors advocate for student educational achievement to the highest attainable standards and support student goals as they uphold the educational mission of the institution.

◇ Advisors advocate for the creation, enhancement, and strengthening of programs and services that recognize and meet student academic needs.

Core Value 5: Advisors are responsible to their educational community.

◇ Many institutions recognize the importance of integrating classroom learning with community experience, study abroad, and programs that bridge the gap between the academic and off-campus environments. Where such programs exist, advisors help students understand the relationship between the institution and local, regional, national, and international communities.

◇ Advisors advocate for students who desire to include study abroad or community service learning into their cocurricular college experience, and they make appropriate referrals to enable students to achieve these goals.

◇ Advisors understand the intricacies of transfer between institutions and make appropriate referrals to enable students to achieve their goals.

Core Value 6: Advisors are responsible for their professional practices and for themselves personally.

◇ Advisors use the Statement of Core Values to guide their professional actions.

◇ Advisors seek opportunities to grow professionally. They identify appropriate workshops, classes, literature, research publications, and groups, both inside and outside the institution, that can keep their interest high, hone professional skills, and advance expertise within specific areas of interest.

◇ Advisors seek cross cultural opportunities to interact with and learn more about ethnic communities, racial groups, religions, sexual preferences, genders, and age levels, as well as physical, learning, and psychological abilities and disabilities found among the general student population.

◇ Advisors recognize that research topics are embedded in academic advising practice and theory. Advisors engage in research and publication related to advising as well as in areas allied with their training and disciplinary backgrounds. Advisors' research agendas safeguard privacy and provide for the humane treatment of subjects.

◇ Advisors are alert to the demands surrounding their work with students and the necessity of taking care of themselves physically, emotionally, and spiritually to best respond to high level demands. They learn how to maintain listen and provide sensitive, timely responses that teach students to accept their responsibilities. Advisors establish and maintain appropriate boundaries, nurture others when necessary, and seek support for themselves both within and outside the institution.

Revised 2005.

Appendix C

Academic Advising Program: CAS Standards and Guidelines

Council for the Advancement of Standards in Higher Education

Part 1. Mission

The primary purpose of the Academic Advising Program (AAP) is to assist students in the development of meaningful educational plans.

AAP must incorporate student learning and student development in its mission. AAP must enhance overall educational experiences. AAP must develop, record, disseminate, implement, and regularly review its mission and goals. Its mission statement must be consistent with the mission and goals of the institution and with the standards in this document. AAP must operate as an integral part of the institution's overall mission.

The institution must have a clearly written mission statement pertaining to academic advising that must include program goals and expectations of advisors and advisees.

Part 2. Program

The formal education of students is purposeful, holistic, and consists of the curriculum and the co-curriculum. The Academic Advising Program (AAP) must identify relevant and desirable student learning and development outcomes and provide programs and services that encourage the achievement of those outcomes.

Relevant and desirable outcomes include: intellectual growth, effective communication, realistic self-appraisal, enhanced self-esteem, clarified values, career choices, leadership development, healthy behaviors, meaningful interpersonal relations, independence, collaboration, social responsibility, satisfying and productive lifestyles, appreciation of diversity, spiritual awareness, and achievement of personal and educational goals.

AAP must provide evidence of its impact on the achievement of student learning and development outcomes.

Both students and advisors must assume shared responsibility in the advising process. AAP must assist students to make the best academic decisions possible by encouraging identification and assessment of alternatives and consideration of the consequences of their decisions.

The ultimate responsibility for making decisions about educational plans and life goals should rest with the individual student.

The table below offers examples of achievement of student learning and development outcomes.

Desirable Student Learning and Development Outcomes	Examples of Achievement
Intellectual growth	Examines information about academic majors and minors; Understands the requirements of an academic degree plan, as well as institutional policies and procedures; Employs critical thinking in problem solving on selection of major and course selection; Uses complex information from a variety of sources including personal experience and observation to form a decision or opinion; Declares a major; Achieves educational goals; Applies previously understood information and concepts to a new situation or setting; Demonstrates understanding of a general education and expresses appreciation for literature, the fine arts, mathematics, sciences, and social sciences
Personal and educational goals	Sets, articulates, and pursues individual goals; Articulates personal and educational goals and objectives; Uses personal and educational goals to guide decisions; Produces a schedule of classes in consultation with advisors. Understands the effect of one's personal and education goals on others
Enhanced self-esteem	Shows self-respect and respect for others; Initiates actions toward achievement of goals; Evaluates reasonable risks with regard to academic course selection and course load when conferring with advisors
Realistic self-appraisal	Evaluates personal and academic skills, abilities, and interests and uses this appraisal to establish appropriate educational plans; Makes decisions and acts in congruence with personal values and other personal and life demands; Focuses on areas of academic ability and interest and mitigates academic weaknesses; Uses information on degree program requirements, course load, and course availability to construct a course schedule; Seeks opportunities for involvement in cocurricular activities; Seeks feedback from advisors; Learns from past experiences; Seeks services for personal needs (e.g., writing labs and counseling)
Clarified values	Demonstrates ability to evaluate personal values and beliefs regarding academic integrity and other ethical issues; Articulates personal values; Acts in congruence with personal values; Identifies personal, work, and lifestyle values and explains how they influence decision making in regard to course selection, course load, and major and minor selections
Career choices	Describes career choice and choices of academic major and minor based on interests, values, skills, and abilities; Documents knowledge, skills, and accomplishments resulting from formal education, work experience, community service and volunteer experiences; Makes the connections between classroom and out-of-classroom learning; Identifies the purpose and role of career services in the development and attainment of academic and career goals
Independence	Operates autonomously by attending advising sessions or programs or by seeking the advice of advisors in a timely fashion; Correctly interprets and applies degree audit information; Selects, schedules, and registers for courses in consultation with advisors

Table continued

Desirable Student Learning and Development Outcomes	Examples of Achievement
Effective communication	Communicates personal and academic strengths and weaknesses that affect academic plans; Demonstrates ability to use campus technology resources; Composes appropriate questions when inquiring about particular requirements, departments, and resources
Leadership development	Articulates leadership philosophy or style; Serves in a leadership position in student, community, or professional organizations; Comprehends the dynamics of a group; Exhibits democratic principles as a leader; Exhibits ability to visualize a group purpose and desired outcomes
Healthy behavior	Exhibits personal behaviors that promote a healthy lifestyle; Articulates the relationship between health and wellness and accomplishing life long goals; Exhibits behaviors that advance a healthy campus and community
Meaningful Interpersonal Relationships	Develops relationships with academic advisors, faculty members, students, and other institution staff to be engaged with the institution in meaningful ways; Listens to and considers others' points of view; Treats others with respect
Collaboration	Works cooperatively with others; Seeks the involvement of others; Seeks feedback from others; Contributes to achievement of group goals; Exhibits effective listening skills
Social responsibility	Understands the requirements of the codes of conduct; Understands and practices principles of academic integrity; Understands and participates in relevant governance systems; Understands, abides by, and participates in the development, maintenance, and orderly change of community, social, and legal standards or norms; Appropriately challenges the unfair, unjust, or uncivil behavior of other individuals or groups; Participates in service and volunteer activities
Satisfying and productive lifestyles	Achieves balance among academic course load requirements, work, and leisure time; Develops plans to satisfy academic requirements, work expectations, and leisure pursuits; Identifies and works to overcome obstacles that hamper goal achievement; Functions on the basis of personal identity, ethical, spiritual, and moral values; Articulates long-term goals and objectives
Appreciating diversity	Selects course offerings that will increase understanding of one's own and others' identity and cultures; Seeks involvement with people different from oneself; Demonstrates an appreciation for diversity and the impact it has on society
Spiritual awareness	Identifies campus and community spiritual and religious resources, including course offerings; Develops and articulates personal belief system; Understands roles of spirituality in personal and group values and behaviors

AAP must be guided by a set of written goals and objectives that are directly related to its stated mission. AAP must:

◇ Promote student growth and development
◇ Assist students in assessing their interests and abilities, examining their educational goals, making decisions and developing short-term and long-term plans to meet their objectives
◇ Discuss and clarify educational, career, and life goals
◇ Provide accurate and timely information and interpret institutional, general education, and major requirements
◇ Assist students to understand the educational context within which they are enrolled
◇ Advise on the selection of appropriate courses and other educational experiences
◇ Clarify institutional policies and procedures
◇ Evaluate and monitor student academic progress and the impact on achievement of goals
◇ Reinforce student self-direction and self-sufficiency
◇ Direct students with educational, career or personal concerns, or skill/learning deficiencies to other resources and programs on the campus when necessary.
◇ Make students aware of and refer to educational, institutional, and community resources and services (e.g., internship, study abroad, honors, service-learning, research opportunities)
◇ Collect and distribute relevant data about student needs, preferences, and performance for use in institutional decisions and policy

AAP should provide information about student experiences and concerns regarding their academic program to appropriate decision makers.

AAP must be (a) intentional, (b) coherent, (c) based on theories and knowledge of teaching, learning and human development, (d) reflective of developmental and demographic profiles of the student population, and (e) responsive to the needs of individuals, special populations, and communities.

AAP should make available to academic advisors all pertinent research (e.g., about students, the academic advising program, and perceptions of the institution).

The academic advisor must review and use available data about students' academic and educational needs, performance, and aspirations.

AAP must identify environmental conditions that may positively or negatively influence student academic achievement and propose interventions that may neutralize negative conditions.

AAP must provide current and accurate advising information to students and academic advisors.

AAP should employ the latest technologies for delivery of advising information.

Academic advising conferences must be available to students each academic term.

Academic advisors should offer conferences in a format that is convenient to the student, i.e., in person, by telephone, or on-line. Advising conferences may be carried out individually or in groups.

Academic advising caseloads must be consistent with the time required for the effective performance of this activity.

The academic status of the student being advised should be taken into consideration when determining caseloads. For example, first year, undecided, under-prepared, and honors students may require more advising time than upper division students who have declared their majors.

Academic advisors should allow an appropriate amount of time for students to discuss plans, programs, courses, academic progress, and other subjects related to their educational programs.

When determining workloads it should be recognized that advisors may work with students not officially assigned to them and that contacts regarding advising may extend beyond direct contact with the student.

Part 3. Leadership

Effective and ethical leadership is essential to the success of all organizations. Institutions must appoint, position, and empower Academic Advising Program (AAP) leaders within the administrative structure to accomplish stated missions. Leaders at various levels must be selected on the basis of formal education and training, relevant work experience as an advisor, personal skills and competencies, knowledge of the literature of academic advising, relevant professional credentials, as well as potential for promoting learning and development in students, applying effective practices to educational processes, and enhancing institutional effectiveness. Institutions must determine expectations of accountability for AAP leaders and fairly assess their performance.

AAP leaders must exercise authority over resources for which they are responsible to achieve their respective missions.

AAP leaders must:

◇ Articulate a vision for their organization
◇ Set goals and objectives based on the needs and capabilities of the population served
◇ Promote student learning and development
◇ Prescribe and practice ethical behavior
◇ Recruit, select, supervise, and develop others in the organization
◇ Manage financial resources
◇ Coordinate human resources
◇ Plan, budget for, and evaluate personnel and programs
◇ Apply effective practices to educational and administrative processes
◇ Communicate effectively
◇ Initiate collaborative interactions between individuals and agencies that possess legitimate concerns and interests in academic advising

AAP leaders must identify and find means to address individual, organizational, or environmental conditions that inhibit goal achievement.

AAP leaders must promote campus environments that result in multiple opportunities for student learning and development.

AAP leaders must continuously improve programs and services in response to changing needs of students and other constituents and evolving institutional priorities.

Part 4. Organization and Management

Guided by an overarching intent to ensure student learning and development, Academic Advising Programs (AAP) must be structured purposefully and managed effectively to achieve stated goals. Evidence of appropriate structure must include current and accessible policies and procedures, written performance expectations for all employees, functional workflow graphics or organizational charts, and clearly stated service delivery expectations.

Evidence of effective management practices must include use of comprehensive and accurate information for decisions, clear sources and channels of authority, effective communication practices, decision making and conflict resolution procedures, responsiveness to changing conditions, accountability and evaluation systems, and recognition and reward processes. AAP must provide channels within the organization for regular review of administrative policies and procedures.

The design of AAP must be compatible with the institution's organizational structure and its students' needs. Specific advisor responsibilities must be clearly delineated, published, and disseminated to both advisors and advisees.

Students, faculty advisors, and professional staff must be informed of their respective advising responsibilities.

AAP may be a centralized or decentralized function within an institution, with a variety of people throughout the institution assuming responsibilities.

AAP must provide the same services to distance learners as it does to students on campus. The distance education advising must provide for appropriate real time or delayed interaction between advisors and students.

Part 5. Human Resources

The Academic Advising Program (AAP) must be staffed adequately by individuals qualified to accomplish its mission and goals. Within established guidelines of the institution, AAP must establish procedures for staff selection, training, and evaluation; set expectations for supervision; and provide appropriate professional development opportunities. AAP must strive to improve the professional competence and skills of all personnel it employs.

Academic advising personnel may be full-time or part-time professionals who have advising as their primary function or may be faculty whose responsibilities include academic advising. Paraprofessionals (e.g., graduate students, interns, or assistants) or peer advisors may also assist advisors.

An academic advisor must hold an earned graduate degree in a field relevant to the position held or must possess an appropriate combination of educational credentials and related work experience.

Academic advisors should have an understanding of student development, student learning, career development, and other relevant theories in education, social sciences, and humanities.

Academic advisors should have a comprehensive knowledge of the institution's programs, academic requirements, policies and procedures, majors, minors, and support services.

Academic advisors should demonstrate an interest and effectiveness in working with and assisting students and a willingness to participate in professional activities.

Sufficient personnel must be available to address students' advising needs without unreasonable delay.

Degree or credential-seeking interns must be qualified by enrollment in an appropriate field of study and by relevant experience. These individuals must be trained and supervised adequately by professional staff members holding educational credentials and related work experience appropriate for supervision.

Student employees and volunteers must be carefully selected, trained, supervised, and evaluated. They must be trained on how and when to refer those in need of assistance to qualified staff members and have access to a supervisor for assistance in making these judgments. Student employees and volunteers must be provided clear and precise job descriptions, pre-service training based on assessed needs, and continuing staff development.

AAP must have technical and support staff members adequate to accomplish its mission. Staff members must be technologically proficient and qualified to perform their job functions, be knowledgeable of ethical and legal uses of technology, and have access to training. The level of staffing and workloads must be adequate and appropriate for program and service demands.

Support personnel should maintain student records, organize resource materials, receive students, make appointments, and handle correspondence and other operational needs. Technical staff may be used in research, data collection, systems development, and special projects.

Technical and support personnel must be carefully selected and adequately trained, supervised, and evaluated.

AAP staff must recognize the limitations of their positions and be familiar with institutional resources to make appropriate referrals.

Salary levels and fringe benefits for all AAP staff members must be commensurate with those for comparable positions within the institution, in similar institutions, and in the relevant geographic area.

AAP must institute hiring and promotion practices that are fair, inclusive, and non-discriminatory. AAP must employ a diverse staff to provide readily identifiable role models for students and to enrich the campus community.

AAP must create and maintain position descriptions for all staff members and provide regular performance planning and appraisals.

AAP must have a system for regular staff evaluation and must provide access to continuing education and professional development opportunities, including in-service training programs and participation in professional conferences and workshops.

AAP must strive to improve the professional competence and skills of all personnel it employs.

Continued professional development should include areas such as the following and how they relate to academic advising:

◇ Theories of student development, student learning, career development, and other relevant theories in education, social sciences, and humanities
◇ Academic policies and procedures, including institutional transfer policies and curricular changes
◇ Legal issues including US Family Education and Records Privacy Act (FERPA)/Canadian Freedom Of Information and Protection of Privacy (FOIPP) and other privacy laws and policies
◇ Technology and software training (e.g., degree audit, web registration)
◇ Institutional resources (e.g., research opportunities, career services, internship opportunities, counseling and health services, tutorial services)
◇ ADA compliance issues

Part 6. Financial Resources

The Academic Advising Program (AAP) must have adequate funding to accomplish its mission and goals. Funding priorities must be determined within the context of the stated mission, goals, objectives, and comprehensive analysis of the needs and capabilities of students and the availability of internal and external resources.

AAP must demonstrate fiscal responsibility and cost effectiveness consistent with institutional protocols.

Special consideration should be given to providing funding for the professional development of advisors.

Financial resources should be sufficient to provide high-quality print and web-based information for students and training materials for advisors. Sufficient financial resources should be provided to promote the academic advising program.

Part 7. Facilities, Technology, and Equipment

The Academic Advising Program (AAP) must have adequate, suitably located facilities, adequate technology, and equipment to support its mission and goals efficiently and effectively. Facilities, technology, and equipment must be evaluated regularly and be in compliance with relevant federal, state, provincial, and local requirements to provide for access, health, safety, and security.

AAP must assure that online and technology-assisted advising includes appropriate mechanisms for obtaining approvals, consultations, and referrals.

Data about students maintained on individual workstations and departmental or institutional servers must be secure and must comply with institutional policies on data stewardship.

Academic advisors must have access to computing equipment, local networks, student data bases, and the Internet.

Privacy and freedom from visual and auditory distractions must be considered in designing appropriate facilities.

Part 8. Legal Responsibilities

The Academic Advising Program (AAP) staff members must be knowledgeable about and responsive to laws and regulations that relate to their respective responsibilities. Staff members must inform users of programs and services and officials, as appropriate, of legal obligations and limitations including constitutional, statutory, regulatory, and case law; mandatory laws and orders emanating from federal, state, provincial, and local governments; and the institution's policies.

Academic advisors must use reasonable and informed practices to limit the liability exposure of the institution, its officers, employees, and agents. Academic advisors must be informed about institutional policies regarding personal liability and related insurance coverage options.

The institution must provide access to legal advice for academic advisors as needed to carry out assigned responsibilities.

The institution must inform academic advisors and students, in a timely and systematic fashion, about extraordinary or changing legal obligations and potential liabilities.

Part 9. Equity and Access

The Academic Advising Program (AAP) staff members must ensure that services and programs are provided on a fair and equitable basis. Facilities, programs, and services must be accessible. Hours of operation and delivery of and access to programs and services must be responsive to the needs of all students and other constituents. AAP must adhere to the spirit and intent of equal opportunity laws.

AAP must be open and readily accessible to all students and must not discriminate except where sanctioned by law and institutional policy. Discrimination must especially be avoided on the basis of age; color; creed; cultural heritage; disability; ethnicity; gender identity; nationality; political affiliation; religious affiliation; sex; sexual orientation; or social, economic, marital, or veteran status.

Consistent with the mission and goals, AAP must take affirmative action to remedy significant imbalances in student participation and staffing patterns.

As the demographic profiles of campuses change and new instructional delivery methods are introduced, institutions must recognize the needs of students who participate in distance learning for access to programs and services offered on campus. Institutions must provide appropriate services in ways that are accessible to distance learners and assist them in identifying and gaining access to other appropriate services in their geographic region.

Part 10. Campus and External Relations

The Academic Advising Program (AAP) must establish, maintain, and promote effective relations with relevant campus offices and external agencies.

Academic advising is integral to the educational process and depends upon close working relationships with other institutional agencies and the administration. AAP should be fully integrated into other processes of the institution. Academic advisors should be consulted when there are modifications to or closures of academic programs.

For referral purposes, AAP should provide academic advisors a comprehensive list of relevant external agencies, campus offices, and opportunities.

Part 11. Diversity

Within the context of the institution's unique mission, diversity enriches the community and enhances the collegiate experience for all; therefore, the Academic Advising Program (AAP) must nurture environments where similarities and differences among people are recognized and honored.

AAP must promote educational experiences that are characterized by open and continuous communication that deepen understanding of one's own identity, culture and heritage, and that of others. AAP must educate and promote respect about commonalties and differences in historical and cultural contexts.

AAP must address the characteristics and needs of a diverse population when establishing and implementing policies and procedures.

Part 12. Ethics

All persons involved in the delivery of the Academic Advising Program (AAP) must adhere to the highest of principles of ethical behavior. AAP must develop or adopt and implement appropriate statements of ethical practice. AAP must publish these statements and ensure their periodic review by relevant constituencies.

Advisors must uphold policies, procedures, and values of their departments and institutions.

Advisors should consider ethical standards or other statements from relevant professional associations.

AAP staff members must ensure that privacy and confidentiality are maintained with respect to all communications and records to the extent that such records are protected under the law and appropriate statements of ethical practice. Information contained in students' education records must not be disclosed without written consent except as allowed by relevant laws and institutional polices. AAP staff members must disclose to appropriate authorities information judged to be of an emergency nature, especially when the safety of the individual or others is involved, or when otherwise required by institutional policy or relevant law.

When emergency disclosure is required, AAP should inform the student that it has taken place, to whom, and why.

All AAP staff members must be aware of and comply with the provisions contained in the institution's human subjects research policy and in other relevant institutional policies addressing ethical practices and confidentiality of research data concerning individuals.

All AAP staff members must recognize and avoid personal conflict of interest or appearance thereof in their transactions with students and others.

All AAP staff members must strive to ensure the fair, objective, and impartial treatment of all persons with whom they deal. AAP staff members must not participate in nor condone any form of harassment that demeans persons or creates intimidating, hostile, or offensive campus environment.

When handling institutional funds, all AAP staff members must ensure that such funds are managed in accordance with established and responsible accounting procedures and the fiscal policies or processes of the institution.

AAP staff members must perform their duties within the limits of their training, expertise, and competence. When these limits are exceeded, individuals in need of further assistance must be referred to persons possessing appropriate qualifications.

AAP staff members must use suitable means to confront and otherwise hold accountable other staff members who exhibit unethical behavior.

AAP staff members must be knowledgeable about and practice ethical behavior in the use of technology.

Part 13. Assessment and Evaluation

The Academic Advising Program (AAP) must conduct regular assessment and evaluations. AAP must employ effective qualitative and quantitative methodologies as appropriate, to determine whether and to what degree the stated mission, goals, and student learning and development outcomes are being met. The process must employ sufficient and sound assessment measures to ensure comprehensiveness. Data collected must include responses from students and other affected constituencies.

AAP must evaluate periodically how well they complement and enhance the institution's stated mission and educational effectiveness.

Results of these evaluations must be used in revising and improving programs and services and in recognizing staff performance and the performance of academic advisors.

About the Authors

JIM BLACK is president and CEO of SEM WORKS, a consulting firm specializing in enrollment management. His areas of expertise include leadership, organizational change, customer service, strategic enrollment management, marketing, recruitment, and retention. He has published widely in the enrollment management field and has served as a consultant for American Association of Collegiate Registrars and Admissions Officers (AACRAO), National Association of Student Personnel Administrators (NASPA), and more than 200 colleges and universities. He is the 2005 recipient of the AACRAO Distinguished Service Award. He earned a bachelor of arts in English education and a master of education in higher education student personnel services from the University of South Carolina. He holds a PhD in higher education curriculum and teaching, with a concentration in business administration from The University of North Carolina at Greensboro.

EVETTE J. CASTILLO is the interim director of multicultural affairs at Tulane University. Castillo is a past board member of the National Academic Advising Association (NACADA) and currently is the National Asian and Pacific Islander Knowledge Community co-chair for the National Association of Student Personnel Administrators (NASPA). She received her EdD in international and multicultural education from the University of San Francisco, an MA in student personnel administration in higher education from New York University, and a BA in sociology from the University of California, Irvine. Her areas of research concern college students of color and leadership in higher education.

JOANNE K. DAMMINGER is the executive assistant to the vice president for student affairs at Rowan University where her work focuses on designing first-year experiences to increase student satisfaction, academic success, intentional learning, social adjustment, and retention. Additionally, she coordinates major events such as first-year and transfer orientations and homecoming and enjoys teaching. Joanne presents nationally on the topics of the first-year experience, creating living/learning communities, and helping students to become intentional learners. She earned her doctorate in education in educational leadership and has a master of arts degree in student personnel services.

RUTH A. DARLING serves as assistant vice chancellor for academic affairs and director of the Student Success Center at University of Tennessee. Previously, Darling was the director of advising services for the College of Arts and Sciences and director of the Thornton Athletic Student Life Center. She has been active at the University in various initiatives related to undergraduate education, student success and retention programs, academic advising, curriculum development, and collegiate athletics. She is past president of the National Academic Advising Association (NACADA) and currently serves on the NACADA Summer Institute advisory board and on the *NACADA Journal* editorial board. She received her doctorate in education in leadership studies in higher education from the University of Tennessee.

JEAN HENSCHEID is a fellow at the National Resource Center for The First-Year Experience and Students in Transition, managing editor of the Jossey-Bass/American College Personnel

Association publication *About Campus*, and an instructor in the Core Curriculum at the University of Idaho. She is a faculty member at the National Learning Communities Summer Institute; has authored and edited monographs, book chapters, and articles on various topics related to the college student experience; and conducts workshops across the US and abroad. Previously, Jean led learning community programs and taught undergraduate and graduate courses in leadership and research methods at Washington State University.

MARY STUART HUNTER is director of the National Resource Center for The First-Year Experience and Students in Transition at the University of South Carolina (USC) where her work centers on providing educators with resources to develop personal and professional skills while creating and refining innovative programs to increase undergraduate student learning and success. In addition to her administrative and teaching responsibilities at USC, she frequently speaks and conducts workshops on the first-year experience, sophomores, faculty development, teaching, and related topics on campuses and at national conferences. Her recent publications focus on these topics as well. As a former academic advisor, she has continued to stay involved with National Academic Advising Association (NACADA) throughout her career.

CHRISTINE JOHNSTON is the director of Rowan University's Center for the Advancement of Learning. For the past 11 years, she has engaged in research on the effects of the Let Me Learn Process in higher education within the US and abroad. Recently, she completed work for the European Union's LML Grundtvig Project, working with higher education populations in Italy, Spain, the United Kingdom, the Czech Republic, Slovenia, Malta, and Holland. Johnston serves on the external advisory board to the University of Wisconsin-Eau Claire's College of Education and Human Sciences and Corporate DuPont's Office of Research and Education. Johnston received her EdD from Rutgers University, her MA from the University of Wisconsin-Milwaukee, and her BA from the University of Wisconsin-Eau Claire.

JENNIFER R. KEUP is the director of Student Affairs Information and Research Office at UCLA. Keup earned her PhD in higher education and organizational change from the UCLA Graduate School of Education and Information Studies and served as a research analyst and project director at the Higher Education Research Institute (HERI) for seven years. Keup is currently the principal research analyst at the UCLA Student Affairs Information and Research Office. Her professional roles, personal research agenda, and publications focus on student development, the impact of college on student outcomes, and assessment in higher education, particularly at points of transition such as the first-year experience, the transfer-student experience, and graduating seniors.

JILLIAN KINZIE is associate director of the National Survey of Student Engagement Institute for Effective Educational Practice at the Indiana University Center for Postsecondary Research. She earned her PhD in higher education with a minor in women's studies at Indiana University Bloomington. Prior to this, she held a visiting faculty appointment in the higher education and student affairs department at Indiana University and worked as an administrator in academic and student affairs for several years. She is co-author of *Student Success in College: Creating Conditions that Matter* (Jossey-Bass, 2005) and *One Size Does Not Fit All: Traditional and Innovative Models of Student Affairs Practice* (Routledge, 2006).

MICHAEL J. LEONARD is the assistant director of Penn State's Division of Undergraduate Studies. He received a master's degree in educational psychology from Penn State and has worked in the field of academic advising for more than 25 years. He is a past chair of the National Academic Advising Association's Technology in Advising Commission and a recipient of its Service to Commission Award. He has presented numerous sessions and workshops at professional conferences, and he has provided consulting services to higher education institutions on the topic of technology in advising. He is also managing editor of *The Mentor: An Academic Advising Journal*, an award-winning electronic publication.

WESLEY P. LIPSCHULTZ is a senior undergraduate studies advisor in Penn State's Division of Undergraduate Studies and has been in the field of academic advising for the past 11 years. He completed several years of PhD work in social psychology and has taken graduate coursework in instructional systems at Penn State, but he is still looking for an academic home. He has served on the steering committee of the National Academic Advising Association's (NACADA) Technology in Advising Commission for five years and has presented numerous sessions and workshops at national and regional NACADA conferences for the past decade.

BETSY MCCALLA-WRIGGINS is director emeritus of the Career and Academic Planning Center at Rowan University where her work focused on integrating academic advising for undeclared and change of major students with career advising for all students. Currently, she is the higher education specialist for the Center for the Advancement of Learning at Rowan. In this role, she supports institutions of higher education as they seek to infuse learning pattern research and strategies into the fabric of the organization so that students are empowered to take responsibility for their learning. She also was the 2001-2003 president of the National Academic Advising Association.

MELINDA MCDONALD is associate director for honors in the Fisher College of Business at The Ohio State University where her work focuses on directing honors programming and advising. Her prior positions were program coordinator for the Alternatives Advising program in University College at Ohio State and program administrator specialist for the Ohio Board of Regents. She completed a BA degree in Spanish education and an MA in counselor education from Rollins College and a PhD degree in counselor education from Ohio State. Her research interests include advisor training, advising high-ability students, and career development and decision making with undecided and major-changing students.

VICTORIA MCGILLIN earned her BS and MS in psychology from Pennsylvania State University and her PhD in clinical psychology from Michigan State University. She has taught and advised at the graduate and undergraduate level at Michigan State University, the University of Connecticut, Clark University, and Wheaton College and has administered faculty advising programs at Clark and Wheaton. She is currently associate provost at Texas Woman's University. McGillin has presented on advising research, assessment, and faculty development at regional and national conferences; served on the board of directors of National Academic Advising Association; and has published extensively in the advising literature.

SHARON PATERSON MCGUIRE has an administrative and teaching career that spans 17 years. Throughout her career, she has designed, implemented, and assessed comprehensive intervention programs that have increased retention and academic performance/success for participants; collaborated and negotiated with faculty, departments, student organizations, and individual students to enrich the campus environment; provided leadership for multiple staff and work teams within a variety of structures; and researched multiple factors that positively and negatively impact college student success. She holds a PhD in sociology, specializing in inequality, work/occupations, and higher education from Virginia Polytechnic Institute and State University.

MICHELLE MOUTON is currently the coordinator of graduate admissions and marketing at the graduate school of the University of North Florida. Mouton is also the advisor of the Graduate Student Organization and serves on the board of the First Coast Higher Education Alliance. She earned her master's degree in higher education and student affairs at the University of South Carolina, where she was a graduate assistant with the National Resource Center for The First-Year Experience and Students in Transition.

CHARLIE NUTT is the associate director of National Academic Advising Association (NACADA) and assistant professor in the counseling and educational psychology department at Kansas State University. Prior to his role at NACADA, Nutt was vice president for student development services and assistant professor of English at Coastal Georgia Community College.

PENNY J. RICE, a first-generation and adult learner, earned her bachelor of science in psychology and women's studies and her master of science in counseling and student personnel from Minnesota State University, Mankato. She anticipates completing her doctoral degree in educational leadership and policy studies in 2008. Rice currently is the director of the Margaret Sloss Women's Center and prior to this position, was the director of off-campus and adult student services at Iowa State University. Before arriving at Iowa State, she was the director of adult and graduate student services at Texas A&M University, College Station.

MARION SCHWARTZ earned an honors degree in modern history and English at the University of Toronto and a doctorate in English literature at Princeton. She taught college English in New York and the Midwest before moving to Penn State in 1987. She has worked with the English department, the Schreyer Honors College, and the Division of Undergraduate Studies as a coordinator of student programs. She has published on general education, undergraduate research, worked with high-achieving students, and presented papers for National Academic Advising Association, Association for General & Liberal Studies, and the National Resource Center for The First-Year Experience and Students in Transition.

CASEY SELF is the executive director of academic advising for University College at Arizona State University (ASU). Self has presented at numerous National Academic Advising Association (NACADA) conferences on LGBTQ issues and served as the LGBTQ commission chair for two years. NACADA leadership positions also include three years on the NACADA council and a three-year term on the NACADA board of directors beginning in October 2006. Self is a founding member of Ubiquity (ASU staff and faculty supporting LGBTQ issues) and served as the LGBTQ student coalition advisor for two years. Self received his masters in college student personnel at Western Illinois University and undergraduate degree from the University of Northern Colorado.

MELISSA SCANDLYN SMITH obtained her bachelor of arts in history from Rhodes College and her master of science in college student personnel from the University of Tennessee. She has worked with the Student Success Center, the Parents Association, the Thornton Athletics Student Life Center, and the Tennessee Career Information Delivery System (TCIDS), all at the University of Tennessee. She is currently coordinator of student services and recruiting for the Knoxville campus of the University of Tennessee College of Pharmacy.

GEORGE E. STEELE is director of educational access at the Ohio Learning Network (OLN). OLN works with those Ohio higher educational institutions interested in the use of technology to improve learning. In this capacity, he focuses on student services issues and links to college access programs. Steele's professional interests include writing, speaking, and conducting workshops on advising undecided and major-changing students as well as the use of technology in advising. Steele received his bachelor's, master's, and doctoral degrees at The Ohio State University in the field of education.

DICK VALLANDINGHAM has been involved with providing services for individuals with disabilities since 1970 when he worked at the Tulsa Center for the Physically Limited. He obtained his bachelor of science degree in speech and hearing science from Oklahoma State University and his master of arts in audiology from the University of Tulsa. After working as an educational audiologist, he completed the doctor of philosophy in rehabilitation counseling from the University of Arizona. His community college career began in disability support services at Johnson County Community College, and he is currently vice president for student development services at Coastal Georgia Community College. He has held positions as chair of the Kansas Commission for the Deaf and Hearing Impaired and as chair of the National Academic Advising Association commission on advising students with disabilities. He is a frequent presenter on services for students with disabilities.

ERIC R. WHITE earned his undergraduate degree in history from Rutgers University and his masters and doctorate in counseling psychology from the University of Pennsylvania. He began his tenure at The Pennsylvania State University as a psychological counselor, was named director of the division of undergraduate studies in 1986, executive director in 1999, and associate dean for advising in 2005. He also serves as an affiliate assistant professor of education at Penn State. He was president of the Association of Deans and Directors of University Colleges and Undergraduate Studies in 1993. White served a four-year term as the National Academic Advising Association's (NACADA) treasurer and was president of NACADA in 2004-2005. White is the recipient of NACADA's Virginia N. Gordon Award for Excellence in the Field of Advising and Penn State's Administrative Excellence Award.

MARIANNE WOODSIDE obtained her doctorate from Virginia Tech University in curriculum and counselor education. Her past positions in higher education include professor of human services and counselor education, coordinator of university studies and first-year studies, and executive assistant to the chancellor. Currently, she is a professor in the Department of Educational Psychology and Counseling, unit leader of Counselor Education, and the co-author of numerous books focused on human service education. Recent conference presentations focus on multicultural cases and applications in counseling and promoting advocacy in counseling.